Lecture Notes in Computer Science 2184

Edited by G. Goos, J. Hartmanis, and J. van Leeuwen

T0216377

Springer

Berlin
Heidelberg
New York
Barcelona
Hong Kong
London
Milan
Paris
Tokyo

Maurizio Tucci   (Ed.)

Multimedia Databases and Image Communication

Second International Workshop, MDIC 2001
Amalfi, Italy, September 17-18, 2001
Proceedings

Springer

Series Editors

Gerhard Goos, Karlsruhe University, Germany
Juris Hartmanis, Cornell University, NY, USA
Jan van Leeuwen, Utrecht University, The Netherlands

Volume Editor

Maurizio Tucci
Università di Salerno
Dipartimento di Matematica e Informatica
via S. Allende, 84081 Baronissi, Italy
E-mail: mautuc@unisa.it

Cataloging-in-Publication Data applied for

Die Deutsche Bibliothek - CIP-Einheitsaufnahme

Multimedia databases and image communication : second international workshop ;
proceedings / MDIC 2001, Amalfi, Italy, September 17 - 18, 2001. Maurizio
Tucci (ed.). - Berlin ; Heidelberg ; New York ; Barcelona ; Hong Kong ;
London ; Milan ; Paris ; Tokyo : Springer, 2001
  (Lecture notes in computer science ; Vol. 2184)
  ISBN 3-540-42587-X

CR Subject Classification (1998): H.5.1, H.3, E.4, C.2, I.7.2, H.4.3

ISSN 0302-9743
ISBN 3-540-42587-X Springer-Verlag Berlin Heidelberg New York

Springer-Verlag Berlin Heidelberg New York
a member of BertelsmannSpringer Science+Business Media GmbH

http://www.springer.de

© Springer-Verlag Berlin Heidelberg 2001
Printed in Germany

Typesetting: Camera-ready by author, data conversion by Christian Grosche, Hamburg
Printed on acid-free paper   SPIN 10840533   06/3142   5 4 3 2 1 0

Foreword

Multimedia technologies are rapidly attracting more and more interest every day. The Internet as seen from the end user is one of the reasons for this phenomenon, but not the only one. Video on Demand is one of the buzzwords today, but its real availability to the general public is yet to come. Content providers – such as publishers, broadcasting companies, and audio/video production firms – must be able to archive and index their productions for later retrieval. This is a formidable task, even more so when the material to be sorted encompasses many different types of several media and covers a time span of several years.

In order for such a vast amount of data to be easily available, existing database design models and indexing methodologies have to be improved and refined. In addition, new techniques especially tailored to the various types of multimedia must be devised and evaluated. For archiving and trasmission, data compression is another issue that needs to be addressed. In many cases, it has been found that compression and indexing can be successfully integrated, since compressing the data by filtering out irrelevancy implies some degree of understanding of the content structure.

Image and audio data cannot be effectively managed with the exclusive use of older, keyword-based search techniques. Video sequences present similar, possibly even harder, problems. As broadband communications become more and more viable for the general public, video data is bound to dominate the data flow on the Internet. The issue of video coding and indexing is therefore of maximum practical usefulness, especially since there is as of yet no general method for content-based video indexing and retrieval.

The 2nd International Workshop on Multimedia Databases and Image Communication (MDIC 2001), which took place in Amalfi, Italy, on September 17–18, 2001, addressed these topics. I am proud to say that we received several interesting contributions by outstanding authors from all around the world.

However, research can hardly improve on its own results if young researchers are not trained in order to follow the lead of the more experienced ones. Education is, in my opinion, an important issue that should not be underestimated. For this reason, MDIC 2001 had an educational side, too – the Summer School on Multimedia Databases and Image Communication.

A word of thanks goes to all the people who contributed towards MDIC 2001: the anonymous referees who donated their time in order to review the numerous submissions; the sponsors who offered financial aid; the researchers and grantees who assisted the organization by managing the accepted papers, maintaining contacts with the sponsors, talking to travel agencies, and in several other ways. In particular, I would like to thank Monica Sebillo, Michele Nappi, and Riccardo Distasi for their precious assistance.

Granted: organizing an international workshop *and* a summer school is no easy task; however, when things eventually work out and the contributions are significant, the reward is definitely worth the effort.

September 2001   Maurizio Tucci

Organization

MDIC 2001 was organized by the Dipartimento di Matematica e Informatica (DMI) of the Università di Salerno.

Workshop Program Committee

Program Chair: Maurizio Tucci (Università di Salerno)

Augusto Celentano (Università di Venezia "Ca' Foscari")
Shi-Kuo Chang (University of Pittsburgh)
Gennaro Costagliola (Università di Salerno)
Erland Jungert (FOI / Swedish Defense Research Agency)
Stefano Levialdi (Università di Roma)
Piero Mussio (Università di Brescia)
Michele Nappi (Università di Salerno)
Gennaro Petraglia (Università di Salerno)
Stan Sclaroff (Boston University)
Monica Sebillo (Università di Salerno)
Genoveffa Tortora (Università di Salerno)
Sergio Vitulano (Università di Cagliari)

Invited Speakers

Shi-Kuo Chang (University of Pittsburgh)
Stan Sclaroff (Boston University)

Summer School Scientific Committee

School Director: Maurizio Tucci (Università di Salerno)

Shi-Kuo Chang (University of Pittsburgh)
Augusto Celentano (Università di Venezia "Ca' Foscari")
Gennaro Costagliola (Università di Salerno)
Athula Ginige (Southwestern University of Sidney)
Erland Jungert (FOI/Swedish Defence Agency)
Michele Nappi (Università di Salerno)
Gennaro Petraglia (Università di Salerno)
Monica Sebillo (Università di Salerno)
Genoveffa Tortora (Università di Salerno)

Summer School Lecturers

Augusto Celentano (Università di Venezia "Ca' Foscari")
Shi-Kuo Chang (University of Pittsburgh)
Athula Ginige (Southwestern University of Sidney)
Erland Jungert (FOI/Swedish Defence Agency)

Summer School Scientific Secretariat

Riccardo Distasi (Università di Salerno)
Luca Paolino (Università di Salerno)

Sponsoring Institutions

Provincia di Salerno
Comune di Amalfi

Table of Contents

V   Video Indexing and Communication

Part I

Invited Talks

MAWC Operations for the Growing Book

Shi-Kuo Chang
Department of Computer Science
University of Pittsburgh, USA
Chang@cs.pitt.edu

Abstract: We describe the conceptual framework for the Growing Book, which is an ever-expanding body of knowledge created by a team of experts, and the basic operations such as Match, Abstract, Weave and Customize, which can be used to extract and organize information from the multi-level, multimedia, multi-lingual book.

1   Introduction

A *Growing Book* is an electronic book co-developed by a group of teachers who are geographically dispersed throughout the world and collaborate in teaching and research. Since the course materials are constantly evolving, the Growing Book must be constantly updated and expanded. The Growing Book is used by each teacher both in the local classroom as well as in the world-wide distance learning environment. Therefore the Growing Book must be accessible by multi-lingual students. The chapters of the Growing Book are owned by different authors who may utilize and/or provide different tools for distance learning, self learning and assessment.

The Macro University provides an experimental test bed for the Growing Book. The Macro University is a distance learning framework consisting of three layers: the micro-university [2], the virtual university, and the macro university. A micro-university is a self-contained learning environment, usually on a single PC (or laptop, notebook, palmtop, PDA, etc.) for a single student interacting with a teacher. A micro-university is designed to serve a single individual, but of course many instances of the same micro-university can be created to serve many students. A virtual university is a collection of individualized learning environments so that students can engage in learning activities from home, remote locations, etc. A virtual university is usually owned and operated by an academic institution and therefore has more administrative functions than a micro-university. The Macro University is a framework such that many virtual universities can pool their resources together, thus creating a very rich learning environment for a large number of students from all over the world.

The structure of the Macro University is illustrated by Fig. 1. As mentioned above, a micro-university is a teaching or learning environment for an individual teacher/student, designed to serve the needs of that teacher/student. In particular, a micro-university may be a Growing Book as shown in Fig. 1, where two of the micro-universities are Growing Books. A virtual university consists of one or more micro-universities. In the limiting case a virtual university is the same as a single micro-university. But usually a virtual university consists of many micro-universities and in

M. Tucci (Ed.): MDIC 2001, LNCS 2184, pp. 3-15, 2001.

addition can perform many complex administrative functions supported by a virtual administration office. The administrative tools include software tools for managing users, curriculum, facilities, resources, plans, etc. Each of the above tools can be used by the authorized users according to their roles and responsibilities in a virtual university. Virtual universities can be small, medium or large. It can be a single software module, a few software modules, or a complex configuration of software modules. For example, the Virtual universities of the Macro University may include: the Growing Book, Virtual Course-room, Virtual Collaboration Room [4], Virtual Laboratory, Virtual Library and Virtual Private Office, each of which can operate on a dynamically changing collection of tele-action objects [1, 3].

In what follows, we describe a conceptual framework on how to design and manage the Growing Book. The basic MAWC (Match, Abstract, Weave and Customize) operations on the Growing Book are then presented.

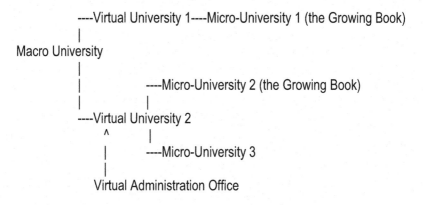

Fig. 1. The Structure of the Macro University.

2   A Multi-level, Multi-lingual, and Multi-modal Growing Book

As described above, the Macro University is a worldwide consortium of Virtual Universities. As such there will be a wide variety of curricula and educational programs for peoples with different linguistic skills, different cultures, and different perceptual preferences. The Growing Book should support the multi-level, multi-lingual and multi-modal usage of the shared content co-developed by many teachers. (a) **Multi-Level Usage**: The same course materials can be organized in different ways to be used in a regular semester course, a short course, an introductory exposition, an advanced seminar, etc. (b) **Multi-lingual Usage**: The same course materials can be transformed into different languages. (c) **Multi-Model Usage**: The same course materials can be used by people with different perceptual preferences and various handicaps.

The Macro University Consortium was established in the Spring of 1999 and now has more than fifteen international members. The participants of the Macro University are currently working together to develop a prototype Growing Book. The prototype Growing Book has the following characteristics: course materials accessible with a browser; common look-and-feel and common buttons; common assessment tool with adjustable granularity [5]; individual tools downloadable as plug-ins; examples in C and later Unicode; adaptive learning with embedded audio/video clips; collaboration in content and tools evaluation, and availability in hard copy and CD.

The prototype Growing Book is intended as a textbook for an undergraduate course on *data structures and algorithms*. The initial version of the Growing Book is available for experimental purposes.

In the Growing Book project, *adaptability*, *scalability* and *universal accessibility* are emphasized, which are driven by both teacher and student, so that the student feels to be actively driving his/her course like a helmsman in a motor boat, requesting explanations, special documents, homework corrections, etc. In this sense *interactivity* is a basic issue in the Growing Book model. We emphasize interactivity in managing all the different type of documents such as images, text, video clips, audio, etc., reflecting a teaching/learning communication model. The teacher may send multimedia documents and, without cumbersome delays, students may request explanations, ad-hoc documents that may enrich the lecture/exercise on a real-time basis. We also emphasize common assessment software tools, plug-ins for common platforms, multi-lingual capability through a button, truly effective distributed teaching, and lively animation and/or visualization of algorithms. The Growing Book thus poses many challenging research issues.

3   Operations for the Growing Book

As discussed in Section 2, students, teachers and authors all need an interactive language built upon some basic operations (triggered as events on specific and specified parts of the multimedia documents) that simplify their response with respect to novel concepts in a given course, retrieving extra documents from virtual libraries, or simply communicating with other students and/or other teachers. In this way there may be an enrichment with respect to a standard series of documents as when a new view is obtained with respect to the processing of a query in a given database management system.

In what follows, the basic operations are divided into several groups. The details of multi-level, multimedia matching, abstraction, weaving and presentation, and the concept of awareness, will be further explained in subsequent sections.

a) Operations for Multi-level, Multimedia Customization

The first group of operations support the matching, abstraction, weaving and customization of multimedia documents. These are called MAWC operations.

MATCH Chapter_No Paragraph: Select a paragraph of the chapter with Chapter_No, and find all documents that match the selected paragraph by keyword matching.

MATCHPAR NumKeyword Threshold YesWords NoWords PathName: This operation allows the user to enter the parameters for the keyword matching algorithm. The meaning of the parameters will be explained later.

ABSTRACT Chapter_No Level_No: Create an abstraction of the chapter with Chapter_No at Level_No. For instance, Level 1 is title and a few keywords, Level 2 is title and immediate sub-sections, Level 3 includes all sub-sections, and Level 4 is the document itself.

WEAVE Chapter_No Tag Tool: Weave the pieces in Chapter_No that are surrounded by < Tag > and < /Tag > into a presentation stream, where Tag is defined for a specific media type.

CUSTOMIZE Chapter_No Tool: Apply Tool to materialize and customize the presentation from a presentation stream created by the WEAVE operation.

b) Operations for Increasing/Updating Awareness

The user can specify an awareness vector, so that he/she can be informed about certain events. The awareness vector is a binary vector where each entry indicates the absence/presence of an awareness attribute. For example, the awareness vector can be $(1,0,1,1,0)$, indicating the user wants to be aware of any changes in fellow students (1st entry), domain experts (2nd entry), centers of excellence (3rd entry), references (4th entry) and tools (5th entry). A user can also set privacy, so that he/she is not included in any awareness information.

AWARE Chapter_No Name Password: In the chapter with Chapter_No, if Name and Password is in Author, Student or Teacher list, display info Name should be aware of.

CHECK_AWARENESS Chapter_No Name Password: In the chapterwith Chapter_No, search Author, Teacher and Student lists for matched Name and Password, and if found, display the Awareness Profile for Name.

SET_AWARENESS Chapter_No Name Password Profile: In the chapter with Chapter_No, search Author, Teacher and Student lists for matched Name and Password, and if found, add or reset the Awareness of Name to Name,Profile.

SET_PRIVACY Chapter_No Name Password: In the chapter with Chapter_No, search Author, Teacher and Student lists for matched Name and Password, and if found, add Name to Privacy list.

CLEAR_PRIVACY Chapter_No Name Password: In the chapter with Chapter_No, search Author, Teacher and Student lists for matched Name and Password, and if found, remove Name from Privacy list.

c) Operations for Communication

Communication operations are for sending messages to authors, teachers and fellow students. A user may not know their exact names and/or e-mail addresses, but he/she still can send messages to the group of people he/she wants to communicate with.

SEND_AUTHOR Chapter_No Message: Send Message to the Author(s) of Chapter_No.

SEND_STUDENT Chapter_No Message: Send Message to the Student(s) of Chapter_No.

SEND_TEACHER Chapter_No Message: Send Message to the Teacher(s) of Chapter_No.

d) Operations for Watermarking

Watermarks can be added or displayed for a multimedia document, including text document.

ADD_WATERMARK Chapter_No Chapter_Password Key Watermark: In the chapter with Chapter_No, if Chapter_Password is correct, add Watermark to the html files of Chapter_No using Key.

DISPLAY_WATERMARK Chapter_No Chapter_Password Key Watermark: In the chapter with Chapter_No, if Chapter_Password is correct, and Watermark provided matches the watermark in the document, display Watermark of the html files of Chapter_No using Key.

e) Operations for Managing the Growing Book

There are many operations for gathering statistics and managing the Growing Book. Some of them are listed here.

ADD_SUBJECT Chapter_No Chapter_password Word: First search for a Word in a chapter and if it is present, add the Word as a new subject of the chapter.

SEARCH_MESSAGE Word Teacher_name Teacher_password: Search for Word in the message file of the Growing Book program.

SEARCH_STUDENT Student_Name Book_Password: Find all chapters that Student_Name is studying.

ENROLLED Chapter_no Teacher_name Teacher_password: List students studying a chapter.

GET_STUDENT_INFO Chapter_no : Produce useful statistics on the students studying a chapter.

ADD_AUTHOR Chapter_No Chapter_Password Author Password: If Chapter_Password is
correct, add Author,Password to the author(s) of Chapter_No.

ADD_CENTER Chapter_No Chapter_Password Center: In the chapter with Chapter_No, if Chapter_Password is correct, add Center to Center_of_Excellence list.

ADD_REFERENCE Chapter_No Chapter_Password Reference: In the chapter with Chapter_No, if Chapter_Password is correct, add Reference to Reference list.

ADD_STUDENT Chapter_No Chapter_Password Student Password: If Chapter_Password
is correct, add Student,Password to the student(s) of Chapter_No.

ADD_TEACHER Chapter_No Chapter_Password Teacher Password: If Chapter_Password is correct, add Teacher,Password to the teacher(s) of Chapter_No.

ADD_TOOL Chapter_No Chapter_Password Tool: In the chapter with Chapter_No, if Chapter_Password is correct, add Tool to Tool list.

ADD_WHO_IS_WHO Chapter_No Chapter_Password Who: In the chapter with Chapter_No, if Chapter_Password is correct, add Who to who_is_who list.

DROP_AUTHOR Chapter_No Chapter_Password Author: If Chapter_Password is correct, drop Author,Password from the author(s) of Chapter_No.

DROP_CENTER Chapter_No Chapter_password Center: Drop center.

DROP_REFERENCE Chapter_No Chapter_password Reference: Drop reference.

DROP_STUDENT Chapter_No Chapter_Password Student: If Chapter_Password is correct, drop Student,Password drop the student(s) of Chapter_No.

DROP_STUDENT_ALL Chapter_No Chapter_Password Student: If Chapter_Password is correct, drop Student,Password drop the student(s) of Chapter_No.

DROP_TEACHER Chapter_No Chapter_Password Teacher: If Chapter_Password is correct, drop Teacher,Password from the teacher(s) of Chapter_No.

DROP_TOOL Chapter_No Chapter_password Tool: Drop tool.

DROP_WHO_IS_WHO Chapter_No Chapter_password who_is_who: Drop who_is_who.

CH_TEA_PWD Name Old_Pwd New_Pwd: Change password

ADD_CHAPTER Chapter_No Chapter_Password Book_password: Add a new chapter.

DELETE_CHAPTER Chapter_No Chapter_password Book_password: Drop an old chapter.

The above described operations are implemented as commands for the customized IC Manager [Chang96] of the Growing Book. When the user submits a command to the Growing Book, the customized IC Manager processes this command. The command consists of a name and its parameters. The command name is treated as a message type by the IC Manager to be passed on, together with the parameters, to the appropriate IC for processing. The Growing Book operations are implemented as "actions" (C programs) of the ICs managed by the IC Manager.

4　Profiles for Awareness

The above described operations assumes that each chapter of the Growing Book is characterized by a Chapter Profile, which is a list of (attribute-name, attribute-value) pairs. As an example, Chapter 1 of the Growing Book has the following Chapter Profile:

Chapter_No: 1
Chapter_Title: Stacks
Author_Affiliation: Knowledge Systems Institute
Author: fthulin@ksi.edu,1234
Chapter_URL: http://www.cs.pitt.edu/~chang/bookds/01htm/chap1.htm
Book_Password: 123
Chapter_Password: sem010
Teacher: chang@cs.pitt.edu,B122L judy@ksi.edu,044hw
Student: jung@cs.pitt.edu,7777x changsk@ksi.edu,xi43w
Who_is_Who: guru@cs.pitt.edu
Center_of_Excellence: www.ksi.edu
Reference: www.branden.edu
Tool: www.abs.com
Awareness: jung@cs.pitt.edu,10111 changsk@ksi.edu,10000

In this example, the awareness attributes are shown in bold face. For each chapter, the interested students, teachers and authors can each have their individual awareness vectors. Taken together, these awareness vectors determine the student profile, teacher profile, and author profile. In other words, a user's profile is shaped by what he/she is aware of or what he/she wants to be aware of.

5   A Scenario

We are now in a position to describe how a user applies the operations on the Growing Book to produce customized books. The following scenario is a generic scenario and can be further specialized.

a) Initial Search: A user can use the MATCH operation to search for similar web pages. From the top page of the Growing Book (Fig. 2), by clicking on a button the user arrives at the table of contents page. The user clicks on "Submit" and then selects a chapter from the table of contents. Suppose Chapter 4 on Searching is selected. The user can highlight a sentence or a paragraph, such as "Search on Array" and click on the button "Show highlighted text and continue". The highlighted text is shown in a text box. When the user clicks on "OK", the search program finds the matching results for every html page in the Growing Book. Pages that match the highlighted text will have a link with the words: "Click here to access the above chapter", such as a link to chapter 9 that discusses "breadth-first search".

Fig. 2. Top Page of the Growing Book.

The search algorithm assumes the various chapters all reside on the local hard disk, so that an efficient search can be conducted. In general, these chapters could be located at other websites. We could keep a local copy of the Growing Book, which includes all the text materials but not the multimedia objects (graphics, images, audio and video). Thus we can search locally to identify the related chapters and web pages.

The user can use the command MATCHPAR to define the five parameters for the matching algorithm. For example, if the parameters entered are 10|1|yes.txt|no.txt|e:/index/, the following results will be displayed:

These are the parameters
First: 10
Second: 5.300000
Third: yes.txt
Forth: no.txt
Fifth: e:/index/

The parameters are stored in the file matchpar.dat in the specified local directory and have the following meaning:

1. NumKeyword: The Number of keywords can be selected in the range 10 to 30.

2. Threshold: The threshold for number of matched keywords is a positive integer.

3. YesWords: The file name for YesWords. Keywords must be selected from the YesWords, which is simply a list of words sorted in alphabetical order such as (*, apple, beet, cake). The special character * is a wild card that matches any word. If we put a * in the YesWords, every word will be considered in the YesWords list, in other words, no restrictions on the keywords.

4. NoWords: The file name for NoWords. Keywords must not be selcted from the NoWords, which is a sorted list of words such as (*, a, an, any, the, some). If we put a * in the NoWords, every word will be considered in the NoWords, in other words, all words are excluded.

5. PathName: The full path name of the local directory where the files YesWords and NoWords can be found. This local directory also stores a local copy of the Growing Book without the image, audio and video files. Therefore, the matching program will only search this local directory for matching. Of course, the full path name may point to a remote directory. The matching program still works but will take a lot more time.

b) Retrieval: Once the related documents are found, as described in Step a), then the user can abstract and weave the information together into a customized book.

b.1) Abstract: The chapters and pages are abstracted at a certain level of abstraction. Both tags such as <h1>, <h2>, etc. and section headings and other semantic clues will be used in the abstraction.

b.2) Weave: The media objects at the specified level of abstraction are weaved together into a presentation stream. We will mainly concentrate on graphics, sound and video.

b.3) Customize: The abstracted, weaved objects are retrieved and stored into the local hard disk. This operation enables the user to create a customized version of the Growing Book with a uniform presentation and at a desirable level of abstraction. Thereafter the user may only be interested in using this customized version, rather than the original version.

c) Set Awareness: Finally, the user sets and/or modify the awareness vectors so that future changes/additions/annotations on the parts of interest to the user can be reported to the user. The user can set awareness vector so that more information can be gathered, or less information will be gathered. This will lead to new ways to customize the Growing Book.

6   Tag Structures for the Growing Book

To facilitate MATCH, ABSTRACT, WEAVE and CUSTOMIZE, we can extend the TAOML language by introducing a number of new tags.

6.1   General Structure of Tags

In the following example we have two objects, ts1 and ts2. ts1 has two objects within it, ts11 and ts12, and ts12 has one object ts121. ts2 has one object which ists21. the structure is kept by the order in which the strings appear in the file, in a top-down manner. so the structure and sequence of the presentation is preserved. The same pattern will be used for the multimedia strings as well.

```
<ts>
 <ts1>.............</ts1>
  <ts11>............</ts11>
  <ts12>............</ts12>
   <ts121>...........</ts121>
 <ts2>.............</ts2>
  <ts21>............</ts21>
</ts>
```

6.2   Parameters for Tags

As a natural extension, let us consider the tags as:

```
<ts1 parameters>
```

The parameters provide more detailed information on the objects. For example:

<ts1 name="chap1" keywords="tree, graph" url="URL_address" type="mixed">

<ts22 name="animated example" keywords="tree search", url="URL_address" type="ani">

<ts31 name="lecture 3" keywords="tree search", url="URL_address" type="audio">

The examples are self-explanatory. The processing algorithms, in general, are as follows:

```
Scan the document for any ts tags;
 If there_are_ts_tags
  Then process the document using ts tags
  Else process the document using the
        heuristics considering the HTML tags, etc.;
```

6.3   A Detailed Example of Tag Structures for Multi-level Documents

1) The input to the Abstractor is several URLs, which is output of Matcher. the format is <qs> URL1 URL2 URL3 ... </qs>. the URL1, URL2, URL3 are the results of matching some interesting terms like "tree, graph".

2) The Abstractor will use every URL to get all the contents for the URL and related URL to generate a HTML page for the user. and also a structure for the Weaver and Customizer to use:

a) Level 1:

```
<ts>
 <ts1 name="chap1" keywords="tree,graph" url="URL_address"></ts1>
 <ts2 name="chap2" keywords="tree search", url="URL_address"></ts2>
</ts>
 (Note: keywords could be null, if the document has none)
```

b) Level 2:

```
<ts>
 <ts1 name="chap1" keywords="tree,graph" url="URL_address">
  <ts11 name="chap11" subsection="stacks" url="URL_address"></ts11>
  <ts12 name="chap12" subsection="Recursion",url="URL_address"></ts12>
  <ts13 name="chap13" subsection="Backtracking",url="URL_address"></ts13>
 </ts1>
 <ts2 name="chap2" keywords="tree search", url="URL_address">
  <ts21 .............................................></ts21>
  <ts22 .............................................></ts22>
```

```
   </ts2>
 </ts>
```

(Note: Notice level 1 tags are also included. Same is true for other levels)

c) Level 3:

```
<ts>
 <ts1 name="chap1" keywords="tree,graph" url="URL_address">
  <ts11 name="chap11" subsection="stacks" url="URL_address">
   <ts111 name="chap111" subsection="The LIFO Nature of Stacks"
        url="URL_address"></ts111>
   <ts112 name="chap112" subsection="reversing with a Stack"
        url="URL_address"></ts112>
  </ts11>
  <ts12 name="chap12" subsection="Recursion",url="URL_address">
   <ts121 name="chap121" subsection="Introduction"
        url="URL_address"></ts121>
   <ts122 name="chap122" subsection="Procedure calls and Runtime stack"
        url="URL_address"></ts122>
  </ts12>
 </ts1>
</ts>
```

d) Level 4:

```
<ts>
 <ts1 name="chap1" url="URL_address">
  <ts11 name="chap11" url="URL_address">
   <ts111 name="chap111" url="URL_address"></ts111>
   <ts112 name="chap112" url="URL_address"></ts112>
  </ts11>
 </ts1>
 <ts2 name="chap2" url="URL_address">
  <ts21 name="chap21" url="URL_address">
   <ts211 name="chap211" url="URL_address"></ts211>
   <ts212 name="chap212" url="URL_address"></ts212>
  </ts21>
 </ts2>
</ts>
```

Notice that it is unnecessary to put the contents, because the contents are indicated by the URL_address. When several subsections have the same URL_address, i.e., they really are part of the same document, we can use URL_address#section1 to refer to the section.

7   Discussion

In this paper we outlined our approach in designing the Growing Book for distance learning in the Macro University framework. The seed project is currently under way, and interested research groups and institutions are invited to join. More information can be found at:

http://www.cs.pitt.edu/~jung/GrowingBook

As explained above, the heart of the growing book is how to make different levels of course materials easily available to people using the MATCH, ABSTRACT, WEAVE and CUSTOMIZE operations. We started with simple version of MAWC operations. MATCH takes care of matching, ABSTRACT takes care of abstraction, WEAVE takes care of multimedia presentation, and CUSTOMIZE takes care of uniform stylization. Our goal is to work out really powerful MATCH, ABSTRACT, WEAVE and CUSTOMIZE operations to develop a rich multi-level book. From the course materials, we can abstract to create a structure, weave it into a desirable stream, and then customize and flesh out into a multi-media presentation.

Some further extension can be considered. The TaoEditor can create a TAOML document. This can be translated into XML for knowledge sharing. TAOML can also be converted into SR grammar, which can be parsed to change the syntactic correction of the TAOML design, i.e., verification. The SR grammar can also be reformulated into a logical language such as Prolog5, so that we can change the semantic correctness of a design, i.e. validation.

References

[1] S.K. Chang, "Visual Languages for Tele-Action Objects", in *Artificial Vision: Image De scription, Recognition and Communication*, V. Cantoni, S. Levialdi, V. Roberto (eds.), Academic Press, 1996, 281-301.
[2] S.K. Chang, E. Hassanein and C.Y. Hsieh, "A Multimedia Micro-University", *IEEE Multimedia Magazine*, Vol. 5, No. 3, July-September 1998, 60-68.
[3] S.K. Chang, "The Sentient Map", *Journal of Visual Languages and Computing*, Vol. 11, No. 4, August 2000, pp. 455-474.
[4] J. Ma, R. Nakatani and R. Huang, "Communications, Management and Manipulations of Objects in a Virtual Collaboration Room", The International Conference on Distributed Multimedia Systems (DMS'99).
[5] T.K. Shih, S.K. Chang, J.H. Ma and R.H. Huang, "Web Learning Assessment and Adaptive Tutoring", Technical Report, Tamkang University, Taipei, 2000.

Motion Mining

Stan Sclaroff, George Kollios, Margrit Betke, and Romer Rosales

Boston University, Computer Science Dept., Boston MA 02215, USA
sclaroff@cs.bu.edu
http://www.cs.bu.edu/fac/sclaroff/

Abstract. A long-term research effort to support data mining applications for video databases of human motion is described. Due to the spatio-temporal nature of human motion data, novel methods for indexing and mining databases of time series data of human motion are required. Further, since data mining requires a significant sample size to accurately model patterns in the data, algorithms that automatically extract motion trajectories and time series data from video are required. A preliminary system for estimating human motion in video, as well as indexing and data mining of the resulting motion databases is described.

1 Introduction

In the last decade, there has been an explosive growth in the number of computer systems that gather data about human motion via video cameras, magnetic trackers, eye trackers, motion capture body suits and gloves, etc. These systems generate streams of 3D motion trajectories or other time series data about human motion that are used in computer human interfaces, computer animation and special effects, analysis of human biomechanics, and surveillance of human activity. Recently, new efforts have formed around the issue of creating archives of human motion data for use as "standard data sets" in the development of new algorithms in the computer science community, as well as for use in studies conducted by researchers from other disciplines (e.g., [22,33,35]).

As these datasets grow, there will be an opportunity to analyze this massive data archive to gain new insights that can be used to improve our understanding and models of human motion. Insights gained through *motion mining* could lead to improved methods for computer-assisted physical rehabilitation, occupational safety, and ergonomics, as well as improved methods for sports training, medicine, and diagnosis. Furthermore, motion mining could lead to improved computer vision and pattern recognition algorithms that are specially tuned to basic patterns or clusters found in human motion databases. It could also enable algorithms that automatically recognize anomalous motions because they are outliers when considered as part of the motion database.

Data mining has emerged as an important discipline in the database field during the last few years. Two reasons can be identified: (1) a huge amount of data is available today and (2) traditional approaches to analyze such data from statistics and machine learning are inadequate to cope with it. The goal of

M. Tucci (Ed.): MDIC 2001, LNCS 2184, pp. 16–30, 2001.

data mining is to efficiently find and describe structures and patterns in large datasets. These patterns are previously unknown and not stored explicitly in the database. Examples of data mining tasks include clustering, identifying patterns, and detecting outliers. Data mining of image databases or databases that store encodings of visual events has received only a small amount of attention [17,30].

Database and data mining methods can be used to discover patterns in databases of human motion data. Such data has a spatio-temporal aspect that must be dealt with, and therefore a major issue here is to develop methods for indexing and mining databases of motion trajectories and time series data. Another important problem is to automatically extract and analyze motion data given motion capture or video sequences. Another promising direction is to develop tracking/recognition algorithms that can learn from the clusters or patterns of motion found in data mining [40]. Through a tight coupling between computer vision and data mining modules, more reliable tracking and recognition algorithms can be achieved. In this paper, we describe a preliminary system for estimating human motion in video, trajectory-based encoding of human activity, as well as trajectory-based retrieval and data mining. This work represents the first step towards our long-term goal of an automatic system for mining databases of human motion data.

2   Related Work

In one approach to motion mining, we can assume that each object's motion is represented as a sequence of multidimensional points that we call a *trajectory*. For instance, the trajectory might consist of the position of the object centroid at each time step. The main reason for using this representation is its simplicity and generality: every motion pattern can be represented as a time series of points moving in a low-dimensional space. Another reason is that simple representations will allow the design of more efficient and robust algorithms. This is very important when working with large datasets. Given trajectories represented in this way, a method for measuring similarity between trajectories is needed.

Perhaps the simplest approach to define the similarity between two sequences is to map each sequences into a vector and then use a p-norm distance to define the similarity measure. The p-norm distance between two n-dimensional vectors $\bar{x}$ and $\bar{y}$ is defined as $L_p(\bar{x}, \bar{y}) = (\sum_{i=1}^{n}(x_i - y_i)^p)^{\frac{1}{p}}$. For $p = 2$ is the well know Euclidean distance and for $p = 1$ the Manhattan distance. The advantage of this simple model is that it allows efficient indexing by a dimensionality reduction technique [1,48,19,15]. On the other hand the model cannot deal well with outliers and is very sensitive to small distortions in the time axis. There are a number of interesting extensions to the above model to support various transformations such as scaling [12,37], shifting [12,21], normalization [21] and moving average [37]. Other recent works on indexing time series data for similarity queries assuming the Euclidean model include [27,26].

Another approach is based on the time warping technique that first has been used to match signals in speech recognition [41]. Berndt and Clifford [3] proposed to use this technique to measure the similarity of time-series data in data mining. The idea is to allow stretching in time in order to get a better distance. Recently, indexing techniques for this similarity measure have been proposed [28,34].

Other techniques to define time series similarity extract certain features (Landmarks [36] or signatures [14]) from each time-series and then use these features to define the similarity. An interesting approach to represent a time series using the direction of the sequence at regular time intervals is presented in [46]. Ge and Smyth [18] present an interesting alternative approach for sequence similarity that is based on probabilistic matching. A domain independent framework for defining queries in terms of similarity of objects is presented in [25].

Note that all the above work deals mainly with one dimensional time-series. An approach to indexing two-dimensional moving object trajectories in video databases was proposed in [11]. The system also provides a sketched-based user interface for formulating trajectory-based queries, but provides no data mining component. Moving blobs are automatically segmented, given a motion-stabilized video sequence as input. Moving blobs are indexed using color and/or texture features. In addition, the series of positions of a blob's centroid in each video frame is stored as a motion trail. This system employs variants of the Euclidean distance metric to enable time-normalized retrieval of similar trajectories. As mentioned earlier, the Euclidean distance measure is sensitive to outliers, and nonlinear distortions of the time axis.

The most related paper to our work is the Bozkaya, et al. [7]. They discuss how to define similarity measures for sequences of multidimensional points using a restricted version of the edit distance. Also, they present two efficient methods to index the sequences for similarity retrieval. However, they focus on sequences of feature vectors extracted from images and not trajectories and they do not discuss transformations or approximate methods to compute the similarity. In another recent work, Lee et al. [31] propose methods to index sequences of multidimensional points. They extend the ideas presented by Faloutsos et al. in [16] and the similarity model is based on the Euclidean distance.

A recent work that proposes a method to cluster trajectory data is due to Gaffney and Smyth [17]. They use a variation of the EM (expectation maximization) algorithm to cluster small sets of trajectories. However, their method is a model based approach that usually has scalability problems. Also, it implicitly assumes that the data (trajectories) follow some basic models which are not easy to find and describe in real datasets.

3   Estimating Human Motion Trajectories

Spatio-temporal indexing of trajectories relies on algorithms that can detect, estimate, and encode relevant information about human motion in image sequences. Since data mining requires a significant sample size to accurately model patterns in the data, algorithms that automatically extract motion trajectories and time series data from video are required. Therefore, a first concern in building our system will be detecting and segmenting changing or moving blobs in video.

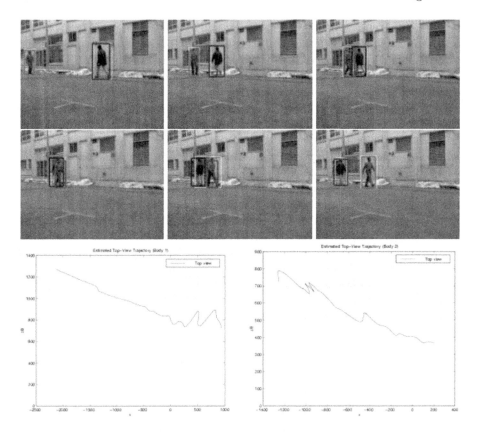

Fig. 1. Trajectory estimation example: Two bodies walking along different trajectories, occluding each other. The estimated minimum bounding boxes (MBRs) for each moving object are shown overlaid on the input video images. The graphs show the recovered trajectories (top view) for the two moving bodies. Note that motion of Body 1 is from right to left. Body 2 goes left to right. Trajectory estimates improve over time, as the extended Kalman Filter converges given more video frames.

We will assume that the time-varying image sequences have been registered and rectified to correct for motion of the camera, as well as normalized for differences in imaging conditions. Given a set of registered images, we can make use of change detection and moving blob segmentation methods that rely on first and second order statistics [39,47] or adaptive mixture models [43]. A connected components analysis is then applied to the resulting image. Initial segmentation is usually noisy, so morphological operations and size filters are applied.

To estimate the motion trajectory for each blob, we can use a predictive tracker [39], which is based on a first order Extended Kalman Filter (EKF) [42]. The EKF has proven to be very useful in recovery of rigid motion and structure from image sequences [9,2,8,38]. Most of these approaches assume rigid motion. One of the first important results on recursive structure and motion estimation was the work of [9]. The formulation of [2] yields improved stability and accuracy of the estimates. In both methods, image feature tracking and correspondence are assumed. In this paper, we present a method that automatically tracks multiple moving objects, and use this information to estimate 3D translational trajectories (up to a scale factor).

To model trajectories, [8] assumed that the surface on which the motions occur was known, and also that this surface was a plane. Each object was represented as a point moving in the plane, partially avoiding problems related to changes in shape. It is also possible to reducing tracking to a plane, if the projective effect is avoided through the use of a top, distant view [24]. It is also possible to use some heuristics about body part relations and motion on image plane like [23]. In our work, we do not assume planar motion or detailed knowledge about the object and our formulation can handle some changes in shape.

In our approach, each blob's tracker T_i contains information about object location, a binary support map, blob characteristics, minimum bounding rectangle (MBR), etc. For this application, we can choose an EKF state $\mathbf{x}$ that models the blob's MBR moving along a piece-wise linear trajectory:

$$\mathbf{x} = (x_0, y_0, x_1, y_1, z\beta, \dot{x}_0, \dot{y}_0, \dot{x}_1, \dot{y}_1, \dot{z\beta}). \tag{1}$$

In the state vector (x_0, y_0) and (x_1, y_1) are the corners of the MBR, z is the relative distance from the camera, and $\beta = \frac{1}{f}$ is the inverse camera focal length. Note that if the focal length is unknown, this formulation does not provide a unique solution in 3D space. However, the family of allowable solutions all project to a unique solution on the image plane. We can therefore estimate objects' future positions on the image plane and their image trajectories given their motion in $(x, y, z\beta)$ space. It is therefore assumed that although the object to be tracked is highly non-rigid, the 3D size of the object's bounding box will remain approximately the same, or at least vary smoothly. This assumption might be too strong in some cases; *e.g.*, if the internal motion of the object's parts cannot be roughly self contained in a bounding box. However, when analyzing basic human locomotion, we believe that these assumptions are a fair approximation.

For our representation a 3D central projection model similar to [44,2] is used:

$$\begin{bmatrix} u \\ v \end{bmatrix} = \begin{bmatrix} x \\ y \end{bmatrix} \frac{1}{1 + z\beta}, \tag{2}$$

where (x, y, z) is the real 3D feature location in the camera reference frame, (u, v) is the projection of it to the camera plane, and $\beta = \frac{1}{f}$ is the inverse focal length. The origin of the coordinate system is fixed at the image plane. This model has proven to be useful when estimating focal length and structure in the structure from motion problem [2]. One important property of this model is that it is numerically well defined even in the case of orthographic projection.

Our EKF process is guided by the following linear difference equation:

$$\mathbf{x}_{k+1} = \mathbf{A}_k \mathbf{x}_k + \mathbf{w}_k, \tag{3}$$

where $\mathbf{x}_k$ is our state at time k, $\mathbf{w}_k$ is the process noise and $\mathbf{A}_k$, the system evolution matrix, is based on first order Newtonian dynamics and assumed time invariant $(\mathbf{A}_k = \mathbf{A})$. If additional prior information on dynamics is available, then $\mathbf{A}$ can be changed to better describe the system evolution [38]. In our case, we use the assumption that trajectories are locally linear in 3D.

Our measurement vector is $\mathbf{z}_k = (u_{0k}, v_{0k}, u_{1k}, v_{1k})$, where u_{ik}, v_{ik} are the image plane coordinates for the observed feature i at time k. The measurement vector is related to the state vector via the measurement equation: $\mathbf{z}_k = h(x_k + v_k)$. Measurement noise is assumed to be additive in our model. The EKF time update equation becomes:

$$\hat{\mathbf{x}}_{k+1} = \mathbf{A}_k \hat{\mathbf{x}}_k \tag{4}$$
$$\mathbf{P}_{k+1}^- = \mathbf{A}_k \mathbf{P}_k \mathbf{A}_k^T + \mathbf{W} \mathbf{Q}_k \mathbf{W}^T \tag{5}$$

where $\mathbf{A}$ represent the system evolution transformation, $\mathbf{Q}_k$ is the process noise covariance. The matrix $\mathbf{W}$ is the Jacobian of the transformation $\mathbf{A}$ with respect to $\mathbf{w}$. Finally, the measurement update equations become:

$$\mathbf{K}_k = \mathbf{P}_k^- \mathbf{H}_k^T (\mathbf{H}_k \mathbf{P}_k^- \mathbf{H}_k^T + \mathbf{V} \mathbf{R}_k \mathbf{V}^T)^{-1} \tag{6}$$
$$\hat{\mathbf{x}}_k = \hat{\mathbf{x}}_k^- + \mathbf{K}_k(\mathbf{z}_k - h(\hat{\mathbf{x}}_\mathbf{k}^-, 0)) \tag{7}$$
$$\mathbf{P}_k = (\mathbf{I} - \mathbf{K}_k \mathbf{H}_k)\mathbf{P}_k^-, \tag{8}$$

where $\mathbf{H}_k$ is the Jacobian of $h(\bullet)$ with respect to the estimate of $\mathbf{x}$ at time k:

$$\mathbf{H}_k = \begin{bmatrix} \frac{1}{\lambda} & 0 & 0 & 0 & -\frac{x_0}{\lambda^2} & 0 & 0 & 0 & 0 & 0 \\ 0 & \frac{1}{\lambda} & 0 & 0 & -\frac{y_0}{\lambda^2} & 0 & 0 & 0 & 0 & 0 \\ 0 & 0 & \frac{1}{\lambda} & 0 & -\frac{x_1}{\lambda^2} & 0 & 0 & 0 & 0 & 0 \\ 0 & 0 & 0 & \frac{1}{\lambda} & -\frac{y_1}{\lambda^2} & 0 & 0 & 0 & 0 & 0 \end{bmatrix}, \tag{9}$$

where $\lambda = 1 + z\beta$. The matrix $\mathbf{V}$ is the Jacobian of $h(\bullet)$ with respect to $\mathbf{v}$, and $\mathbf{R}_k$ is our measurement noise covariance at time k. In this formulation, the general assumptions are: $\mathbf{w}$ is a Gaussian random vector with $p(\mathbf{w}_k) \sim N(0, \mathbf{W}\mathbf{Q}_k\mathbf{W}^T)$, and $\mathbf{v}$ is also Gaussian $p(\mathbf{v}_k) \sim N(0, \mathbf{V}\mathbf{R}_k\mathbf{V}^T)$. For more detail, see [39,42].

Another problem is occlusion, a problem that cannot be ignored in the segmentation of multiple moving objects. Occlusion can occur when another object partially (or completely) obstructs a camera's view of the human; e.g., two people's paths cross in the image yielding a temporary occlusion of one person from that camera's viewpoint. Therefore, any general system must include algorithms that can reliably detect and maintain the tracking of moving objects before, during, and after an occlusion. Fortunately, given our EKF-based approach, occlusion time can be estimated using the EKF predictions and estimates of MBR's velocity and position.

3.1   Estimating Trajectories of Human Body Components

Estimation of trajectories of locomotion is one possible source of human motion databases. Trajectories of different components of the human body are also important in applications ranging from computer human interfaces to motion studies. Methods for automatic and robust detection, tracking, and interpretation of human body components and their motion in video under normal lighting conditions have been developed [4,5,20]. The goal is to reliably estimate the motion trajectories of, for example, a finger, foot, or facial feature in real-time and interpret them as a communication of the computer user.

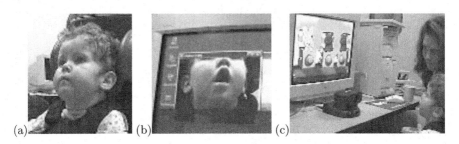

Fig. 2. (a) Thirty-month old *Camera-Mouse* user with cerebral palsy. (b) The vision system's view of the user. (c) The user playing with educational software (video camera is below the user computer's monitor).

One application of this approach is found in the "Camera Mouse" system [20], which has been developed to provide computer access for people with severe disabilities. The system tracks the computer user's movements with a video camera and translates them into the movements of the mouse pointer on the screen. Fig. 2 shows a thirty-month old user of the Camera Mouse system and her tracked face on the monitor of the vision computer. Here the vision algorithm is tracking her lower lip.

In Fig. 3 we show an example of three trajectories of mouse pointer movements that correspond to human facial movements tracked with Camera Mouse system. These trajectories were obtained from a non-handicapped user of the system. The Camera Mouse was used with a spelling program. The three trajectories were created when the computer user spelt out some words by moving the mouse pointer to an area on the screen that corresponds to a particular letter and selecting the letter ("clicking" the mouse) by lingering over the area for about a second. The figure represents the output of vision algorithms (data sets) used in evaluating preliminary versions of a data mining system.

4   Motion Mining

Given various types of human motion trajectories, our attention now returns to the issue of data mining. Many data mining tasks require a similarity model (or a distance function) for the objects stored in the database. The problem is non-trivial. Most of the current methods in the data mining community are based on mapping the time-series with n elements to a vector in an n-dimensional space.

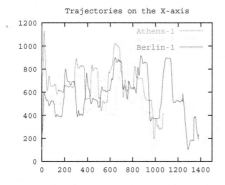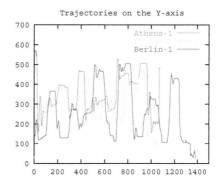

Fig. 3. Trajectories of mouse pointer movements that correspond to human facial movements tracked with Camera Mouse system. The motion on X and Y axis during the spelling of two words – Athens (twice) and Berlin (once) are shown.

They then use a p-norm distance function to define the similarity measure. As explained in Sec. 2, the p-norm is inadequate to deal with trajectories.

A general way to address these issues is to use the Longest Common Sub-Sequence ($LCSS$) model [6]. The basic idea is to try to match two sequences by allowing them to stretch without rearranging the sequence of values. The $LCSS$ is a variation of the Time Warping model [3,41], which has been proved very effective in other domains, for example in speech and gesture recognition, robotics, medicine, etc. In addition, the $LCSS$ model is more robust than time warping with respect to outliers. Next we present some simple similarity models and then we proceed with a discussion on how to use these model to index and cluster sets of trajectories. For this discussion, we assume that objects are points that move on the (x, y)-plane and time is discrete. However, our techniques are general and can be applied to objects moving in an n-dimensional space.

Let $A = ((a_{x,1}, a_{y,1}), \ldots, (a_{x,n}, a_{y,n}))$ and $B = ((b_{x,1}, b_{y,1}), \ldots, (b_{x,m}, b_{y,m}))$ be two trajectories of moving objects with size n and m respectively. For a trajectory A, let $Head(A) = ((a_{x,1}, a_{y,1}), \ldots, (a_{x,n-1}, a_{y,n-1}))$.

Definition 1. *Given an integer δ and a real number $0 < \epsilon < 1$, we define the $LCSS_{\delta,\epsilon}(A, B)$ as follows:*

$$
LCSS_{\delta,\epsilon}(A, B) = \begin{cases} 1 + LCSS_{\delta,\epsilon}(Head(A), Head(B)) & \text{if } |a_{x,n} - b_{x,m}| < \epsilon \text{ and} \\ & |a_{y,n} - b_{y,m}| < \epsilon \text{ and} \\ & |n - m| \leq \delta \\ \max(LCSS_{\delta,\epsilon}(Head(A), B), & \\ \quad LCSS_{\delta,\epsilon}(A, Head(B))) & \text{otherwise} \end{cases}
$$

The constant δ controls how far in time we can go in order to match a given point from one trajectory to a point in the another trajectory. The constant ϵ is the match threshold.

Definition 2. *We define the similarity function* $S1$ *between two trajectories* A *and* B, *given* δ *and* ϵ, *as follows:*

$$S1(\delta, \epsilon, A, B) = \frac{LCSS_{\delta, \epsilon}(A, B)}{\min(n, m)}$$

This first similarity function is based on the $LCSS$ and the idea is to allow time stretching. Then, objects that are close in space at different time instants can be matched if the time instants are also close.

We use this function to define two new similarity measures that are more suitable for trajectories. The first one is based on approximating the trajectory with a signature, which is similar to the Landmarks model [36]. Given a time period τ we compute the location of the object every τ time instants $(0, \tau, 2\tau$, etc.) Then, we approximate the trajectory with a piecewise-linear curve by connecting the consecutive points with a line segment. Next, we compute the direction of each line segment by projecting the segment on to the (x, y)-plane and find the angle of the segment with respect to the x-axis. If ϕ is the angle of a segment s and $i * \frac{2\pi}{k} \leq \phi < (i+1) * \frac{2\pi}{k}$, we replace the segment s with the value i. Doing the same for every segment, we get a sequence of symbols, one for each segment. Thus, we represent the trajectory of a moving object as a sequence of symbols. We only need $k+1$ symbols, one for each angle range and one more to represent static object. We call the above sequence the *motion signature* of the trajectory. An example of a motion signature for a trajectory is shown in Fig. 4. In the example k is equal to 4. Using the motion signatures we now define the similarity of two trajectories by computing the $LCSS$ of the signatures.

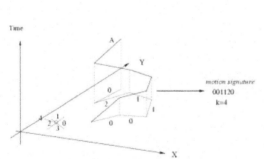

Fig. 4. Motion Signature of A.

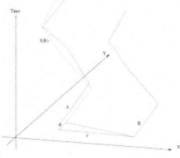

Fig. 5. Translation of Trajectory B.

Definition 3. *Let* A *and* B *be two trajectories with motion signatures* $A' = (a'_1, \ldots, a'_{n'})$ *and* $B' = (b'_1, \ldots, b'_{m'})$, *where* $a'_i, b'_j \in (0, \ldots, k)$. *Then, given an* *integer δ we define the similarity function S2 as follows:*

$$S2(\delta, A, B) = \frac{LCSS_\delta(A', B')}{\min(|A'|, |B'|)}$$

where,

$$LCSS_\delta(A', B') = \begin{cases} 1 + LCSS_\delta(Head(A'), Head(B')) & \text{if } a'_{n'} = b'_{m'} \text{ and} \\ & |n' - m'| \leq \delta \\ \max(LCSS_\delta(Head(A'), B'), \\ \quad LCSS_\delta(A', Head(B'))) & \text{otherwise} \end{cases}$$

Using the above method we can detect objects with similar movements even if these objects move in different locations and their movement is not synchronized. Another interesting point is that we can use only $log_2 k$ bits to represent each symbol and the signature is usually much smaller in size than the original trajectory. Therefore, the computation of the similarity is very efficient.

To create a more accurate measure, we define similarity based on exact trajectories. First, we consider the set of translations. A translation simply shifts a trajectory in space by a different constant in each dimension. Let $\mathcal{F}$ be the family of translations. Then a function $f_{c,d}$ belongs to $\mathcal{F}$ if $f_{c,d}(A) = ((a_{x,1} + c, a_{y,1} + d), \ldots, (a_{x,n} + c, a_{y,n} + d))$. Next, we define a second notion of the similarity based on the above family of functions.

Definition 4. *Given δ, ϵ and the family $\mathcal{F}$ of translations, we define the similarity function S3 between two trajectories A and B, as follows:*

$$S3(\delta, \epsilon, A, B) = \max_{f_{c,d} \in \mathcal{F}} S1(\delta, \epsilon, A, f_{c,d}(B))$$

By allowing translations, we can detect similarities between movements that are parallel in space, but not identical. In addition, the $LCSS$ model allows stretching and displacement in time, so we can detect similarities in movements that happen with different speeds, or at different times. In Fig. 5 we show an example where a trajectory B matches another trajectory A after a translation is applied. Note that the value of parameters c and d are also important since they give the distance of the trajectories in space. That can be a useful information when we analyze trajectory data.

To compute the similarity functions S1 and S2 we have to run a $LCSS$ computation to the two sequences. The $LCSS$ can be computed by a dynamic programming algorithm in $O(n^2)$ time. However, we only allow matchings when the difference in the indices is at most δ, and this allows the use of a faster algorithm. We can show that given two trajectories A and B, with $|A| = n$ and $|B| = m$, we can compute the S1 and S2 distances in $O(\delta(n + m))$ time. For the S3 distance we use an approximation algorithm that can find the distance between two trajectories A and B with error smaller than β in $O((m+n)\delta^3/\beta^2)$ time. Given trajectories A, B with lengths n, m respectively, and constants δ, β, ϵ, the approximation algorithm is as follows:

1. *Using the projections of A, B on the two axes, find the sets of all different translations on the x and y axis.*
2. *Find the $i\frac{\beta(n+m)}{2}$-th quantiles for each set, $1 \le i \le \frac{4\delta}{\beta}$.*
3. *Run the $LCSS_{\delta,\epsilon}$ algorithm on A and B, for each of the $(\frac{4\delta}{\beta})^2$ pairs of translations.*
4. *Return the highest result.*

4.1   Indexing Trajectories of Moving Objects

Given some distance measure, we need to design new index methods to store and retrieve trajectories of moving objects using this method. Indexing methods play a very important role in exploratory data mining, where the analyst makes hypotheses about the data and asks queries for validation. Considering the size of the datasets and the on-line nature of the analysis, a system with no indexing capabilities will be of limited use.

An important observation for the $S2$ distance measure is that for trajectories of equal size it is actually a metric (that is, the triangle inequality holds). A metric distance function is important for indexing, because we can prune a large part of the dataset during the query phase based on the triangle inequality. Therefore, our method is to divide first the different trajectories into groups of equal (or almost equal) length and then index each group separately. One approach is to use indexing methods for general metric spaces, e.g., the M-tree [13] or the vp-tree [45].

Another approach to index a set of trajectories is to embed them into a normed space $\mathcal{D}$ and try to keep the pairwise distances as close as possible to the original ones. Ideally, $\mathcal{D}$ will be a low dimensional Euclidean space $\Re^d$, where d is small. An interesting embedding method is presented in [32]. The basic idea is to select a set of subsets of S. Let X be a subset of S. Then we find the minimum distance of a given trajectory t to X, $D(t, X) = min_{x \in X} d(x, t)$. This number defines the coordinate of t for the dimension that corresponds to X. Using d number of subsets, $X_1, X_2, \ldots, X_d$, we map each trajectory $t \in S$ to a vector $[D(t, X_1), D(t, X_2), \ldots, D(t, X_d)]$. The distance between two vectors is defined using the l_1 or l_2 norm. However, the problem with this approach is that the distortion in the pairwise distances can be large and we may have many false negatives.

For the $S3$ distance, indexing is more challenging since this measure is not a metric. However, we can still use the embedding approach and get approximate answers. Another alternative is to cluster the set of trajectories and then use the clusters to answer nearest neighbor queries. That is, given the clusters and a query trajectory, find the clusters that have a representative point closer to the query trajectory and then report the trajectories in these clusters, possibly sorted by the distance to the query.

Another type of useful query is the *subsequence match query*, where we specify a part of a trajectory S_p and we ask the system to find the trajectories that have a similar subsequence. To solve this problem we can partition the original trajectories into smaller ones and we can index these subsequences.

4.2   Motion Clustering and Outlier Detection

A very important data mining task is to cluster set of objects in a large dataset. Therefore, it is important to design clustering methods for large sets of trajectories using various distance functions. The results of a clustering task can be used directly to characterize different groups of objects and summarize their main characteristics. The clusters will be used for re-training the classification and prediction algorithms in the Computer Vision sub-system. Also, hierarchical clustering algorithms can be used for indexing large datasets for similarity queries as we mentioned above.

One of the few methods to cluster trajectory data taking into account the special properties of trajectories has been proposed in [17]. They use a variation of the EM (expectation maximization) algorithm to cluster small sets of trajectories. A problem with this approach is its scalability. Also, the distance measure is based on the probabilistic model which may not be the most appropriate for some specific applications.

Another important task in a data mining system is to identify outliers. An outlier is an object that behaves in an unusual and unpredictable manner. Outlier mining has been used in fraud detection, by detecting unusual usage of credit cards or telecommunication services [10]. In our type of applications we are interested to find unusual or strange motion patterns. Actually, these patterns are sometimes more interesting for further analysis.

The first issue in outlier detection is to define what data is considered as an outlier for a given dataset. The statistical approach to define outliers is to assume that the distribution of the objects in the dataset follows a specific model and then try to identify objects that deviate from this model. Unfortunately, finding an appropriate model for datasets of trajectories is very difficult and usually real datasets do not follow general statistical models. Another definition of outliers uses a different approach that extends the distance based outlier definition by [29]. In particular, given a function that describes a distance between any two objects in the database, we say that an object O is a $DT(k, \xi)$ outlier, if there are at most k objects in the database the have a distance to O smaller than ξ. The challenge then is to find efficiently all the outliers, given some values for k and ξ. An alternative approach is to find the distance of each object to its k-th closest object and report a list of the objects ordered by this distance. Clearly, objects that are "far" from the others will appear first in the list.

5   Conclusion

We have described preliminary work towards a *motion mining* system for content-based retrieval and pattern discovery in video databases of human motion. The proposed methods are tailored to capture the spatio-temporal nature of human motion data. Two approaches to automatic estimation of human motion trajectories were described and tested. Since data mining requires a significant sample size to accurately model patterns in the data, algorithms that automatically extract motion trajectories and time series data from video are required. We defined trajectory representations that can be used in computing similarity between motion trajectories based on the LCSS method. This preliminary system enables ongoing and future work in the areas of spatio-temporal indexing, clustering, and outlier detection for large databases of human motion. A key issue in the immediate future will be evaluating the retrieval and mining methods on large video databases.

In future work, we plan to investigate alternative representations for trajectories. In particular, the use of a probabilistic model, e.g., Hidden Markov Models (HMMs) or Semi-Markov Models [18]), seems like a promising direction to pursue. However, in this case distance measures needed for indexing, mining, and retrieval are more difficult to compute in an efficient manner given current techniques. The embedding approaches described in Sec. 4.1 should prove quite useful in this regard.

Acknowledgments

This work was supported in part through US ONR Young Investigator Award N00014-96-1-0661, and NSF grants IIS-9624168 and EIA-9623865.

References

1. R. Agrawal, C. Faloutsos, and A. Swami. Efficient Similarity Search in Sequence Databases. *In Proc. of the 4th FODO*, pages 69–84, October 1993.
2. A. Azarbayejani and A. Pentland. Recursive estimation of motion, structure, and focal length. *IEEE Trans. on Pattern Analysis and Machine Intelligence (PAMI)*, 17(6), 1995.
3. D. Berndt and J. Clifford. Using Dynamic Time Warping to Find Patterns in Time Series. *In Proceedings of KDD Workshop*, 1994.
4. M. Betke and J. Kawai. Gaze detection via self-organizing gray-scale units. In *Proc. IEEE International Workshop on Recognition, Analysis, and Tracking of Faces and Gestures in Real-Time Systems*, 1999.
5. M. Betke, B. Mullally, and J. Magee. Active detection of eye scleras in real time. In *Proc. IEEE CVPR Workshop on Human Modeling, Analysis and Synthesis*, 2000.
6. B. Bollobas, G. Das, D. Gunopulos, and H. Mannila. Time-Series Similarity Problems and Well-Separated Geometric Sets. *In Proc of the 13th SCG, Nice, France*, 1997.
7. T. Bozkaya, N. Yazdani, and M. Ozsoyoglu. Matching and Indexing Sequences of Different Lengths. *In Proc.of the Intern. Conf. on Information and Knowledge Management, Las Vegas*, 1997.
8. K. Bradshaw, I. Reid, and D. Murray. The active recovery of 3D motion trajectories and their use in prediction. *IEEE Trans. on Pattern Analysis and Machine Intelligence (PAMI)*, 19(3), 1997.
9. T. Broida and R. Chellappa. Estimating the kinematics and structure of a rigid object from a sequence of monocular images. *IEEE Trans. on Pattern Analysis and Machine Intelligence (PAMI)*, 13(6):497-513, 1991.
10. M. Cahill, F. Chen, D. Lambert, J. Pinheiro, and Don Sun. *Detecting Fraud in the Real World*. Klewer, 2000.

11. S.F. Chang, W. Chen, J. Meng, H. Sundaram, and D. Zhong. A fully automated content based video search engine supporting spatio-temporal queries. *IEEE Trans. on Circuits and Systems for Video Technology*, 8(5), 1998.

12. K. Chu and M. Wong. Fast Time-Series Searching with Scaling and Shifting. *ACM Principles of Database Systems*, pages 237–248, June 1999.

13. P. Ciaccia, M. Patella, and P. Zezula. M-tree: An efficient access method for similarity search in metric spaces. In *In Proc. of the 23rd Conference on Very Large Data Bases, Athens, Greece*, pages 426–435, August 1997.

14. C. Faloutsos, H.V. Jagadish, A. Mendelzon, and T. Milo. Signature technique for similarity-based queries. *In SEQUENCES 97*, 1997.

15. C. Faloutsos and K.-I. Lin. FastMap: A fast algorithm for indexing, data-mining and visualization of traditional and multimedia datasets. *In Proc. ACM SIGMOD*, pages 163–174, May 1995.

16. C. Faloutsos, M. Ranganathan, and I. Manolopoulos. Fast Subsequence Matching in Time Series Databases. *In Proceedings of ACM SIGMOD*, pages 419–429, May 1994.

17. S. Gaffney and P. Smyth. Trajectory Clustering with Mixtures of Regression Models. *In Proc. of the 5th ACM SIGKDD, San Diego, CA*, pages 63–72, August 1999.

18. X. Ge and P. Smyth. Deformable Markov model templates for time-series pattern matching. *In Proc ACM SIGKDD*, 2000.

19. A. Gionis, P. Indyk, and R. Motwani. Similarity search in high dimensions via hashing. *In Proc. of 25th VLDB*, pages 518–529, 1999.

20. J. Gips, M. Betke, and P. Fleming. The camera mouse: Preliminary investigation of automated visual tracking for computer access. In *Annual Conf. of the Rehabilitation Eng. and Assistive Tech. Soc. of North America (RESNA)*, July 2000.

21. D. Goldin and P. Kanellakis. On Similarity Queries for Time-Series Data. *In Proceedings of CP'95, Cassis, France*, September 1995.

22. J. Hodgins. Digital Muybridge: A Repository for Human Motion Data. http://www.interact.nsf.gov/cise/abst.nsf/awards/0079060, May 2000.

23. L. Davis I. Haritaouglu, D. Harwood. W4s: A realtime system for detecting and tracking people in 2.5d. In *Proceedings of Third European Conference on Computer Vision*, 1998.

24. S. Intille and A. F. Bobick. Real time close world tracking. In *Proc. IEEE Conf. on Computer Vision and Pattern Recognition (CVPR)*, 1997.

25. H. V. Jagadish, Alberto O. Mendelzon, and Tova Milo. Similarity-based queries. *In Proc. of the 14th ACM PODS*, pages 36–45, May 1995.

26. T. Kahveci and A. K. Singh. Variable length queries for time series data. In *Proc. of IEEE ICDE*, pages 273–282, 2001.

27. E. Keogh, K. Chakrabarti, S. Mehrotra, and M. Pazzani. Locally adaptive dimensionality reduction for indexing large time series databases. In *Proc. of ACM SIGMOD*, pages 151–162, 2001.

28. E. Keogh and M. Pazzani. Scaling up Dynamic Time Warping for Datamining Applications. *In Proc. 6th Int. Conf. on Knowledge Discovery and Data Mining, Boston, MA*, 2000.

29. E. Knorr and R. Ng. Algorithms for Mining Distance Based Outliers in Large Databases. *In Proceedings of VLDB, New York*, pages 392–403, August 1998.

30. G. Kollios, S. Sclaroff, and M. Betke. Motion mining: Discovering spatio-temporal patterns in databases of human motion. In *ACM SIGMOD Workshop on Research Issues in Data Mining and Knowledge Discovery*, May 2001.

31. S.-L. Lee, S.-J. Chun, D.-H. Kim, J.-H. Lee, and C.-W. Chung. Similarity Search for Multidimensional Data Sequences. *In Proceedings of ICDE*, pages 599–608, 2000.

32. N. Linial, E. London, and Y. Rabinovich. The geometry of graphs and some of its algorithmic applications. In *In Proc. of the 35th IEEE FOCS*, pages 577–591, 1994.

33. C. Neidle, S. Sclaroff, and V. Athitsos. Signstream: A tool for linguistic and computer vision research on visual-gestural language data. *Behavior Research Methods, Instruments and Computers*, (to appear).

34. S. Park, W. Chu, J. Yoon, and C. Hsu. Efficient Searches for Similar Subsequences of Different Lengths in Sequence Databases. *In Proceedings of ICDE*, pages 23–32, 2000.

35. W. Park, X. Zhang, C.B. Woolley, J. Foulke, U. Raschke, and D.B. Chaffin. Integration of magnetic and optical motion tracking devices for capturing human motion data. In *Proc. SAE Human Modeling for Design and Engineering Conference*, 1999.

36. S. Perng, H. Wang, S. Zhang, and D. S. Parker. Landmarks: A New Model for Similarity-based Pattern Querying in Time Series Databases. *In Proceedings of ICDE*, pages 33–42, 2000.

37. D. Rafiei and A. Mendelzon. Querying Time Series Data Based on Similarity. *IEEE Transactions on Knowledge and Data Engineering, Vol. 12, No 5.*, pages 675–693, 2000.

38. D. Reynard, A. Wildenberg, A. Blake, and J. Marchant. Learning dynamics of complex motions from image sequences. In *Proceedings of Third European Conference on Computer Vision*, 1996.

39. R. Rosales and S. Sclaroff. Improved tracking of multiple humans with trajectory prediction and occlusion modeling. In *Proc. IEEE Workshop on the Interpretation of Visual Motion*, June 1998.

40. R. Rosales and S. Sclaroff. Specialized mappings and the estimation of body pose from a single image. In *IEEE Human Motion Workshop. Austin, TX*, 2000.

41. H. Sakoe and S. Chiba. Dynamic programming algorithm optimization for spoken word recognition. *IEEE Trans. Acoustics, Speech and Signal Processing*, ASSP-26(1):43–49, February 1978.

42. H.W. Sorenson. Least-Squares Estimation: From Gauss to Kalman. *IEEE Spectrum*, Vol. 7, pp. 63-68, 1970.

43. C. Stauffer and W.E.L. Grimson. Adaptive background mixture models for real-time tracking. In *Proc. IEEE Conf. on Computer Vision and Pattern Recognition (CVPR)*, 1999.

44. R. Szeliski and S. Bing Kang. Recovering 3D shape and motion from image streams using non-linear least squares. In *Proc. IEEE Conf. on Computer Vision and Pattern Recognition (CVPR)*, 1993.

45. J. Uhlmann. Satisfying general proximity / similarity queries with metric trees. *IPL: Information Processing Letters*, 40:175–179, 1991.

46. X. Wang and A.R. Hanson. Parking lot analysis/ visualization using multiple aerial images. In *Workshop on Applications of Computer Vision*, page Session 1B, 1998.

47. C. Wren, A. Azarbayejani, T. Darrell, and A. Pentland. Pfinder: Real time tracking of the human body. *IEEE Trans. on Pattern Analysis and Machine Intelligence (PAMI)*, 19(7):780-785, 1997.

48. B.-K. Yi and C. Faloutsos. Fast Time Sequence Indexing for Arbitrary Lp Norms. *In Proceedings of VLDB, Cairo Egypt*, September 2000.

Part II

Image and Visual Computing Applications

The Riddles of Murecine: The Role of Anthropological Research by Images and Visual Computing

Andrea F. Abate[1], Giuseppe Sasso[2], Anthony C. Donadio[3], and Francesco S. Sasso[3]

[1] Dipartimento di Matematica e Informatica, Università di Salerno, 84081 Baronissi, Italy
abate@unisa.it
[2] S.G.C. Diagnostic Imaging and Radiotherapy Centre
viale Cavalleggeri d'Aosta 26, 80124 Naples, Italy
giuseppe.sasso@ieo.it
giuseppesasso@tiscalinet.it
[3] Second University of Naples, Diagnostic Imaging, Emergency Radiology and
Radiotherapy Department, piazza Luigi Miraglia 2, 80138 Naples, Italy
francescos.sasso@unina2.it

Abstract. This paper shows the use of a visual environment for retrieval of images on the basis of similarity in the context of anthropological research. The aim of the project is to correlate physiognomic data to craniological data through faces represented in artistic work found in Pompei and faces of actual inhabitants of the same area.

1 Introduction

The discovery of ancient humans features, habits of life and health status is one of the most exciting historical riddle. Life at the time of Pompei continues by our studies, and the ancient inhabitants are still alive through the images and the findings of modern excavations.

A great interest was reserved to the anthropological aspect of the inhabitants, and several studies by physiognomists, craniometrists, cephaloscopists and others were based on the findings promptly collected in the Royal Borbonic Museum. Since then many new victims of the plinian eruption were discovered but only last year on the right side of Sarno river an archeological site was object of study by the most advanced techniques of archaeopathological analysis: the site of Murecine.

1.1 Historical Overview

Poli (1829) asserts that through Vesuvius in 79 b. C. and after Borbonic Kingdom preservation of excavations of Ercolano and Pompei, an archaeological heritage was obtained, saved from collectionism.

In 1853 Stefano delle Chiaie confirms that thanks to the decision of Carlo III to note down all the human findings since the beginning of the archaeological adventure in Pompei and Ercolano, a great improvement was furnished to the history of these cities and to description presented by anatomists.

M. Tucci (Ed.): MDIC 2001, LNCS 2184, pp. 33–41, 2001.

Under researchers' solicitation and through Mons. Apuzzo, President of the General Council of Public Education of Borbonic State, with a Royal Note on April 17th 1851, the King decided that first bones unearthed were brought to the Anatomic Museum of Royal University of Naples; these were 60 persons unearthed before 1853 and 20 persons in the same year; among these, 27 persons in Pompei and 1 in Ercolano were holding objects. Stefano delle Chiaie began an organic study on these findings and recognized three types of skull morphology: globose, ovoidal and oblong, that he related with different races, referring to the well-known presence of slaves. On morphological data he stated that 30% of subjects presented characteristics of intertropical populations, of Africa and Middle East, with a major antero-posterior diameter of these skulls.

Wounds: an example of the lesions related to wars is furnished by classical studies of paleopathologists, based on literary documents of Ancient Greek. Particularly were observed 147 wounds due to: stones, sword, lance, arrows; head wounds were always mortal, even if the warrior had a helmet; 13 out of 16 neck wounds were mortal; 67 out of 79 trunk wounds; 2 out 10 upper limb and 1 out of 11 lower limb wounds were mortal. It seems that no sword injured survived.

1.2   Purpose of the Study

A series of bones (skulls) from Pompei were brought in 1851 by Mons. Apuzzo in the Anatomical Museum of the University, founded by the Minister Marchese Santangelo, and actually patrimony of the Second University of Naples (SUN); Pompeian skulls were studied by Stefano delle Chiaie, which reported his data on September 15th 1853. A research group of the University is actually studying these skulls with *digital* radio-diagnostic methodologies to evaluate possible pathologies, together with a study of ancient DNA and the possibility to obtain the physiognomy; this research program was possible thanks to SUN contribution. Recently 5 skulls and several bones of 16 (sixteen) humans, most of them child or teenagers, were found at the so-called "Grand Hotel Murecine", already known since 1959 but since one year is a site of excavation. After these news our group asked and obtained from the Sopraintendenza Archeologica of Pompei the assignment of these findings to obtain craniometric, digital radio-diagnostic and bio-molecular studies in collaboration with the research group guided by prof. Antonio De Simone from the Historical Disciplines Department of the "Federico II" University of Naples. The findings were collected by the researchers in the excavation of Murecine, in a flooded field. These were immediately isolated in proper containers and transferred in a cold chamber to preserve their microenvironment. For microbiological and ancient DNA (aDNA) study, and for radio-diagnostic evaluation, adhesive material of a skull was extracted with several withdrawals for its culture or for the culture of the material inside accessible bony cavities and of two teeth of superior arch for extraction of aDNA undergoing amplification with PCR. One of the skulls, probably of a 40 years old man, was utilized for three-dimensional CT and virtual endoscopy reconstruction. This very recent technique allows to follow a route inside human body cavities, after acquisition of digital images of close sections, usually with CT; with actual reconstruction algorithms these endoscopic visions are easily obtained through rapid computerized system capable to evaluate extensive database of digital images; the operator chooses the virtual route that wants to follow and his observation passes through the edge of the selected cavity. Generally to furnish indices to images and consequently easily handle them in the management of database we associate two types of descriptors, the first based on explicit information of image content and the second based on implicit information correlated to spatial relation of its "pictorial" elements, of their morphology and geometrical measures among image elements. So "pictorial indices " can be utilized, giving an index to icons.

With a Query by Pictorial Example approach (Q-PE) image index is an iconic image representing visual information contained in primary image, suitable to the several levels of abstraction and to the contest of its management .A database system must integrate an image management technique to uniformly comply with the capacities of the database model, also with spatial indices methodology; moreover it must furnish a video interface easy to use to let the operators a facilitated management of images through a visual selection that easily sails in the database. We realized such a system in collaboration with the informatics research group directed by professors Tortora and Tucci from the Salerno University and permits imaging manipulation in an extensive database with approximate research through imaging content. This is a visual environment integrated to load digitalized images, to process them to extract acceptable spatial indices, to easily save and recall them, with visual interface. The system applies an index-images methodology by virtual images that allows access on informative contents and imaging recall on the basis of similarity. To realize an effective and efficacious database system the device includes 4 basic processes in an integrated graphic environment:

1. Extraction of imaging characteristics by processing (profile remark and segmentation)
2. Representation of imaging content and indices.
3. Loading and recall methodologies: for efficient imaging spatial access by a process of identification or exclusion.
4. Easy to manage interface (graphic environments, language through visual question, etc.)

To obtain an efficient imaging access is important to have a Spatial Access Method (SAM) that organizes several imaging descriptions in a data structure allowing a faster research than sequential traditional research: the data structure of our system is based on "k-d-trees". The systems needs of homogeneity elements in relation to approximately "equal" contents and this seems possible because we are interested in anatomical aspects. Databases of craniometric tracing and their physiognomic features allow "ideal" reconstructions with reference to the actual individuals database with craniometric characters "equal or similar to" those of skulls of the victims examined. Comparison of actual thickness of soft tissues of face and skull in database of several CT exams will represent a further evaluation element for the "reconstruction" of physiognomic features of individuals whose skulls are studied, in comparison with artistic –scientific technique of Manchester. A valid collection of physiognomies in classical arts contemporary to eruption can be valid for comparison of physiognomic reconstruction.

Scenes and subjects related to mythological or heroic figures, but characterized as national "native types" correlated physiognomic data to craniologic data, through faces represented in artistic work found in Pompei: Nicolucci believes that local models and subjects inspired artists and supposes that the "Pompeian type" portrays a common "faces" similar to those still visible in Pompei, Torre Annunziata, Scafati, Angri, Bosco Reale (all sites are close to Murecine).

2   Materials and Methods

2.1   State of the Art

The past 20 years have seen tremendous changes in imaging techniques: new modalities and protocols are rapidly expanding the available digital image data. Advances in imaging techniques have been mirrored by advances in the use of computers to extract and interpret image data: helping researchers to make effective use of this superabundance of information is a key aim of scientific software research. Yet a framework for gathering, managing, and using different archives of images and related information in integrated database environment is missing.

Inexpensive, convenient database to store digital radiological and photographic images of multiple formats or creating teaching files from it, are available [1,2]. These systems still need to be customized to the user to optimize its use in special medical application such as: image processing, compression and display; picture archiving and communication systems, computer-aided reconstruction and comparison.

Goal of our project is to develop multi-archives database environmental system for query-retry comparison between different image modalities on the basis of their hierarchical similarity.

2.2   The Project

Lack of supporting infrastructure and inability to index images by contest are the main immediate issues affecting the building of image database systems. An effective and efficient image database system should include some fundamental issues in an integrated graphical environment. These are: image content representation and indexing, storage and retrieval methodologies for efficient spatial access to images by exact and/or inexact match, and last nor least, user friendly interface (graphical environments, visual query languages, etc.).

In many database applications the usefulness and understandability of a system is considerably enhanced if the information is represented in multimedia forms, such as images (photo and radiographic), audio and video annotations [3]. This is especially true for applications where multimedia objects naturally play a central role. In particular, the usability of a large image database system can be considerably improved if non-expert users are provided with an intuitive and simple visual interface that allows them to manipulate the images easily. Moreover, several applications of image databases require content-based access, but a raster image is too complex and too large to be suitably described by traditional indexing methods, based on user-supplied alphanumeric descriptors. Indeed, PACS (Picture Archiving and Communication System) have become a basic research topic in computer science due to need of new techniques developed to provide quickly delivery and easy access to images, video, text and associated information, using appropriate representations for the intended tasks [4,5].

To index an image we can associate it with two kinds of descriptors: explicit information about its contents (in textual form), and implicit information related to the spatial arrangement of its pictorial elements and their morphological and geometrical measures. Then picture icons can be used as picture indexes, following an iconic indexing methodology [6,7,8,9]. With this Query-by-Pictorial-Example approach [10,11], the index of an image is an iconic image itself, which represents the visual information contained in the image in a suitable form for different levels of abstraction and management. An image database system should then integrate an image management technique to access information uniformly and consistently according to a powerful database model, and a spatial image indexing methodology that allows efficient content-based access. It should also offer a user-friendly visual interface to help users in storing and retrieving images by means of a visual browser that easily navigates the database. The proposed system consists of an integrated visual environment for loading digitized images from different archives, processing them to extract suitable spatial indexes, and storing and retrieving such images easily thanks to a user-friendly visual interface. The system applies an image indexing methodology, based on *virtual images* [12], that provides content-based access and similarity retrieval in a very efficient and reliable way.

A user-friendly visual interface lets users issue store–retrieve commands by simply editing real and iconic images by means of a palette of image processing tools and a palette of graphical objects. To achieve an efficient access to images, it is important to have a Spatial Access Method (SAM) that organizes large collections of image descriptions in a data structure that allows faster searching than sequential. The data structure used to manage the index for images is based on k-d trees [13,14].

2.3   System's Characteristics

The system is an experimental environment for the management of images with content-based access. It is based on the system called IME (Image Management Environment) [15]. It supports any application domain where the spatial relationships among objects are the primary keys to index the images. To achieve user-friendliness, it incorporates a visual interface that merges the query-by-pictorial-example and query-by-sketch paradigms. The user interface was conceived as a typical Windows application. In particular, for a given image a physician has to identify common characteristic, consider their spatial relationships, and evaluate their morphological and geometrical features; in other words, a scientist has to evaluate the semantic contents of the image based on his/her personal knowledge to formulate a similarity criteria. The personal knowledge of a scientist is typically based on remembering similar features of previously examined images. In order to obtain a similarity match he has to perform three complex operations:

1. import and define the images object of the study (identifying the hot spots);
2. retrieve related images by similarity from his/her mnemonic database (experience) or from a very large archive of images;
3. formulate similarity criteria.

Therefore, it would be helpful for him/her to have more support in accessing images and related data of cases with similar characteristics (normal features and abnormalities).

Unlike alphanumeric text, medical images usually require a long time to be accessed, processed, stored, retrieved and distributed, because of their size and internal complexity. Thus, an electronic database should meet the requirement of effectively handling the above time-consuming operations. [16]

The image processing tools integrated in the system allow hot spots and canonical objects extraction by means of an entropy based method for segmentation and edge detection [17], applying a such method archeological images of human skulls.

Before storing the image in the database, it must be processed to extract the key features to be used for indexing. In this phase the visual interaction with the physician is particularly useful to assign the correct meaning to the patterns in the image and to select the significant ones.

As previously stated, records of alphanumeric descriptors are automatically extracted from the image, such as spatial relationships, morphological and geometrical measures of each hot spot. When considering an image, a scientist may want to retrieve some similar images from the available archives in database and compare them to the first one in order to be supported assess the physiognomic similarity based reconstruction. Therefore, he first asks for edge detection from the image, and then selects the objects by which he wants to formulate a query. All the images in the database with a similar features or abnormality approximately in the same relation and position will be retrieved.

The system was tested at the Second University of Naples on a database with a large number of lung CT scan images (chosen from digital archives of Diagnostic Imaging, Emergency Radiology and Radiotherapy Department and S.G.C. Diagnostic Imaging and Radiotherapy Centre), finding it sensible and specific. It should be noted that such a set of images are relative to the same human body district (chest), and then all contain approximately the same objects in the same positions. The only relevant difference between two images is related to the presence or absence of a similar abnormality, owing to several possible lung pathologies.

Frequently used evaluation criteria to measure effectiveness of retrieval system are the *recall* and the *precision*: the *recall* is the capability of system to retrieve all relevant images; the *precision* is the capability of system to retrieve only relevant images. We have chosen an extension of the former, namely the *Normalized Recall* (NR), introduced in to assess the performances of IME. [18]

Normalized Recall (NR) ranges from 1 for the best case (perfect retrieval) to 0 for the worst case.

3   Discussion

3.1   Comparison Literature Data

The palaeopathological observation of Stefano delle Chiaie on skull is a frequent hypertrophic thickening in the frontal area, but also in the parietal and occipital areas with deep vascular grooves and wide vascular foramina at the base; also in mastoid cells was noted down the presence of "limestone molecules". Caries and their complication were noted down during archaeopathological research: particularly caries of a tooth at the right hemimaxilla complicated by the involvement of the maxillary sinus and destruction of the external profile of the alveolar process. Giustiniano Nicolucci described Pompeian skulls in an edition red at the Reale Accademia delle Scienze Fisiche e Matematiche (Royal Academy of Physic and Mathematics Sciences), on January 14th 1882. His study was carried out on 600 skeletons. He states, referring to the relation of engineer Michele Ruggiero, that dead found in an enclosed space showed scattered bones among various materials, while dead found in an open space were into a print formed by their bodies covered by ashes and lapilli. Nicolucci studied ethnic groups present in Pompei at the moment of eruption, as the Osci, of the Etruschi there are no certain data, and the Greeks, that are hypothesized by Nicolucci, even if he didn't find their morphological characteristics; he studied 100 skulls, 55 male and 45 female, mainly 60-90 years old, based on the state of teeth and sutures. 11% presented medio-frontal suture (metopic) (5 males and 6 females) versus an ordinary frequency of 7% in Italian population with a major width between orbits and with a wider forehead. Volume of skull cavity in male metopics is above average. Metopism is more common among European races. Skulls are dolicocephalic in 14%, mesaticephalic in 43% and brachicephalic in 43%, with a prevalence of dolicocephalic among men (18.18%); brachicephaly is more common in female skulls (46.67%); morphology is defined by Nicolucci as almost similar to the Pompeian or Osco-Campano type. This population is characterized by an oval shape; anteriorly there are well-developed frontal protuberances, while skullcap is gently rounded till occiput, similar to a hemicircumference. On a plane without mandible the skull insists either upon occiput or teeth of upper arch. Forehead is curved posteriorly, as the entire skull profile. Occipital spine is prominent. Anteriorly skullcap profile is almost ogival (the author thinks this pattern is common to osco-sannitic skulls); frontal sinuses are not well developed. Frontal malar apophyses are prominent with deep temporal hollows and rounded orbits. Nasal opening presents a narrow root; zygoma are not well developed without extending anteriorly beyond the lateral orbital profile. Superior teeth arch is almost semicircular. The chin is prominent, with a moderately developed mandible with a parabolic lower profile, defining a slightly oval face.

3.2   Preliminary Observations

Radiological study with digital technology by CT of the skull from Murecine revealed an opaque stratification of sinusal cavities, leveled in a similar pattern in all cavities.

In lower portion of left maxillary sinus the leveled opacity seems remarkable, with a pseudo-level image more elevated than right maxillary sinus. There is the persistence of radicular residuals of the fifth and sixth left superior and a periapico-radicular cavity of the left fifth superior; it is present a wide periapicoradicular cavity of sixth left superior connected to left maxillary sinus, due to extension of inflammation and infection to the bone and the sinus. It could be supposed the presence of opacities in the sinusal cavities of this subject, even if "sediment", comparing other Pompeian skulls.

We examined the skull of similar age from the collection of the Museo di Anatomia (Anatomic Museum) of SUN and finding dense material in maxillary sinusal cavities, especially on the left side, where we observe a small hyperdense particle. Probably this skull of Museum was not immersed in water like the one of Murecine, but both contain in maxillary sinusal cavities something "powdery". We must remember the description of Plinio il Giovane about the death of his uncle, Plinio il Vecchio and about "the atmosphere full of ashes obstructing the throat, that used to be always swelling and inflamed". We suppose that powdery materials were inhaled, especially fine ashes and we begun analysis of material radiological evident in sinusal cavities of skulls from Murecine and the collection of the Anatomic Museum of the Second University of Naples. In the Pompeian skull from the Anatomic Museum of the Second University of Naples is evident the difference between maxillary sinuses of the two sides: on the right side there is a lesser quantity of material, probably due to an inflammation of the cavity, but this point must still be confirmed by further studies. The skull found in Murecine showed a deep and brief cut on external diploe at the right lateral frontal level, probably due to a sharp arm; on digital radiographic study with CT this lesion appears completely healed by reparative bony gathering: was he a warrior? In this skull was present the metopic suture. Studies must include radiography on standard planes with "telecranic technique"; another possibility for craniometric data (points, lines, angles, distances) is represented by CT with thin slices and 3D reconstruction with a dedicated program, elaboration of volumetric images and "virtual" endoscopy.

4   Conclusion

The use of a visual environment for retrieval of images was very helpful. The possibility to connect various (visual) databases and to obtain different kind of images as response of a query speeded up the research. In adjunct we are interested in discovery the Pompeian faces. Nicolucci indicates the necessity to correlate physiognomic data to craniologic data through faces represented in artistic work found in Pompei: they show scenes and subjects related to mythological or heroic figures, but characterized as national "native types". He believes that local models and subjects inspired artists, supposing that the "Pompeian type" portrays a common "face" similar to those still visible in Pompei, Torre Annunziata, Scafati, Angri, Bosco Reale.

We are in contact with the authorities to extend the study to the plaster "mould" of eruption victims (moulds of Fiorelli): these moulds probably contain skeleton parts integrated into a real surface profile. Analyzing in the same subject both the profile of plaster mould and the skull image obtained by CT acquisition (with thin slices correlated to an "individual" reconstruction), will give us a chance to confirm with a "direct" validation the process of face reconstruction in relation to craniometry. Moreover, a valid collection of physiognomies in classical arts contemporary to eruption can be valid for comparison of physiognomic reconstruction, excluding the representation of members of imperial family or other important personalities because their features were usually idealized.

References

1. Tran THD, Roach NA, O'Kane PL and Thune M. Creating a Digital Radiographic Teaching File and Database Using a PC and Common Software. AJR 2000; 175:325-327.
2. Maldjian JA and Listerud J. Automated Teaching File and Slide Database for Digital Images. AJR 2000; 175:1249-1251.
3. Sinha U, Dai B, Johnson DB, Taira R, Dionisio J, Tashima G, Golamco M and Kangarloo H. Interactive software for generation and visualization of structured findings in radiology reports. AJR 2000; 175:609-612.
4. Narasimhalu AD. Multimedia databases. Multimedia Systems 1996; 4:226–249.
5. Schnep A, Du DHC, Ritenour ER. Building future medical education environment over ATM networks. Communications of the ACM. 1995; 38(2):54–69.
6. Chang SK, Shi QY, Yan CW. Iconic indexing by 2-D string, IEEE Trans. Pattern Anal. Machine Intell. 1987; 9(3):413–428.
7. Chang SK, Yan CW, Dimitroff DC, Arndt T. An intelligent image database system. IEEE Trans. Software Engineering. 1988; 14:681–688.
8. Lee SY, Hsu FJ. 2D C-string: a new spatial knowledge representation for image database systems. Pattern Recognition. 1990; 23:1077–1087.
9. Tanimoto L. An iconic symbolic data structuring scheme, in: Pattern Recognition and Artificial Intelligence. Academic Press, New York, 1976; 452–471.
10. Chang SK, Hou TY, Hsu A. Smart image design for large image database, Journal of Visual Languages and Computing. 1992; 3:323–342.
11. Chang SK, Hsu A. Image information systems: where do we go from here? IEEE Transaction on Knowledge and Data Engineering. 1992; 4(5):431–442.
12. Petraglia G, Sebillo M, Tucci M, Tortora G. A normalized index for image databases, in: Chang SK, Jungert E, Tortora G (Eds.), Intelligent Image Database   Systems, World Scientific Publishing, Singapore. 1996; 43–69.
13. Bentley L, Friedman JH. Data structures for range searching. ACM Computing Survey. 1979; 11(4):397–409.
14. Ullman JD. Principles of Database and Knowledge-based Systems. Computer Science Press, Rockville, Maryland, USA, 1988.
15. Abate A.F., Nappi M., Tortora G. and Tucci M., "IME: An Image Management Environment with Content-based Access", Image and Vision Computing, 17 (1999) 967–980, Elsevier Science.
16. Jungert E, Chang SK. An image algebra for pictorial data manipulation. CVGIP: Image Understanding. 1993; 58(2):147–160.
17. Di Ruberto C, Nappi M, Vitulano S. Different methods to segment biomedical images. Pattern Recognition Letters. 1998; 18(11/13):1125–1131.
18. Salton G, McGill MJ. Introduction to Modern Information Retrieval. McGraw Hill, 1983.

Information Retrieval from Medical Database

Angelo Balestrieri[2], Antonella Balestrieri[2], Aristide Barone[1],
Andrea Casanova[2] and Matteo Fraschini[2]

[1] Dipartimento di Radiologia, Seconda Università di Napoli
P.za L. Miraglia 2, 80124 Napoli, Italia
[2] Dipartimento di Scienze Mediche Internistiche, Università di Cagliari
via San Giorgio 12, 09100 Cagliari, Italia
casanova@unica.it

Abstract. Digital images are a convenient media for describing and storing
spatial, temporal, spectral, and physical components of information contained in
a variety of domains (e.g. aerial/satellite images in remote sensing, medical
images, etc.). In the paper we address the problem of efficiently and accurately
retrieving images from a medical database purely based on shape analysis. The
detection of mass lesions on mammograms can be a difficult task for human
observers or machines. The potential variability and heterogeneity of normal
breast tissue often produces a number of localized findings that may simulate
mass lesions or, depending on the observer, create distractions, during the
search process. The tool we'll test in this paper represents contours and textures
by a vector containing the location and the energy of the signal maxima. The
main contribute of this work shows how the method works as information
retrieval from image dataset and also as Cad system.

1   Introduction

In the U.S. invasive breast cancer is diagnosed in more than 180.000 women each
year, and over 40.000 deaths of this disease annually. If these tumours can be
identified while confined to the breast, then breast cancer usually can be cured by
means of local treatment. It is distant metastatic disease, and the destruction of other
organ systems, that cause death in women with breast cancer [1]. Indeed, the results
of randomized controlled trials of screening [2, 3] have demonstrated that if breast
cancer can be detected and treated before becoming metastatic, death due to breast
cancer can be avoided.

Over the last decade or so, many investigators have carried out basic studies and
clinical applications toward the development of modern computerized schemes for
detection and characterization of lesion in radiologic images, based on computer
vision and artificial intelligence. These methods and techniques are generally called
computer-aided diagnosis (CAD) schemes.

The development of CAD has now reached a new phase, since the first commercial
unit for detection of breast lesions in mammograms was approved in June 1998, by
the Food and Drug Administration (FDA) for marketing and sale for clinical use in
the United States.

M. Tucci (Ed.): MDIC 2001, LNCS 2184, pp. 42-52, 2001.
© Springer-Verlag Berlin Heidelberg 2001

CAD may be defined as a diagnosis made by a physician who takes into account the results of the computer output as a 'second opinion' [4, 5]. In radiology, the computer output is derived from quantitative analysis of diagnostic images. It is important to notice that the computer is used only as a tool to provide additional information to clinicians, who will take the final decision as to the diagnosis of a patient. Therefore, the basic concept of CAD is clearly different from that of 'automated diagnosis', which had been investigated in the 1960s and 1970s.

The purpose of CAD in radiology is to improve the diagnostic accuracy as well as the consistency of radiologist's image interpretation by using the computer output as a guide. The computer output can be very helpful because a radiologist's diagnosis is made on subjective judgement and because radiologist tend to miss lesions such as lung nodules in chest radiographs, and micro calcifications and masses in mammograms. More over, variations in diagnosis, such as inter-observer and intra-observer variations, can be large.

M. P. Rosen in his paper [6] compares the diagnosis, of two different groups of radiologists, on 80 patients, where the first group has the 87.3% and the second one the 82.8% of certainty.

Usually, two types of general approaches are employed in computerized schemes for CAD. One is to find the location of lesions such as lung nodules in chest images by searching for isolated abnormal patterns with a computer. Another is to quantify the image features of normal and/or abnormal patterns, such as lung texture.

Computerized schemes for CAD generally include three basic components which are based on three different technologies. The first component is image processing for enhancement and extraction of lesions. It is important to notice that the image processing involved in CAD schemes is aimed to facilitate the computer, rather than the human observer, to pick up the initial candidates of lesions and suspicious patterns. Various image-processing techniques have been employed for different types of lesions. Some of the commonly used techniques include filtering based on Fourier analysis, wavelet transformation, morphological filtering, different image technique, and artificial neural networks.

The second component is the quantization of image features such as the size, contrast, and shape of the candidates selected in the first step. It is possible to define numerous features based on some mathematical formulas that may not be easily understood by the human observer. However, it is generally useful to define, at least in the initial phase of CAD development, image features that have already been recognized and described subjectively by radiologists. This is because radiologist' knowledge is based on their observation of numerous cases over the years, and their diagnostic accuracy is generally very high and reliable. One of the most important factors in the development of CAD schemes is to find unique features that can distinguish reliably between a lesion and other, normal anatomic structures.

The third component is data processing for distinction between normal and abnormal patterns, based on the features obtained in the second step. A simple and common approach employed in this step is a rule-based method, which may be based on the understanding of lesion and other normal patterns. Therefore, it is important to notice the rule-based method may provide useful information for improving the CAD schemes.

The main aim of the present paper is to utilize, as CAD scheme, a new image indexing system, which can deal with both contour and texture information in a homogeneous way. The method is based on a hierarchical entropy-based representation (HER) [8], which transforms 2-d visual signals such as contour and texture into a 1-d representation.

The structure of the paper is as follows. Section 2, Related works, compares the most used CAD systems. Section 3 explains how an intrinsically 2-d signal can be turned into a 1-d time series and then illustrates our tool and the hierarchical signal representation it is founded upon. The experimental results are presented and discussed in section 4, and a few remarks finally conclude the paper in section 5.

2   Related Works

Computer-aide analysis for digital mammograms is widely reputed as a remarkable goal, and several methods have been proposed in literature.

Zheng in his paper [9] compares two independent CAD schemes for mass detection in digitized mammograms that have been developed in his laboratory [10, 11]. The two schemes use independent approaches to select the initial suspicion and then to analyse image features in those regions. The first scheme detects the suspicion region on the bases of Gaussian band pass filtering and multilayer topographic feature analysis [12], and the second scheme applies five filtering-based stages to search for a specific type of suspicious region at each stage [13].

Mammogram films were acquired using a MinR screen and MRE-I film combination and were digitized using a laser film digitizer with a pixel size of 100x100 micron and 12-bit grey-level resolution. After digitization, the images were sub sampled by a factor of four in both dimension to make the size of digitized mammograms approximately 600x450 pixels. All images were acquired during the breast examination of 178 patients at the University of Pittsburgh Medical Centre.

Using the two CAD schemes separately, they achieved 96% and 94% sensitivity with the false-positive detection rate of 0.79 and 1.69 per image, respectively.

One of the early methods achieving significant clinical results is that of Davies [14] with experiments performed over 50 test images, half of which contained no clusters. The authors report a 96% of sensitivity with an average of 0.18 false positive per image. However, the authors detect suspicious areas by using a local threshold and, to such an end, the selected regions are limited by size criteria; further, those with an irregular shape are discarded.

The method due to Dengler [15] exploits a two-stage algorithm for spot detection and shape extraction, based on Gaussian filter detection followed by morphological restriction. They report 70% of sensitivity and 0.3 false positive per image. Such a result is tested using a number of mammograms evaluated through the judgments of expert radiologists, although mammograpies are not publicly available and their outcome cannot be compared with other methods.

Shen [16] proposes a multi-tolerance region growing method. The resulting regions are then given an input to a neuronal network for classification. The results are the following: in mammograms containing benignant tumours, that have simple shape, they achieve 81% of sensitivity and zero false positive, while 85% of sensitivity and 29 false positive of malignant cases are reported. It has been noticed that the experiments, albeit biopsy proved, have been performed on a very low number of images, four real mammograms, which are not publicly available.

Other methods aim at incorporating a priori knowledge within the analysis phase [17]. The method exploits structural geometric knowledge and it relies upon Bayesian techniques and upon the application of random field images.

Recently, multi-scale methods based on the wavelet have been introduced [18-21]. In particular, [19] is appealing as regards both the results achieved and the methodology. Tumour detection is directly accomplished within the transformation domain, relying on a thresholding of the wavelet coefficients to produce a dection/no detection result. However, the threshold is experimentally chosen as a fixed percentile of the histogram of each channel, thus limiting the approach in the capability of dealing with varying conditions due to image formation and digitization process, noise level, etc.

3   Theory

Three modules form whole process:
1. Low level segmentation
2. HER used for edge analysis and classification
3. Texture analysis

Low-level segmentation module [22, 23] is based on the similarity of criteria between the histograms of a domain and a sub domain. Quad-tree has been applied for both domain segmentation and topologic representation.

To compare histograms, is used the distance computed with HER system.

By HER any signal can be represented by means of a vector containing the energy values related to its most important points. The result is obtained by these steps:
1. Compute signal total energy;
2. Find the signal maxima and put then in a queue Q in decreasing magnitude order, along with their x-axis position;
3. Compute the relative energy $Er(ik)$ of the first maximum, say $x(ik)$, in Q and remove it from Q;
4. Compute the standard deviation relative to the current maximum;
5. The energy in the surrounding area of the current maximum has been accounted for, therefore, set the input signal to zero in the surrounding area of the maximum and update the total energy;
6. Go back to step 3 until the fraction of the total energy remaining in the signal falls below a given threshold.

We can now apply the proposed model to signals in order to analyze and classify closed contours of objects and regions of a pictorial scene.

We first need to obtain a 1-D representation of a 2-D contour. In order to do so, we choose our frame of reference to be a coordinate system centred in the centre G of the object under consideration.

Next, we compute the distance d-four between the centre G and the uppermost leftmost pixel of the contour. After repeating the application for all contour pixels according to a predefined direction we obtain a representation of the contour in curvilinear coordinates. Such a representation is univocal, since it is possible to reconstruct the original 2-D contour shape without loss of information.

If we apply HER method we have just described the contour, we observe that the maxima of 1-D signal correspond to the points of the contour having the greatest distance from the centre G.

The entropy associated to each maximum in the 1-D signal can be interpreted as the 'signature' of the distribution of contour pixels in the surrounding area of the considered maximum.

HER for shape contours has several nice invariance properties. In particular, we list the most important ones: translation invariance, rotation invariance, reflection invariance and scaling invariance.

Now we'll use a bi-dimensional space where we have distances in x-axis and entropy in y-axis. Each contour can be represented by as many points as its maxima are. Similarity index between contours is the sum of the Euclidean distance from each maximum.

HER shows signals in hierarchical way along the x-axis. Hierarchy is established by means of the distance compute with the reference signal.

In conclusion, HER represents the signals by mean of its maxima, their position in time space and their entropy.

In the entropy space we have some classes built on the bases of signal similarity.

The main idea of the tool is to transform an image from 2-D signal to 1-D signal.

The 1-D representation of texture data is obtained by drawing a spiral-shaped path on the texture partition element and considering the pixels in the order they are touched. The spiral starts at the upper left corner of the tile and goes inward clockwise.

In the case of textures, the spiral method used to obtain a 1-D dataset, has these invariance property: rotation, reflection, translation, contrast, luminosity, and optical zoom.

The data used for experimentally assessing were contours and texture from various application domains. The experiments, also compared with other significant methods, reveal a high discriminating power, which in turn yields a high-perceived quality of the retrieval results.

4   Experimental Results

The method is widely experimented with some heterogeneous database: for instance, textures, human cells, heterogeneous database (fish, rabbit, RMN signals), etc. In this work we'll show two different applications of the method: information retrieval from medical databases; Cad.

The databases here proposed for the experiment are the following:

1. the first database is composed of 1296 samples drawn from mammograpies acquired with a digital mammography, with 150 pixel/inch and 8 bits. 60% of these samples are diagnosed as pathologic by radiologist.

2. the second database is composed of 625 samples obtained from slides mammograpies with 150 pixel/inch and 8 bits. 50% of these samples are diagnosed as pathologic by radiologist.

3. the third one is composed of 625 samples obtained from slide mammograpies with 150 pixel/inch and 8 bit; 45% of the samples were cancer diagnosed on "skull-caudal" mammograms and confirmed by biopsy; 5% of the samples were cancer diagnosed on oblique projection; 50% were normal.

The frequency and width set sample has been decided for these reasons. Since the human eye is able to perceive only a few tens of grey tones and is not able to perceive statistical variations of orders higher than the second, we suggest using 8 bit in the digital images. We have to remark that the greater is the number of bit/inch the lower is the image contrast.

As the size of human cell is about 20 micron and the pixel size change from 40 to 100 micron, we collected 150 pixel/inch slides mammograpies.

Fig. 1 shows mammography cancer diagnosed by biopsy with dimension 1cm x 2cm.

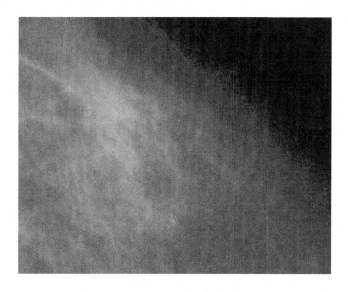

Fig. 1. Mammography Image (Slides).

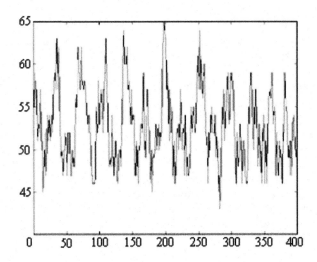

Fig. 2. Signal Obtained from Normal Breast.

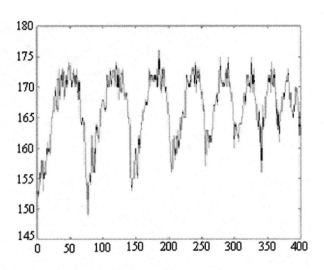

Fig. 3. Signal Obtained from Pathologic Breast (Carcinoma).

Fig. 2 and Fig. 3 show, with good obviousness, the contrast difference between a signal obtained from a pathologic breast and a non-pathological one.

In Fig. 2, non-pathological breast, the maximum of the signal is at 65 tones, while in Fig. 3, pathological case, the signal is between a minimum tone of 150 and a maximum one of 175.

The comparison between the signal in Fig.2 and Fig. 3 also shows a considerable difference between the corresponding behaviour.

We believe that it is easier, for a human observer, to compare one-dimensional signal rather than two-dimensional signal.

A considerable characteristic of this method is to allow a linear transformation from bi-dimensional signals to mono-dimensional signal. We believe that the analysis between signals obtained from pathological samples, as in Fig. 2, and not pathological samples, as in Fig. 3, is not only visually easier but is also possible to obtain some measures (i.e. width signal, periodicity, maximal and minimum high frequency, signal range, topologic information, etc) which could not be obtained from image and would need really complex algorithm.

We performed several queries on the third database, each time specifying one of the 625 samples as a query object. The graph, Fig. 4, shows the sorted distance between each of the 625 samples in the database and the query pathological sample. As can be seen by observing Fig. 4, the dataset is sharply partitioned into three bins and inside each one the distance from the query is nearly constant. In the first bin there are 300 samples corresponding to the "skull-caudal" pathological samples; in the second bin we have 25 samples corresponding to the oblique pathologic samples and in the last one there are 300 samples corresponding to no pathologies.

Table 1. Comparison between Different Methods.

Case n.	Biopsy	Results	Fd image	Material	Author	Bit n.	Analysis
80	No	87.3		Slide	Rosen	8	Radiology
80	No	82.8		Slide	Rosen	8	Radiology
178	No	96	0.79	Slide	Zheng	12	Gauss filter
178	No	94	1.69	Slide	Zheng	12	5 filter
50	No	96	0.18	Slide	Davies		wavelets
		70	0.3	Slide	Dengler		Gauss filter
low	No	81	0	Slide	Shen		Multi toll
low	No	85	29	Slide	Shen		Multi toll
1296	No	96	0.03	Digital	Distasi	8	HER
625	No	98	0.02	Slide	Distasi	8	HER
625	Yes	98	0.04	Slide	Distasi	8	Proposed
625	Yes	100	0	Slide	Distasi	8	Proposed
625	Yes	94	0.06	Slide	Distasi	8	Proposed
625	Yes	98	0.04	Slide	Distasi	8	Proposed
625	Yes	100	0	Slide	Distasi	8	Proposed
625	Yes	99	0.02	Slide	Distasi	8	Proposed

In Table 1 we show the comparison between the Cad system we proposed and some recent Cad systems. In the first column there are the number of samples for each methods; the second column document biopsy; the third column contains the per cent obtained from the experimentation; the fourth is the per cent of errors for each image; the fifth shows the use of slide mammography or digital images; the sixth column contains the first Author's name of the work; the last two explains respectively the number of bits used on the digitalisation and the way used for each methods or eventual check from radiologist.

The last 6 rows show the results we obtained, with different queries, on the third dataset.

Testing suggests two different utilizations:

– information retrieval: considering a medical dataset this method allows to use as queries the signal contour of our lesions. From signal obtained using spiral we can have as queries the band, the number of maximum, the energy of the signal, etc. The method gives in output a hierarchical ordering of all the samples of the dataset with reference of the query.

– Cad system: graphic on Fig. 4 can be explained like a clustering, in fact, is possible to represent each bin like a class, in an energy-position space, where co-ordinates are the energy of the bin and its ranking position of the middle element, as regards to the hierarchical ordering.

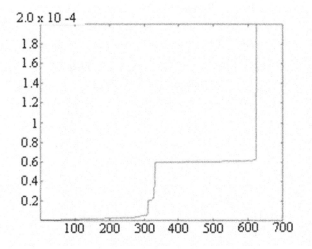

Fig. 4. Data Trend with Pathological Image.

Considering a medical dataset and a query (not included on dataset), which we would like to know possible pathology by means clustering process we can associate a pathology to the query.

5   Conclusion

The method proposed in this work has been widely tried on several kinds of dataset. The experimental results on medical dataset has shown the sound quality of the proposed method and also the fallowing invariance: brightness, contrast, rotation, mirror and linear scaling.

This method has also shown noise sensitivity, in fact noise change the signal behavior with consequent negative influence on the comparison between signals.

We think that the main contribution, of this paper is to show how the method works on medical datasets. As a matter of fact testing has shown good efficiently, low time consuming, high robustness if compared to the most recent methods in literature.

Future work will try to obtain a more user-friendly system by means of visual languages. So, for instance, to have a view of image and corresponding signal in just one screen, we can select the area of interest with the mouse and obtain iconic representation for signal and for contour, etc.

A second step for next experiments will be to research multi-centric lesions on the same breast.

At present this tool, Cad, in is use at the Policlinic of Cagliari, I° and II° Policlinic of Naples and a CNR center in Naples.

References

1.   Tabar, L., Fagerberg, G., Duffy, S.W. et al: Update in the Swedish two-country program of mammografic screening for breast cancer. Radiol. Clin. North Am. (1992) 30: 187-210
2.   Smart, CR., Byrnes, C., Smith, R.A. et al: Twenty-years follow-up of the breast cancers dignosed during the breast cancer detection demonstration project. Ca Cancer I. Clin. (1997) 47:135-149
3.   MacMahon, H., Doi, K. et al: Computer-aided-diagnosis in chest radiology. J. Thoracic Imaging, (1990) 5:67-76
4.   Doi, K., Giger ML et al: A useful clinical tool for CAD diagnosis by quantitative analysis of radiografic images. Acta radiology (1993) 34:426-39
5.   Rosen, M.P., Levine, D. et al: Diagnostic accuracy with US: remote radiologists versus On-site radiologists interpretation. Radiology (1999) 210:733-736
6.   Vyborny, C.J., Tekeshi Doi et al: Breast cancer: importance of spiculation in CAD. Radiology (2000) 215:703-707
7.   Distasi, R., Vitulano, S. et al: Context: A Technique for image retrieval Integrating Contour and Texture Information. To appear in Prooc. ICIAP01, (2001)
8.   Distasi, R., Vitulano, S. et al: A Hierarchical Representation for Content-based Image Retrieval. Journal of Visual Language and Computing (2000) 11:369-382
9.   Zheng, B., Chang, H.Y. et al: Mass detection in digitized mammograms using two indipendent CAD schemes. AJR (1996) 167:1421-24
10.   Chan, H.P. et al: CAD of mammografic microcalcification: pattern recognition with an artificial neural network. Med. Phys (1995) 22:1555-67
11.   Wei, D. et al: Classification Of mass and normal breast tissue on digital mammograms: multiresolution texture analysis. Med.Phys (1995) 22:1501-13
12.   Zheng, B. et al: Computirized detection of masses in digitized mammograms using single-image segmentation and a multilayer topographic feature analysis. Acad. Radiol. (1995) 2:959-66

13. Chang, Y.H. et al: Computerized identification of suspicious regions for masses in digitized mammograms. Invest. Radiol. (1996) 31:143-50

14. Davies, D.H. et al: Automatic computer decision of clustered microcalcification in digital mammograms. Physics in Medicine and Biology (1999) 35:1111-18

15. Dengler, J. et al: Segmentation of microcalcification in mammograms. IEEE Tran. On Medical Imaging (1993) 12:634-44

16. Shen, L. et al: Application of shape analysis to mammographic calcifications. IEEE Trans. On Medical Imaging (1993) 13:263-74

17. Karsseme, I.J. et al: Adaptive noise equalization and recognition of microcalcification cluster in mammograms. Int. Journal of Pattern Recognition and Artificial Intell. (1993) 7:263-74

18. Dinten, J.M. et al: A global approach for localization and characterization of microcalcification in mammograms. Digital mammography (1996) Elsevier:235-38

19. Chitre, Y. et al: Adaptive wavelet analysis and classification of mammographic calcification. Digital mammography (1996) Elsevier:323-26

20. Strckland, R.N. et al: Wavelet transform for detecting microcalcification in mammograms IEEE Trans. On Medical imaging (1996) 218-29

21. Wang, T.C. et al: Detection of microcalcification in digital mammograms using wavelet. IEEE Trans. On Medical Imaging (1998) 498-509

22. Vitulano, S. et al: Different methods to segment biomedical images. Pattern Recognition Letters (1997) 18:1125-31

23. Vitulano, S. et al: edge detection: local and global operators. International Journal of Pattern recognition and Artificial Intelligence (1998) 12:677-93

Part III

Multimedia Technology

M-CODD: A Technique for the Conceptual Design of Multimedia Databases

Gennaro Costagliola, Rita Francese, Annamaria Musto, and Giuseppe Polese

Dipartimento di Matematica ed Informatica
Università di Salerno
{gcostagliola,francese,musto,gpolese}@unisa.it

Abstract. The modeling of multimedia databases in the context of multimedia information systems is a complex task. The designer has to model the structure and the dynamic behavior of multimedia objects, together with possible user interactions on them. These can include content based queries, and dynamic presentations, which might both require the construction of special index structures on the stored data. We have extended the *Unified Modeling Language (UML)* to enable the modeling of multimedia information systems, and have provided refinement techniques to extract the underlying multimedia database. The way a designer can exploit the conceptual specification depends upon the target multimedia DBMS (MDBMS), and its associated data model. In particular, in this paper we describe refinement techniques relying on extended relational DBMS.

1. Introduction

In the last years there has been a considerable proliferation of methods for developing multimedia applications. This is due to the expectation that multimedia information processing will be widely used in future information systems. Many of the methods and tools available today are specialized multimedia frameworks and authoring tools, which provide ad hoc models, direct manipulation tools, and scripting languages to support the rapid development of multimedia applications. However, the development of small specialized multimedia applications will only be part of the problem. We believe that there will be the need to integrate multimedia information processing within large industrial information systems. Thus, there will be the need to have multimedia software engineering (MSE) methodologies and CASE tools to support the analysis and design of large information systems that include some kind of multimedia information processing. Moreover, as most industrial information systems, also multimedia information systems (MIS) might need extensive database support. Thus, MSE should also support the design and implementation of multimedia databases (MDB) according to some multimedia DBMS (MDBMS), for which there is no widely accepted architecture and data model yet.

In order to facilitate the migration from alphanumeric information systems, it will be desirable to integrate the modeling and development of MIS within existing software engineering methodologies. To this aim, in this paper we have chosen UML

M. Tucci (Ed.): MDIC 2001, LNCS 2184, pp. 55-66, 2001.

[14] as the basis for creating notations and development processes for MIS. We have extended UML models to enable the modeling of MIS. In particular, new symbols have been added to the UML class diagram to enable the specification of classes managing multimedia information. These are successively modeled through new state diagrams highlighting their graphical aspects, together with spatial and timing constraints at conceptual level. Also, sequence diagrams are extended to include special events related to multimedia interactions. Moreover, we have provided mapping rules exploiting the information stored within these new diagrams to produce an appropriate multimedia database schema and the associated manipulation functions. We aim to provide an high level methodology for the conceptual design of multimedia databases that is independent from the target database model, like ER diagrams can be used to conceptually model relational as well as hierarchical, and network database schemes. Indeed, other than the direct mapping onto object database models we highlight how to map our conceptual models onto canonical relational and extended relational logic database models based on SQL3 [9].

A prototype of a CASE Tool has been implemented by using visual language compiler generators [3]. The tool allows us to easily customize the visual notations of UML, define its syntax, and implement the mapping rules by defining an appropriate set of semantic routines.

The paper has been organized as follows: Section 2 discusses the related work, in Section 3 we describe UML extensions for conceptually modeling multimedia database applications, and a case study; in Section 4 we show some mapping rules for translating the information contained into extended UML diagrams into an extended relational data schema. Finally, Section 5 contains the conclusions and further research.

2. Related Work

In the last decade many methods for modeling multimedia applications have been proposed. A number of such models are based on Petri-Nets [5, 7, 8, 13]. As an example, the OCPN model [8] allows us to specify the data to be shown and the exhibition length, whereas in DTPN [13] the user interaction is modeled by typical user interaction actions, such as *stop*, *play*, *pause*, etc. Another Petri-Net based model is presented in [7]. The basic Petri-Net model is extended to enable the specification of spatial relations of multimedia objects other than their synchronization relations. These methods lack high level design models, which can yield some scale-up problems. This problem is somehow faced in Gnets [5] and in OMMMA-L [15]. Gnets provide an hybrid hierarchical model for specifying multimedia applications. In particular, Petri-Nets are used to specify the dynamic aspects of classes within Class Diagrams of Object Oriented Design Methodologies. Thus, the Object-Oriented methodologies enable the modular modeling of large applications, and each single module is detailed through a simpler local Petri-Net. OMMMA-L extends the Class and Sequence diagrams of UML, which are combined with specific Presentation Diagrams to enable the modeling of interactive multimedia applications. Both Gnets and OMMA-L do not provide specific techniques for mapping the high level diagrams onto lower level multimedia database schemes.

Another model for specifying multimedia application is the Teleaction Object (TAO) model [1, 2]. This model allows the specification of multimedia objects at a medium level of abstraction, by using an hypergraph to describe the structure of the objects, including their spatial and timing constraints. Moreover, it uses an active index to specify the reactions of objects to external and internal events. It has been shown that TAOs can be translated into equivalent Petri-Nets [2]. The model does not address database design and database manipulation issues. Moreover, the model needs to be supported by higher level design mechanisms to cope with large multimedia applications.

Hypercharts [11] extend Statecharts [6] with timing and synchronization mechanisms to enable the formal and graphical specification of hyperdocuments.

The work by I. F. Cruz and W. T. Lucas [4] describes Delaunay, a visualization framework for quering and presenting multimedia information in distributed databases. There a virtual document is defined as a sequence of viewable pages. Each page is formed by a number of multimedia objects stored into a distributed database. The user has the possibility to specify the data forming the document through a query and to define a template describing how the data are shown.

3. The M-CODD Methodology

In this section we show how the notations of UML diagrams [14] have been extended to enable the modeling of multimedia applications. Some of these extensions aim to enrich the object-oriented specification with information to enable the extraction of multimedia database logical schemes. In particular, these new notations capture information that can be used to produce mapping rules for different underlying data models.

3.1   Extended Class Diagrams

We have extended the Class Diagram of UML to include a new Class symbol for modeling entities of the real world containing multimedia information (MClasses). Moreover, we have introduced new types of relationships and their associated symbols for modeling sharing permissions and dependencies between multimedia objects belonging to different classes, and for modeling spatial and temporal relationships.

The symbol for MClasses is depicted in Figure 1.

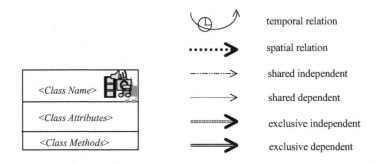

Fig. 1. Symbol for MClasses.   **Fig. 2**. Symbols for New Relationships.

This symbol has the twofold goal to notify that the class has multimedia content, and to instruct a CASE tool to undergo a specific design and translation process for this type of classes. In fact, we will use different diagrams to model the dynamic aspects of MClasses, which will also affect the mapping process. The symbols for the new types of relationships are depicted in Figure 2.

Spatial relations between MClasses are needed to specify the relationships of multimedia objects in the two dimensional space. Examples of spatial relations are *vertical, horizontal, diagonal, overlap*, etc. The temporal ordering of multimedia objects is usually specified by *temporal relations*, such as *co_start, co_end, meet, before, equal, overlap, during*, etc [12]. Moreover, it is possible to specify sharing properties of objects belonging to certain classes and dependencies between related classes. In fact, there might be the need to share certain objects across multiple composite multimedia objects. Thus, we also need to specify whether the existence of a class instance makes sense when a parent or children instance related to it is deleted.

We have introduced four symbols for expressing *Shared* and *Exclusive* multimedia objects, which can be *Dependent* or *Independent* [12]. The *Shared/Exclusive* property indicates the possibility to share or not the referenced object. The *Dependent/Independent* option indicates the type of dependency that holds between related instances.

An example of extended class diagram describing a publishing house is shown in Figure 3. The classes *MMBook, MMChapter*, and *Media* contain multimedia objects and therefore they are modeled through MClasses, whereas the other classes are modeled through the standard class notation. Some of the new relationships shown in Figure 2 have been used. Part-of hierarchies are used to model the structure of multimedia classes. For instance, a book is composed of chapters, which are related through the *before* temporal relation, indicating that they are sequenced in a publication.

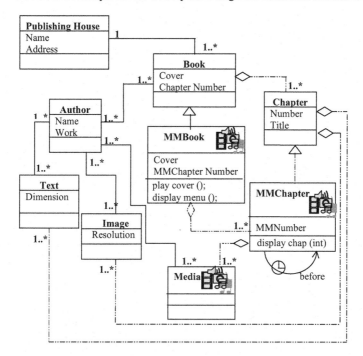

Fig. 3. MClass Diagram for Multimedia Editions.

3.2   Extended UML State Diagrams

In this section we present an extension of the UML State Diagram, the Multimedia State Diagram (MSD) that allows a designer to model the dynamic aspects of a multimedia application. A standard UML State Diagram shows the sequences of states that an object goes through during its life in response to received stimuli, together with its responses and actions. States are represented by state symbols and the transitions are represented by arrows connecting the state symbols. States may be simple states or superstates. The latter can in turn be described in detail through their own state diagram, forming an homogeneous hierarchy of Diagrams. In MSD we also represent spatial aspects of multimedia applications. In fact, simple states are represented in MSD by a box containing:

- Icons for multimedia objects (picture, sound, video, etc) spatially arranged according to dynamic constraints such as horizontal(object1, object2), where object1 is on the left of object2, vertical(object1, object2), where object1 is over object 2, Overlap(object1, object2), where object1 overlaps object 2, etc.

- Interaction button icons for representing special events related to the multimedia domain, such as play, forward, back, pause, stop, rewind, etc. that are depicted inside a bar placed on the bottom of the state symbol. Figure 4 shows the MSD interaction button icons and their meaning.

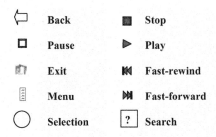

⇐	**Back**	■	**Stop**
☐	**Pause**	▶	**Play**
🗋	**Exit**	◄◄	**Fast-rewind**
▤	**Menu**	►►◄	**Fast-forward**
○	**Selection**	?	**Search**

Fig. 4 - MSD interaction button icons and the Selection icon.

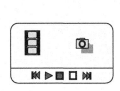

Fig. 5. A MSD Simple State.   **Fig. 6.** A Superstate in MSD.

Figure 5 shows an example of simple state containing a video and a picture icon related by the *horizontal* spatial constraint and its interaction button icons *play*, *pause*, *stop, fast rewind* and *fast forward*.

In MSD we use a different symbol for representing superstates, as shown in Figure 6. They are annotated by icons representing multimedia objects arranged according to spatial constraints that reflect their arrangement during their evolution inside the associated state diagram. Interaction buttons at this level are said *global interaction buttons*. As an example, Figure 6 shows a superstate *S* modeling the behavior of a multimedia presentation containing two videos, video1 and video2, and a text, txt, obeying to the following spatial constraints: horizontal(video1, txt), vertical(txt, video2). The interaction button bar shows the global interaction icons, such as *exit*, to leave the presentation, *back*, to jump to the previous state in the presentation, *pause* , to suspend the presentation, and *stop* to terminate.

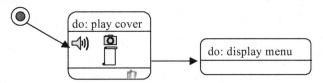

Fig. 7. A MSD Diagram for an MMbook Presentation.

The behavior of a multimedia presentation belonging to the MMbook class can be described by a hierarchical MSD diagram. A portion of an high level diagram is shown in Figure 7: the method *play_cover* of the MClass *MMBook* is invoked and a sound starts while a picture and a text appear in a vertical arrangement. In this state we can only decide to leave the presentation, since the *leave* button is the only one available. When the sound ends, the state *display menu* becomes active. Its behavior is described at a lower granularity level as shown in Figure 8.

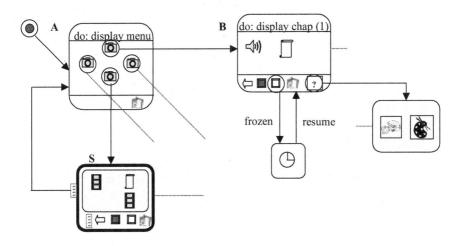

Fig. 8. A MSD for Multimedia Book Consultation.

The state A contains four images, namely the *selection* icons, which are associated to the four book chapters. A transition from this state occurs either when one of the possible chapter or the exit door is chosen. The transition associated to the first image activates the simple state B, where a sound and a text are presented. Five interactivity buttons are available. The back button activates a transition towards the previous state, that is, the *display_menu* state; the *pause* button freezes the presentation in the *suspended* state until the pause button is clicked again. This state is entered every time the pause button is clicked. When the sound ends there is a transition towards the state describing the behavior of chapter two and so on. The state associated to chapter four is the superstate S depicted in Figure 8. The behavior of this state is exploded into another MSD diagram, as shown in Figure 9. Here the state A starts immediately, whereas the state C starts after a delay of δ. When the video of state A ends, a transition occurs causing state B to be activated, and a new video starts with the same spatial relationships as the video in S. A synchronization bar signals an outgoing transition from the superstate S when both B and C complete their playing. The interactivity buttons available during the play of a movie are *stop, play, fast-forward, pause,* etc. If the stop button is clicked while in state A, the video halts and the state B starts. If the pause button associated to the video A is clicked, then state C continues its playing until it ends. In any case, there is a change of state only when the two paths join.

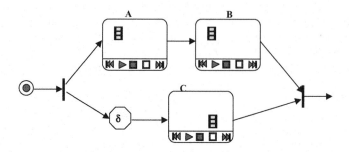

Fig. 9. MSD Associated to Superstate S of Fig. 8.

3.3   Extended UML Sequence Diagrams

The sequence diagram of UML has been extended to model interactions that are specific to Multimedia Information Systems. In particular, we aim to explicity model requests of content based queries on the database associated to the MIS being designed. Thus, we have introduced specific icons to model events representing queries to the multimedia database. In particular, the canonical arrow is enriched with icons to represent the type of content based query. We have classified them as *spatial*, *chromatic, sound,* and *temporal* content based queries, depending upon the nature of the query. For instance, a spatial query might request to retrieve images with a house and a tree to its right; chromatic queries might request pictures with a percentage a certain color; sound queries might request to retrieve video clips containing a song obeying a given sound pattern. These types of queries can be combined. Thus, we might request to retrieve a video in which a photogram with certain chromatic characteristics temporally precedes one having a house with a tree to its right. Figure 10 shows a portion of the multimedia sequence diagram (MSQD) for our case study. A user might perform a *spatial/chromatic* (indicated by a palette icon and an icon with a spatial arrangements of two objects) content based query on the MClass MMBook. This will instruct the designer to provide such a method within the MClass to handle the content based query. When refining the Object-Oriented specification, the designer will have to verify whether the underlying MDBMS provides specific support mechanisms for spatial and chromatic indexing, or if they have been provided within the application. Notice that the invocation of this search method causes the MClass MMBook to forward the request to all the objects of the MClass MMChapter related to the given object of MMBook. This multiple invocation is indicated through a '*' on the arrow symbol. Similarly, MMChapter forwards the query to the objects of the MClass Image.

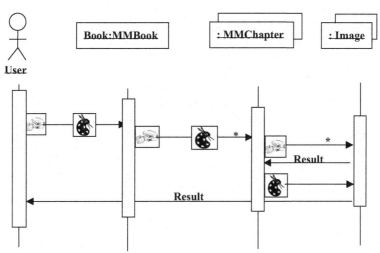

Fig. 10. MSQD Modeling User Interaction with MClass MMBook.

4. Mapping Extended UML Diagrams into Extended Relational Multimedia Databases Schemes

The information captured at the conceptual level in M-Codd is sufficiently rich to allow the definition of mapping rules for different logical data models. We have also provided information to manage the definition of special indexes to enable content based retrieval multimedia objects from the database. For our description we have chosen an extended relational data model, since DBMSs based on this data model provide a universal server that allows us to extend the data types and the function handled within the DBMS.

4.1 Mapping Multimedia Class Diagrams onto Extended Relational Data Schemes

We provide mapping rules to generate an Extended Relational Data Schema by analyzing static information of MClass diagrams (MCD) and subsequently refining it through information contained within MSD and MSQD.

The translation of classes into tables is performed according to the following general rule:

- For each multimedia class create a table with the same name, and a column for each attribute with the same name and the same type.

A generalization/specialization hierarchy can be easily mapped onto an extended relational schema by using the UNDER clause of SQL3. For example, the inheritance relationship between the classes *MMChapter* and *Chapter* in the Figure 2 is mapped as following:

CREATE TABLE MMChapter UNDER Chapter
(MMNumber INTEGER);

The mapping of Part-Of hierarchies is performed as follows:

- aggregate and component classes are mapped singularly;
- the table associated to the aggregate class is linked to the tables associated to the component classes through the mechanism of the foreign keys;
- the different types of dependencies are translated in SQL3 by using the construct of trigger. These triggers are activated when the deletion or update events occur [12].

For example, a portion of the SQL3 statements generated for mapping the part-of relation with shared independent constraint between the classes MMChapter and Media of the MMCD shown in the Figure 2 are:

```
// Create the user-defined Abstract Data Type media_t
CREATE TYPE media_t
(PUBLIC
name CHAR(20),
.........
)
```

```
//Create a table Media in order to store persistent instances of class Media
CREATE TABLE Media
(mediadata media_t);
```

```
//Create the user-defined Abstract Data Type mmchapter_t that is a subtype of
//type Chapter. The member data Mediaobjs is used to map the part-of relation with
//molteplicity one-many with class Media
CREATE TYPE mmchapter_t UNDER chapter
(PUBLIC
 MMNumber Integer,
 Mediaobjs SET(Media);
....
)
```

```
//Create a table MMChapter in order to store persistent instances of  class
//MMChapter
CREATE TABLE MMChapter
(mmchapter_data mmchapter_t);
```

//This trigger is an example of deletion of an object of class Media that is related to
//a shared indipendent link with an object of class MMChapter. The procedure

//set_foreign_key sets to Null the value of the foreign key into the tuples of
//MMChapter referencing the object under deletion, and modifies the value of
//the foreign key into the tuples associated to objects of other classes referencing it.
CREATE TRIGGER delete_Media
BEFORE DELETE ON Media
EXECUTE PROCEDURE set_foreign_key ('Set Null')

4.2   Mapping MSD and MSQD

So far we have described how to map static constraints of the MCD diagrams on an
extended relational data schema. The latter is refined by examining the dynamic
models developed during the conceptual design phases [10]. For instance, the types of
interactions shown in the MSQD and the state descriptions of the MSD, other than
causing the addition of methods to MClasses suggest the creation of indexes to enable
content based retrieval. However, this process depends on the characteristics of the
underlying MDBMS. If it provides support for special index structures there might be
a direct mapping, otherwise everything will have to be realized through application
programs. We believe that extended relational DBMSs can be extended to include
present and future multimedia indexing techniques [12]. New User Defined Types
and Functions (UDT and UDF) can be defined within the universal server of a last
generation RDBMS to store media types and special manipulation functions. For
instance, we might define an *image* UDT, with UDFs for extracting different types of
indexes for content based retrieval.

5. Conclusion and Future Development

We have described a methodology for the conceptual modeling of multimedia
information systems with mapping rules to extract an extended relational multimedia
database schema. The conceptual diagrams have been derived as an extension of
UML Class, Sequence, and State diagrams. The methodology naturally extends
approaches for the design of traditional information systems. In this way it can be
used to design systems that have alphanumeric as well as multimedia processing. In
fact, the distinction between Classes and MClasses allows the designer to undergo
additional design steps for MClasses. In this way we think there can be a softer
paradigm shift from the design of traditional to multimedia information systems.

In future we would like to work on the target extended data model to define data
types embedding special multimedia handling functions. We will proceed this by
using the mechanisms of User Defined Types and functions provided by extended
relational DBMSs implementing universal servers.

We also intend to extend our approach to the Web. The definition of Web classes
might push the designer through a design process to allow the design of web clients
and database server applications that are to be used from web clients.

References

1. T. Arndt, A. Cafiero, A. Guercio, "Multimedia Languages for Teleaction Objects", Proceedings of IEEE Symposium on Visual Languages, Capri, Italy, September 1997, pp. 322-331.
2. S. K. Chang, "Extending Visual Languages for Multimedia", IEEE Multimedia Magazine, no. 3, 1996, pp. 18-26.
3. G. Costagliola, A. De Lucia, S. Orefice and G. Tortora, "A Parsing Methodology for the Implementation of Visual Systems", IEEE Trans. On Software Engineering, Vol. 23, 1997, pp. 777-799.
4. I. F. Cruz and W. T. Lucas, "Delaunay^{MM}: A Visual Framework for Multimedia Presentation", Proceedings of IEEE Symposium on Visual Languages, Capri, Italy, September 1997, pp. 216-223.
5. Y. Deng and S.K. Chang, "A G-Net Model for Knowledge Representation and Reasoning", IEEE Trans. on Knowledge and Data Engineering, Vol. 2, no. 3, September 1990, pp. 295-310.
6. D. Harel, "Statecharts: A Visual Formalism for Complex Systems", Science of Computer Programming", Vol. 8, 1987, pp. 231-274.
7. Y. Kwon, E. Ferrari and E. Bertino, "Modeling Spatio-Temporal Constraints for Multimedia Objects", Data & Knowledge Engineering, Vol. 30, 1999, pp. 217-238.
8. T. Little and A. Ghafoor, "Synchronization and Storage Models for Multimedia Objects", IEEE J. Selected Areas in Comm. ACM, Vol. 8, no. 3, April 1990, pp. 413-427.
9. J. Melton and N. Mattos, "An Overview of SQL3 – the Emerging New Generation of the SQL Standard", Tutorial no. T5, VLDB, Bombay, September 1996.
10. A. Musto, G. Polese, A. Pannella and G.Tortora, "Automatic Generation of RDBMS based Applications from Object Oriented Design Schemes", Proceedings of ACM SAC2000, Como, Italy, 2000.
11. F. B. Paulo, P. C. Masiero, M. C. F. de Oliveira, "Hypercharts: Extended Statecharts to Support Hypermedia Specification", TSE, Vol. 25, no.1, 1999, pp 33-49.
12. G. Polese, A. Pannella and G. Tortora, "An Extended Relational Data Model for Multimedia DBMSs", Journal of Visual Languages and Computing, Vol. 11, 2000, pp. 663-685.
13. B. Prabhakaran, S.V. Raghavan, "Syncronization Models for Multimedia Presentation with User Interaction", Proc. ACM Multimedia'93, California, 1993, pp. 157-166.
14. J. Rumbaugh, I. Jacobson and G. Booch, "The Unified Modeling Language Reference Manual", Addison Wesley, 1999.
15. S. Stefan and G. Engels, "Extending UML for Modeling Multimedia Applications", 1999 IEEE Symposium on Visual Languages, Tokyo, Japan, September 1999.

Controlling Concurrent Accesses in Multimedia Database Systems

Woochun Jun

Dept. of Computer Education
Seoul National University of Education
Seoul, Korea
wocjun@ns.seoul-e.ac.kr

Abstract. In this paper, a locking-based concurrency control scheme is presented in multimedia databases. The proposed scheme deals with composite objects. The proposed scheme is developed using access information on composite objects so that it incurs less locking overhead than existing works under any circumstances. In this work, the correctness of the proposed scheme is proven. Also, it is shown theoretically that the proposed scheme performs better than existing schemes.

1   Introduction

Multimedia databases provide the database capabilities of accessing, concurrent sharing of multimedia information. When we consider multimedia datatypes, there is a natural association of object-oriented concepts with multimedia as follows [6]. At first, object-oriented databases (OODBs) attempt to model the real world as closely as possible. This is also the goal of multimedia applications. Second, multimedia datatypes have a specific set of operations that are applicable to each datatype. The association of operations with a "type" is a fundamental paradigm in object-orientation. The third reason is due to organizational aspect of object-orientation and multimedia. That is, objects are organized in various collections. The multimedia object can be a subpart of many graph-structured object spaces.

Concurrency control is a mechanism used to coordinate access to the multi-user database so that the consistency of the database is maintained [1,2]. A concurrency control scheme allows multi-users rapid access to a database but incurs an overhead whenever it is invoked. This overhead may have a critical effect on OODBs where many transactions are long-lived [5]. Thus, reducing the overhead is vital to improve transaction response time.   Concurrency control usually meets the database consistency by enforcing some form of correctness criterion. The most widely used criterion is serializability [1]. Transactions are serializable if the interleaved execution of their operations produces the same output and has the same effects on the database as some serial execution of the same transactions.

There are two major relationships among objects in multimedia object, IS-A relationship and IS-PART-OF relationship, respectively [4]. IS-A relationship

M. Tucci (Ed.): MDIC 2001, LNCS 2184, pp. 67-76, 2001.

supports inheritance so that a subclass inherits definitions defined on its superclasses. Also, an instance of a class is a specialization of its superclasses. On the other hand, IS-PART-OF relationship supports notion that an object is part of another object. For example, automobile object consists of engine, door and drivetrain as composite objects.

A composite object has composite root object. The root object has a number of component objects. In turn, each component object is either simple object, which has no component object, or another component objects. These composite objects form a hierarchy, called composite object hierarchy.   Fig. 1 shows a composite object hierarchy.

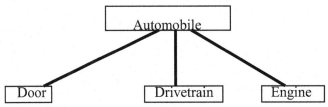

Fig. 1. A Composite Object Hierarchy.

In this paper, a locking-based concurrency control scheme is presented for composite objects. There have been some works in the literature that deal with composite objects, which will be discussed in Section 2. These approaches may work well only for specific applications. The proposed scheme is based on access information for each class so that it induces less locking overheads than existing schemes. It is also shown that the proposed scheme performs better than existing works.

This paper is organized as follows. In Section 2 related works are discussed. In Section 3 the proposed scheme for composite objects is presented. In Section 4 the superiority of the proposed work to existing works is shown. The paper concludes with plans for future research in Section 5.

2   Related Works

There have been some works for dealing with composite object hierarchy in the literature. Those works are summarized as follows.

In [4,7], a locking scheme is presented. In this work, a composite object is considered a single lockable unit. The scheme can be applicable for the shared composite reference (two different instances can reference the same component object) as well as the exclusive composite reference (two different instances cannot reference the same component object). In order to lock an entire composite object, the scheme works as follows: the root object is locked in S or X mode while the root class is locked in IS, IX, SIX or X mode, accordingly. For the exclusive references, the component classes are locked in ISO, IXO, S, SIXO, or X mode. For the shared references, three additional lock modes are necessary, ISOS (intention shared object-shared), IXOS (intention exclusive object-shared), and SIXOS (shared intention exclusive object-shared), corresponding ISO, IXO, SIXO, respectively.

[9] presents a locking protocol, called MGL, for the composite objects. The scheme is based on [4,5], and provides more lock modes so that the higher concurrency is achieved. In their scheme, a composite object can be locked in one of five lock modes, S, X, IS, IX, SIX, instead of two modes in [4,5]. Also, when a composite object is locked, one of its parent objects should be locked accordingly. That is, before requesting an S (or IS) lock on a composite object, at least one of it parent object is locked in IS mode. On the other hand, before requesting an X (IX or SIX) lock, at least one of its parent objects should be locked in IX mode. Also, before requesting X or S mode on a composite object, the shared component object should be locked in X or S mode. In order to request S, X, IS, IX, or SIX mode on a composite object hierarchy, all its component classes should be locked in S^*, X^*, IS^*, IX^*, or S^*, SIX^* mode, respectively.

For example, consider the composite object hierarchy in Fig. 2. Assume that composite objects, a, b, c, d, e, and f belong to classes A, B, C, D, E and F, respectively. Also, composite object b and c have the shared object f. Assume that a transaction is to update the composite object rooted at composite object b. Two schemes, Orion and MGL, work as follows.

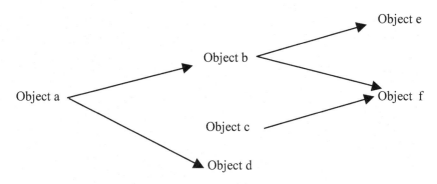

Fig. 2. Illustrative Composite Objects with Shared References.

- Orion

1) Lock class B in IX mode
2) Lock composite object b in X mode
3) Lock the component class E in IXO mode
4) Lock the component class F in IXOS mode

- MGL

1) Lock class B in IX mode
2) Lock composite object a, which is one of parent object of object b, in IX mode
3) Lock the composite object b in X mode

4) Lock the composite object f, which is the shared object between b and c, in X mode
5) Lock the component class E in IX* mode
6) Lock the component class F in IX* mode

MGL scheme can achieve the higher concurrency by using more lock modes. For example, from above example, Orion locks the component class F in IXOS mode while MGL locks F in IX mode. Note that IXOS in Orion is incompatible with IS, IX, S, SIX, X modes. On the other hand, IX mode in MGL is incompatible only with S, SIX, X modes. But, both schemes incur locking overhead when a composite object to be accessed, say C, is near root in the deep hierarchy. This is due to that those schemes need to get locks all component classes of C.

3   The Proposed Scheme

3.1   The Proposed Scheme for Composite Objects

The basic idea for the proposed scheme is that, for component classes, set locks only on some designated classes instead of every component class as in existing works. In order to achieve this objective, some component classes are selected as MFA (more frequently accessed) classes. Informally, a MFA class is a component class accessed frequently. How to decide if a component class is a MFA or not will be discussed in Section 4

For the proposed scheme, in order to reduce locking overhead on component classes, locks are set as follows. Assume that a composite object c, which belongs to class C, is accessed. In this case, for component classes of C, locks are set only from direct component class of C to the first MFA through each component class chain. If there is no such MFA class, locks are required for every class through the chain. Note that, in existing schemes, locks are required on every component class. Thus, locking overhead is reduced compared to existing works. Also, if the direct component class of C is a MFA class, a lock is required on only the MFA class so that locks are reduced than existing works

The proposed locking scheme is based on two-phase locking. For a given lock request on a component object c of class C, locks are set on C and all component classes on the composite object hierarchy as follows. For simplicity, I adopt strict two-phase locking [8] which requires each transaction to release all the locks at the commitment time.

Step 1) (Intention lock)
- For each MFA class from the root to class C through component class chain, check conflict and set intention locks. An intention lock on a class indicates that some lock is held on a component class of the class [8]. It is used to help detecting possible conflicts earlier.

Step 2) locking on composite object c
- Check conflicts and set an appropriate lock on the composite object c.

Step 3) Locking on composite class C

• Check conflicts and set an appropriate lock on the composite class C
Step 4) Locking on component classes of C
- • If the direct component class of C is a MFA class, check conflicts with locks set by other transactions and set lock on the component class.
- • If the direct component class of C is not a MFA class, from the direct component class to the first MFA class through the component class chain, check conflicts and set locks. If there is no such MFA class, set locks from the direct component class to leaf through the chain.
- • (Shared reference) If any component class of C has the shared object, check conflict and set lock on the class.
  - •If class C has more than one component class, perform the same step 4) for each component chain of C.

For example, consider the following lock request by a transaction T, which is to update composite object rooted at instance *a* belonging to class A on a composite object hierarchy in Fig. 3. Let LS be a lock mode LS set by transaction T. Assume that class E and H are MFAs. As seen in Fig 3.a and 3.b, 11 and 5 locks are required for T by existing works and the proposed scheme, respectively.

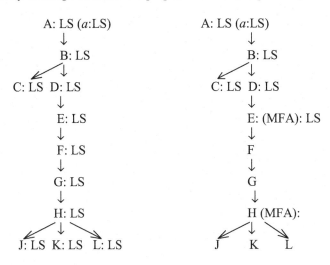

Fig. 3a. Locks by Existing Works.   **Fig. 3b.** Locks by the Proposed Work.

3.2   Correctness of the Proposed Scheme

The proposed scheme is based on two-phased locking. Since it is shown that two-phase locking is correct (it satisfies serializability [3]), it is sufficient to show that, for any lock requester, its conflict with a lock holder (if any) is always detected.

There are three cases depending on how the class to be accessed by lock requester, say R, is related to the class locked by lock holder, say H.

Case 1) H is neither superclass nor subclass of R.

Fig. 4 shows such a case. In this case, there is no conflict between the lock holder and the lock requester. If R and H have the shared object in the hierarchy, the conflict will be detected on the shared component class.

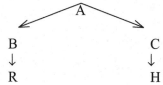

B   C
↓   ↓
R   H

Fig. 4. A Composite Object Hierarchy of Case 1.

Case 2) R is a superclass of H in the hierarchy.

In this case, there are two subcases. If there exists a MFA between R and H, then conflict is detected on the first MFA through the component chain (case 2.1). Otherwise, the conflict is detected on H (case 2.2). In case 2.1, as shown in Fig. 5.a, a conflict (if any) is checked on MFA_1, which is the first MFA of the class R through the chain, since the holder has an intention lock on MFA_1 and the requester is supposed to lock on MFA_1. On the other hand, in case 2.2, for subcase a, a conflict (if any) is checked on H as in Fig. 5.b since H does not have any intention locks through the chain of R and the lock requester needs to set a lock on H. For subcase b, conflict (if any) is checked on H as in Fig 5.c since intention locks on all MFAs through the superclass chain of H are supposed to be compatible and the requester needs to set a lock on H.

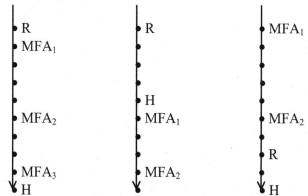

Fig 5a. Case 2.1.   **Fig. 5b.** Subcase a of Case 2.2.   **Fig. 5c.** Subcase b of Case 2.2.

Case 3) R is a subclass of H in the hierarchy.

In this case, there are two cases in which conflicts will be detected. If there exists some MFAs between R and H, the conflict is detected on the first MFA to H through the subclass chain of H such as MFA_2 in Fig. 6.a (case 3.1). Otherwise, conflict is detected on the class R as in Fig. 6.b (case 3.2).

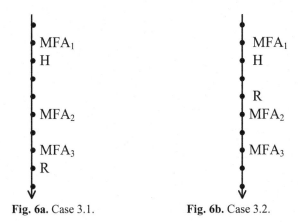

Fig. 6a. Case 3.1.   **Fig. 6b.** Case 3.2.

From cases 1), 2) and 3), it is concluded that, for any lock requester, it is guaranteed that its conflict with a lock holder (if any) is always detected. In turn, since the proposed scheme is based on two-phase locking, serializability is always guaranteed [3,8].

4   Performance Evaluation of the Proposed Scheme

4.1   MFA Assignment

Assume that the stable number of access to each class by various transactions is known in advance. Based on this stable number of access information for each class, we can determine if a class in the hierarchy is assigned as a FMA or not as follows.

// Starting from each leaf class until all classes are checked. //
Step 1) If a class is a leaf, then designate it as a non- MFA.
        If a class C has not been considered for MFA assignment and all component
        classes of C have been already determined in assignment, then do the
         followings
        For class C and all of the component classes,
          Calculate the number of locks (N_1) when the class is assigned as a MFA
          Calculate the number of locks (N_2) when the class is not assigned as a MFA

Step 2) Designate a class as a MFA only if $N_1 < N_2$. That is, the class can be a MFA
        only if the number of locks can be reduced by assignment.

For example, consider a composite object hierarchy as in Fig 7.a and assume that the number of access information on the hierarchy is known as in Fig. 7.b. The numbers represent the numbers of access to the class by all kinds of transactions. In MFA assignment scheme, since C_6 and C_7 are leaf classes in the hierarchy, they are not designated as MFAs. At the class C_4, if C_4 is designated as MFA, the number of locks needed for class C_4, C_5, C_6 and C_7 are 150 (for C_4), 200 (for C_5) and 400 (for

C_5), 250 (for C_7), respectively, resulting 1,000 locks for the four classes. On the other hand, if C_4 is not designated as a MFA, then the total number of locks needed for classes C_4, C_5, C_6 and C_7 are 950 locks, where 300 locks are for C_4, 200 locks are for C_5, 200 locks are for C_6, and 250 locks are for C_5. Thus, class C_4 becomes a non-MFA. Similarly, MFA class assignment for remaining classes can be performed. Fig. 7.c shows the result of the MFA assignment scheme based on access frequency information.

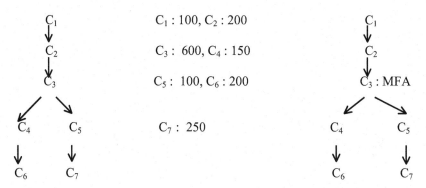

Fig. 7a. A Class Hierarchy.   **Fig. 7b.** Access Information.   **Fig.7c.** Result of Assignment.

4.2   Performance Evaluation

In this section, it is shown that the proposed scheme performs better than existing schemes. Assuming that access frequency for each class is stable in the composite object hierarchy, it is sufficient to show that the proposed scheme incurs less or at least equal number of locks than existing works. The proof is based on induction.

Claim: Assuming that access frequency for each class is stable, the proposed scheme performs better than existing works.
Proof: Proof is based on induction as follows. Let n be the number of classes assigned in MFA assignment scheme so far. Let N_P and N_E be the number of locks by the proposed scheme and the existing schemes, respectively, at given time.

• n =1 : $N_P = N_E$
• n=2 : In this case, without loss of generality, two classes are formed as follows.

C_1 (MFA) C_1 (non-MFA)
↓   ↓
C_2 (leaf) C_2 (leaf)

case a)   case b)

If C_1 is a MFA class as in case a), then $N_P \leq N_E$ otherwise C_1 would not be a MFA class. On the other hand, if C_1 is not a MFA class as in case b), it is concluded similarly that $N_P \leq N_E$.
Assume that the proposed scheme works up to n = K.

• n = K+1: without loss of generality, it is assumed that (K+1)th class as a root of the classes assigned for MFA assignment. Let x be a root (i.e., (K+1)th class) and $x_1...x_m$ be the first m MFAs through the composite chains of x as in Fig. 8. Also, Let N (x:MFA) and N (x:non-MFA) be the numbers of locks required in the proposed scheme when a class x is assigned as a MFA and a non-MFA, respectively (it is assumed that all component classes of x have been assigned in the MFA assignment scheme).

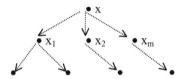

Fig. 8. A Composite Object Hierarchy with K+1 Classes.

Case a) x is a non-MFA

In this case, N (x:MFA) > N (x:non-MFA). Now, prove that $N_P \le N_E$. For the proposed scheme, locks are required for each class from x to $x_1...x_m$. On the other hand, locks are required from x to every component class of x by existing schemes. Also, for locks required for classes other than x, $N_P \le N_E$ by induction assumption.

Case b) x is a MFA

In this case, N(x:MFA) < N(x:non-MFA). There are two cases under this situation.
subcase b.1) $N_P \le$ N(x:non-MFA). Otherwise, x would not be a MFA by the MFA assignment scheme.
subcase b.2) N(x:non-MFA) $\le N_E$. In the proposed scheme, locks are needed from x to $x_1...x_m$ as in Fig. 8. But locks are required from x to every component class of x in existing schemes. For locks required for classes other than x, $N_P \le N_E$ by induction assumption. Thus, $N_P \le N_E$.

From cases a) and b), with stable number of access to a given composite object hierarchy, it is concluded that the proposed scheme incurs less or at least equal number of locks than existing works.

5   Conclusions and Further Works

In this paper, a locking-based scheme is proposed for composite objects in multimedia databases. The proposed scheme is to reduce locking overhead than existing works. Assuming that the number of access for each class is stable for each composite object hierarchy, the proposed scheme always performs better than existing works.

Currently I am preparing simulation study in order to compare the proposed scheme with existing works. Also, I am trying to develop new class hierarchy locking scheme in order to combine it with the proposed composite object locking scheme.

References

1. Bernstein, P., Hadzilacos, V. and Goodman, N., *Concurrency Control and Recovery in Database Systems,* Addison-Wesley, (1987).
2. Cart, M. and Ferrie. J., Integrating Concurrency Control into an Object-Oriented Database System, 2nd Int. Conf. on Extending Data Base Technology, Venice, Italy, Mar., (1990), 363 - 377.
3. Eswaran, K., Gray, J., Lorie, R. and Traiger, I., The notion of consistency and predicate locks in a database system, Communication of ACM, Vol. 19, No. 11, Nov., (1976), 624 – 633.
4. Garza, J. and Kim, W., Transaction Management in an Object-Oriented Database System, ACM SIGMOD Int. Conf. on Management of Data, Chicago, Illinois, Jun., (1988), 37 - 45.
5. Jun, W., Semantic-Based Locking Technique in Object-Oriented Databases, Journal of Information and Software Technology. Elsevier Science Press, Vol. 42, Issue 8, May (2000), 523 – 531.
6. Khoshafian, S., Dasananda, S., and Minassian, M., *The Jasmine Object Database: Multimedia Applications for the Web*, Morgan-Kaufmann Publishers, Inc., (1999).
7. Kim, W., Bertino, E., and Garza, J., Composite Object Revised, ACM SIGMOD RECORD, Vol. 18, No. 2, Jun., (1989), 337-347.
8. Korth, K. and Silberschartz, A., *Database System Concepts*, 2nd Edition, McGraw Hill, (1991).
9. Lee, L. and Liou, R., A Multi-Granularity Locking Model for Concurrency Control in Object-Oriented Database Systems, IEEE Trans. on Knowledge and Data Engineering, Vol. 8, No. 1, Feb., (1996), 144 - 156.

Transformation Dataflow in Multimedia Software Engineering Using TAO_XML: A Component-Based Approach

Paolo Maresca[1], Angela Guercio[2], Tim Arndt[3], and Pasquale Donadio[4]

[1] Dipartimento di Informatica e Sistemistica(DIS), University "Federico II", Napoli
paomares@unina.it
http://maresca.ing.unina.it
[2] Dipartimento di Matematica ed Informatica (DMI), University of Salerno
[3] Departments of Computer and Information Science (DCSI), Cleveland State University
[4] Alcatel Italia S.p.A
pasquale.donadio@alcatel.it

Abstract. Multimedia Software Engineering (MSE) is a new frontier for both Software Engineering (SE) and Visual Languages (VL). In fact multimedia software engineering can be considered as the discipline for systematic specification, design, substitution and verification of patterns that are often visual. Visual Languages give such contributions to MSE as: Visual notation for software specification, design and verification flow charts, ER diagram, Petri Net, UML visualization, visual programming languages etc. Multimedia Software Engineering and Software Engineering are like two sides of the same coin. On the one hand, we can apply software engineering principles to the design of multimedia systems. On the other hand, we can apply multimedia technologies to the practice of software engineering. In this paper we deal with the first of these topics. The aim of this paper is to demonstrate how it is possible to design and implement complex multimedia software systems using a TeleAction Object (TAO) transformer based on XML technology with a component-based multimedia software engineering approach. The paper shows a complete process of dataflow transformation that represents TAOs in different ways (text, TAO_XML, etc) and at different levels of abstraction. The transformation process is a reversible one. We will also show the first experiences conducted jointly from DIS, DCSI, and DMI laboratories using a tool named TAO_XML_T. The tool's component-based architecture is also discussed in the paper.

1. Introduction

For many years, in the industrial and in the academic community the need to represent data in a portable way has been growing. In the past, data was kept in a format that couldn't be read on another machine and applications couldn't be run on different software or hardware platforms.

Nowadays, with the spread of computer networks, we have the necessity to enforce portability and interoperability so that data can flow through many nets and subnets in a way transparent to the user.

M. Tucci (Ed.): MDIC 2001, LNCS 2184, pp. 77-89, 2001.
© Springer-Verlag Berlin Heidelberg 2001

During the transmission from sender to receiver, data gets represented several times at different levels of abstraction so that it can be easily handled by the hardware or software devices and transmitted across the net [1]. Often information or data are used as representations of other information in order to permit reuse.

The concept of information that describes some other information is known as *metadata*. Using metadata it is possible to take a structured text document (if it is not structured it can be given a structure), parse it, and store the contents in a database or an application, local or remote. In this way, the document assumes an exchangeable, structured form in which all parts of it may be reused. This concept can be extended to all textual and multimedia applications for independent information interchange from hardware and software platforms. In this context it is easy to understand why XML [2] has been accepted as a new generation of languages that has promoted data and application portability with the possibility to run them on the most widespread browsers, moreover offering the possibility to handle information exchange in a better way for the net. It's interesting to think that the advantages brought by software engineering and XML could be immediately tested in *Multimedia Software Engineering* (MSE). It's worth noting that MSE is really a new frontier for both Software Engineering (SE) and Visual Languages (VL). In fact, multimedia software engineering can be regarded as the discipline for systematic specification, design, substitution and verification of patterns that are often visual [3]. Visual Languages give such contributions to MSE as: Visual notation for software specification, design and verification flow charts, ER diagrams, Petri Nets, UML visualization, visual programming languages, etc. The good news is that we can apply software engineering principles to the design of multimedia systems [3]. At this point we can start experimenting with multimedia methodologies, techniques and languages. But what is multimedia?

In [1] *Multimedia* was defined as composition of two contributions: *Multiple Media* and *Hypermedia*

$$Multimedia = Multiple\ Media + Hypermedia.$$

Multiple Media means different media (audio, video, text, etc.) while *Hypermedia* means objects + links.

The described formula has inside the conceptual model for MSE applications: the *multidimensional language* (ML).

A multidimensional language is a language where the primitives are objects of different media types and the operators are both spatial and temporal ones. Because of the importance of such spatial/temporal operators, we prefer to call such languages multidimensional languages rather than multimedia languages, although the multidimensional languages can be used to specify multimedia applications. From this viewpoint, a multimedia application is strictly related to a multidimensional language ML. We think that four fundamental aspects describe an ML language and it's worthwhile to outline them here:

    ✂ **Syntactic**. A multimedia application is constructed from a collection of multimedia objects. The primitive objects are media objects of the same media type. The complex multimedia objects are composed of these primitive objects and in general are of mixed media types. The syntax of ML describes how the complex multimedia objects are constructed from the other multimedia objects. Spatial and temporal composition rules must be taken into consideration.

✗ **Semantic**. Multimedia applications nowadays are seldom passive. A static ML can specify a passive multimedia application, but a dynamic multimedia application requires the system to take actions in response to user input or internal/external stimuli. The semantics of ML describes how the dynamic multimedia objects are derived from other multimedia objects when certain internal/external events occur. Since an important characteristic of multimedia is the ability to create links and associations, the semantics of ML must take that into consideration.

✗ **Pragmatic**. Multimedia applications are heavily content-based and require a lot of hard, manual work to put together. Tools are needed to assist the designer in building a multimedia application in a timely fashion. The pragmatics of ML can be based upon the patterns for various multimedia structures or sub-structures, such as navigation structures, content-based retrieval structures, etc. Once such structures and sub-structures are identified, they can be used as building blocks in putting together a multimedia application.

✗ **Systems.** Last but not least, the systems aspects of multimedia applications must be considered. Multimedia applications require the support of distributed multimedia systems. The systematic design, specification, analysis and optimization of distributed multimedia systems will improve the performance of multimedia applications. Both QoS (quality of service) and QoP (quality of presentation) must be considered in systems design.

An example of a Multimedia Language, used in the distance-learning activity, is the TeleAction Object paradigm (TAO) [4a]. The language had evolutions improving the expressivity [4b], [5], [6], [7], [8] and portability in other languages such as HTML [9].

The authors believe that the conjunction between the expressive power of the TAO hypergraph and the interoperability offered by the XML language creates a new MSE paradigm: the TAO_XML language [10], [11]. This last approach seems to be very promising especially for the portability characteristics. For these reasons many experiments have been developed in order to define an architecture for rapid prototyping tools able to design and develop an MSE application. One of these is described in [12]. It is also true that this system design requires new software process models and paradigms, such as the object-oriented approach and RUP-UML process [13], [14]. But the authors believe that one of the SE techniques useful for MSE is the Component-Based Software Engineering (CBSE) paradigm because the paradigm is one of the fast ways to implement reusable Multimedia components that respect the foundations of Object Oriented technology in multimedia software development. Component-Based Multimedia Software Engineering (CBMSE) [15] enables the ability to reuse those parts in other multimedia applications and makes it easier to maintain and to customize those parts to produce new functions and features [16]. CBMSE should provide both a methodology and tools for developing components that work continuously, handle exceptional cases safely, and operate without corrupting other interrelated components. This approach employs top-down design to subdivide a Multimedia Software system into modules and objects that can be easily implemented.

A valid application of the CBSE approach in Multimedia Software Engineering is represented by the complex transformations of the TeleAction Object based on the TAO_XML language.

In this paper we will address the problem of the transformation of multimedia data using a CBSE approach. The paper is structured as follows: the second section shows the TAO_XML Multimedia Software Architecture. Section 3 shows the dataflow transformation process from multimedia objects into TAO_XML language. Section 4 illustrates a case study and finally section 5 states conclusions and lays out future work.

2.   The TAO_XML Multimedia Software Architecture

The TAO_XML Multimedia Software Architecture is based on six basic entities that are represented in figure1. In the next section we will show an instance of this architecture. It is worth while to point out that the architecture in fig. 1 shows a component based architecture in which the different parts are integrated together in order to obtain the main objective: transforming the multimedia flow into TAO_XML languages.

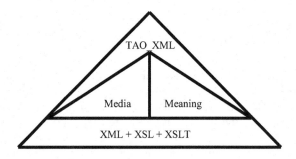

Fig. 1. Multimedia Software Architecture TAO_XML Based.

We briefly describe the components of the architecture in fig. 1.

- Extensible Markup Language (XML) [17], ratified by the World Wide Web Consortium (W3C) [2], is quickly becoming the standard way to identify data, describe data and exchange machine-understandable information on the web; XML describes a class of data objects called XML documents and provides a mechanism that maximizes the interoperability among different platforms.
- Extensible Style sheet Language (XSL) [18] Working Draft describes a vocabulary recognized by a rendering agent to reify abstract expressions of format into a particular medium of presentation. An XML document can have more than one XSL style sheet applied, each style sheet producing a possible (usually) different result (e.g. txt/html/PDF format document or a generic format dependent on custom visualization).
- XSL Transformations (XSLT) 1.0 [19] Recommendation describes a vocabulary recognized by an XSLT processor so that it can transform information from a source file organization into a different one, suitable for continued downstream processing. The main goal of an XSLT processor is to transform an XML source into an abstract hierarchical result. Furthermore the result is serialized into a desired standard format.
- Media that represents the form and technology used to represent and to communicate information. Multimedia presentations, for example, combine sound, pictures, and videos, all of which are different types of media.
- Meaning that represents the concept and the sense of the information that will be transferred.
- TAO_XML that represents the TeleAction Object paradigm [4] based on XML [11] technology. It is fundamentally composed of two parts: a hypergraph which specifies the multimedia objects which constitute the TAO_XML and their relations, and a knowledge structure which describes the environment and the actions of the TAO_XML.

The following section describes the CBSE - TAO_XML dataflow transformation process based on the Multimedia Architecture described.

3.   TAO_XML Dataflow Transformation Process

In the previous section we have analyzed the TAO_XML environment architecture, in this section we will describe the scenario where it will be possible to use such architecture. Among the various possible usage scenarios, the authors have identified two, related to the usage mode of the dataflow transformation: stand-alone and distributed. In the stand-alone scenario the main dataflow transformation process is local. The stand-alone workstation loads the TAO_XML/XSLT engine and delivers a combination of the style sheet and the source information to be transformed to the same workstation. The results are various media formatted as requested by the user (e.g. PDA format, video format, audio format, etc.).

In the distributed scenario the main dataflow transformation process is distributed: the server can distribute the TAO_XML/XSLT engine and provides the transformation process to the clients that require it.

The client forwards the TAO_XML document or an equivalent generic dataflow to the TAO_XSLT server; furthermore it also provides the data transformation request of and the desired output data format. The server loads the TAO_XSLT processor and delivers a combination of the style sheet and the source information to be transformed to the recipient's platform. In the distributed scenario not only is the use of style sheet documents and TAO_XSLT transformation for receiving a desired media format possible, but it's also possible to receive a data flow opportunely formatted for other distributed systems like the Wireless Application Protocol terminal, Personal Digital Assistant terminal, etc. The following describes the TAO_XML dataflow transformation process based on a distributed scenario.

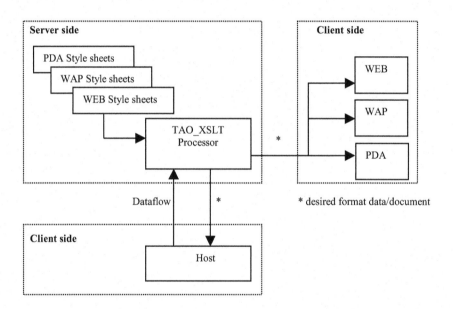

Fig. 2.   TAO_XML Based Dataflow Transformation Process: Distributed Scenario.

The TAO_XML dataflow transformation process is composed of two main subprocesses, described in figure 3:

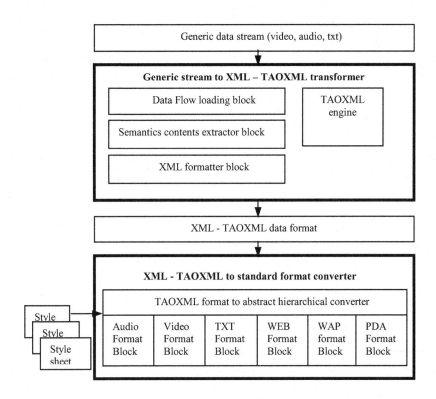

Fig. 3. TAO_XML Based Dataflow Transformation Process: Architecture.

The first sub-process, called "Generic stream to XML-TAO_XML transformer" implements the extraction of the semantic contents and gives a TAO_XML document in output. The following functional blocks compose it:

- Data flow loading block: loads the generic data stream from a generic source.
- Semantics contents extractor block: parses the generic data source and extracts from it the valid semantic contents.
- XML formatter block: loads the semantic contents retrieved in the previous step and write it in a well-formed TAO_XML format.
- TAO_XML engine: provides the manipulation of the document that satisfies the requirements described in the TAO standard.

The following functional blocks compose the second sub-process, called "XML-TAO_XML to standard format converter":

- TAO_XML format to abstract hierarchical converter, which transforms the document from the XML format to an application-independent representation of it.
- Several functional blocks that depend on the data format desired in output.

The following section gives a case study based on the TAO_XML transformation process, and presents the Java-based prototype developed by the authors.

4.   A Case Study

In this section we will illustrate on the one hand, a complete process for the dataflow transformation Component MSE based, and on the other hand our experience that is incorporated in a complete Java based prototype named TAO_XML_T.

The process for the TAO_XML based generic data stream manipulation is principally composed of two main transformations:

- Transformation from generic data format not hierarchically organized, to well-formed XML/TAO_XML format.
- Transformation from XML/TAO_XML format to document format (e.g. txt, doc, PDF, html etc) or media format (e.g. audio, video).

The prototype developed reflects this organization. The modular approach adopted allows us to obtain a standard format document with a modular prototype, which can be reused or extended in a very easy manner in other similar Java-based applications.

The main driver of "Transformation from generic data format to well-formed XML/TAO_XML format" is the SAX API validating Java parser [20]. It parses an input data stream and prints it out in XML format; moreover it generates events that correspond to different features found in the parsed XML document. In this context SAX API Java parser is superior to the DOM API Java parser [20] in many aspects of runtime performance. The SAX API parser used in this prototype is the Java-based open-source tool called Xerces produced by the open-source Apache XML project team [21].

The main driver of "Transformation from XML/TAO_XML format to document or media format" is the XSLT processor. The XSLT processor reads in both the XML document and the XSLT style sheet.

The XSLT style sheet describes a set of patterns to match within the XML document and the transformations to apply when a match is found. Pattern matches are described in terms of the tags and attributes for elements found within an XML document. Transformations extract information from the XML document and format it into desired format. Each match-transformation pair is called an XSLT template.

The XSLT transformation process works in a way very analogous to the way scripting languages such as Python or Perl operate - apply regular expressions to an input stream and then transform the elements that were found to an output stream. In that sense XSLT could really be called a scripting language, especially since it contains elements of control flow similar to a scripting language.

The XSLT processors used in this prototype is an excellent Java-based, open-source tool called Xalan product of the above Apache XML project [21].

The following figure 3 explains the entire component-based structure of the dataflow transformer prototype.

Two main layer compose the TAO_XML_T prototype architecture:

- The Graphic User Interface (GUI) layer that represents the human-machine interface of the prototype
- The Engine layer that represents the core of the prototype.

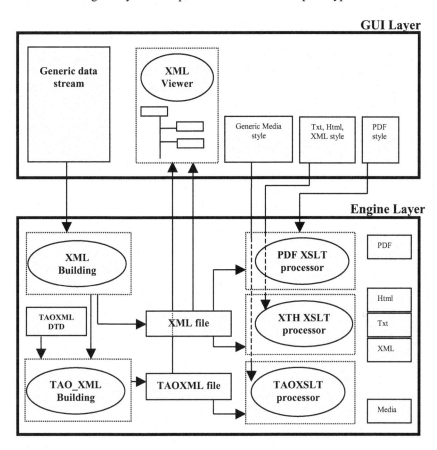

Fig. 4. Dataflow Transformation Process: Prototype Architecture.

- The first component, called "XML building" implements the "Generic stream to XML transformer", described in the above "Dataflow transformation process" section. This mechanism builds an XML file (well formed) from a generic data flow. This mechanism is based on the Xerces SAX API Java parser.

- The second component, called "TAO_XML building" implements part of the "TAO_XML engine", described in the above "Dataflow transformation process" section. This mechanism builds a TAO_XML file (well formed) from the corresponding TAODTD file and the XML file produced in the previous step.
- The third component, defined at the GUI level, is called "XML viewer". It implements an XML display that shows the hierarchic objects of an XML file. It uses a DOM Parser that analyses XML tags and converts it into a hierarchic tree representation.
- The fourth component, called "PDF XSLT processor", implements a part of "XML format to abstract hierarchical converter" and the "PDF format Block" described in the above "Dataflow transformation process" section. It implements the sub layer strictly dependent on the PDF format desired. It uses an independent XSLT processor that transforms XML format into PDF format with two steps:

> ✂ The first step transforms XML format into an intermediate Format Object (FO) representation.
> ✂ The second step transforms the FO representation into PDF format.

The implementation of this component is based on FOP routine, a print formatter driven by XSL Formatted Objects. It is a Java application that reads a formatting object tree and then turns it into a PDF document.

The formatted object tree, can be in the form of an XML document (output of XSLT Xalan engine) or can be passed in memory as a DOM documents or Sax events. FOP is a part of Apache project.

- The fifth component, called "THX XSLT" processor implements a part of the "XML format to Abstract hierarchical converter", and the Html, Txt, XML format blocks described in the above "Dataflow transformation process" section. It provides a common API sub layer, independent from document formats and a particular sub layer strictly dependent on the format of desired document. It uses the XSL style sheets previously defined and an XSLT engine. The implementation of this component is based on an XML Parser and an XSL Processor provided by EZ/X routines. EZ/X is a collection of fast, highly conformant, and easy to use XML foundation technologies.
- The sixth component called "TAOXSLT processor" implements part of the TAO_XML engine described in the above "Dataflow transformation process" section. It realizes a sub layer strictly dependent on the media format desired in output and uses the XSL style sheet previously defined. The TAOXSLT processor works in conjunction with the desired media style sheet and loads and synchronizes the desired media across the XSL script commands.

The prototype, completely developed in the Java language, is under experimentation at laboratories of DIS, DCSI, DMI and is an example of how it is possible to transform a generic multimedia data flow into an XML format. The XML_TAO format can be considered only a particular case of this transformation. Moreover using the TAOXSLT processor it is possible to define a desired media output as a generic XSLT.

5.   Conclusions and Future Work

In this work we have shown the design and implementation of complex multimedia software systems, like Dataflow Transformation mechanisms, with a Component-Based Software Engineering approach.

The goals of the authors were to emphasize the following main aspects:

- Interoperability of a standard process based on a standard language for metadata treatment: TAO_XML, directly obtained by use of the XML language and DTD.
- Reusability of the entire system, because of the CBSE approach.
- Reuse of the XML paradigms in the TAO_XML environment.

The authors have also implemented a Java-based prototype named TAO_XML_T, which demonstrates the main functions of the data flow transformer implemented in terms of TAO_XML basic functions. The prototype is now under experimentation, however the first data was collected and in figure 5 we show an example of output obtained with the CBSE based prototype.

The authors are planning a future development to extend component-based Multimedia software engineering approach to the CORBA environment. In particular, we'll be transforming the TAO multimedia application into metadata in order to have a more portable platform in which to represent multimedia educational material so that it can be transferred on a CORBA channel in a complete secure client server application. This activity can enable us to reuse a lot of material coming from different universities and with different formats.

Acknowledgements

This work has been developed with funds provided by MURST as part of the program "Progetti Cluster", Cluster 16: Multimedialità.

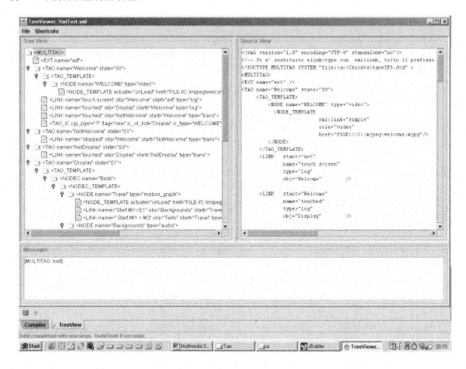

Fig. 5. An Example of Output Obtained with the TAO_XML CBSE Based Prototype.

References

1. P. Maresca, A. Guercio, "Logical Approach For The Construction Of Tools For Multimedia Representation And Simplification", World Multiconference on Systemic, Cybernetics and Informatics, July 23-26, 2000, Orlando (FL), U.S.A.
2. T. Bray, J. Paoli, C. M. Sperberg-McQueen eds. "Extensible Markup Language (XML) 1.0" W3C Recommendation 10 February 1998. http://www.w3.org/TR/1998/REC-xml-19980210
3. S. K. Chang, "Multimedia Software Engineering", 24th IEEE Computer Software and Application Conference, Compsac 2000, October 2000.
4. a) H. Chang, S. K. Chang, T. Hou and A. Hsu, "The Management and Applications of Tele-Action Objects", ACM Journal of Multimedia Systems, Springer Verlag, Volume 3, Issue 5-6, 1995, 204-216.
   b) S. K. Chang, "Towards a Theory of Active Index" J. Visual Languages and Computing, vol. 6, pp.101-118, 1995.
5. T. Arndt, A. Guercio and S.K. Chang "Visual Tools for a Multimedia IC Development Environment (MICE)", in Proceedings 1998 IEEE Symposium on Visual Languages.
6. T. Arndt, A. Guercio and S.K. Chang "Formal Specification and Prototyping of Multimedia Applications", in Proceedings of SEKE '99, Germany, 17-19 June 1999.

7. S. K. Chang, G. Tortora, A. Guercio, Bing Yu "Icon Purity - Toward a Formal Theory of Icons", International Journal of Pattern Recognition and Artificial Intelligence, Vol. 1, No. 3&4, 1987, pp. 377-392.
8. S. K Chang and C. S. Ho, "Knowledge Tables as a Unified Knowledge Representation for Office Information System Design", IEEE TC on Office Automation Newsletter, Vol. 3, No. 1, Feb. 1989, pp. 12-25.
9. S. K. Chang "Extending Visual Languages For Multimedia", IEEE Multimedia, vol. 3, pp. 18-26, 1996.
10. P. Maresca, T. Arndt, A. Guercio, "Unifying Distance Learning Resources: The Metadata Approach ", to appear in International Journal of Computers and their Applications, June 2001.
11. C. Marmo, "Un linguaggio XML-based per i TeleAction Object: Progettazione e Realizzazione di un Ambiente TAO_XML" Laurea degree thesis, 1999, Università degli studi di Napoli and Università degli studi di Salerno.
12. P. Maresca, A. Guercio, "Multimedia Software Engineering Collaboratory", workshop on Multimedia Computing on the World Wide Web in IEEE Conference on Visual Languages, Seattle, USA, September 14, 2000.
13. Booch, Jacobson, Rumbaugh, "Rational Unified Process with UML", Addison Wesley 2000.
14. P. Krutchen, , "Rational Unified Process", Addison Wesley, 2001
15. W. W. Agresti, "New Paradigms for Software Development", IEEE Computer Society Press, 1986
16. David A. Taylor, " Object Oriented Technology - A Manager Guide" Servio 1990
17. J. Bosak, T. Bray "XML and the Second-Generation Web" Scientific American May 1999.
18. Kal Ahmed et al. Professional Java XML, Addison Wesley 2001.
19. M. Kay, XSLT: Programmer's Reference, Wrox Press, 2000.
20. Rajiv Mordani, "Java API for XML Processing" - Sun Microsystems 2001
21. Apache Project, http://www.apache.org

Monitoring Electromagnetic Pollution: A GIS-Based Visual Approach

Luca Paolino, Monica Sebillo, Genoveffa Tortora, and Giuliana Vitiello

Dipartimento di Matematica e Informatica
Università degli Studi di Salerno
Baronissi (SA) 84081- Italy
{paolino,msebillo,tortora,gvitiello}@unisa.it

Abstract. In the last years, the attention of the public community on electromagnetic pollution has continuously grown. In this paper we argue that the use of Geographic Information Systems in this domain should be encouraged as a valid support to the monitoring activities related to this phenomenon. In particular, our proposal of a visual environment, the Metaphor GIS Query Language is shown to provide a fruitful combination of GIS technology and visual languages, which have the double advantage of assisting electromagnetism experts in the measurement tasks, and facilitating non-expert users who might be interested in the level of EMF pollution in a given area.

1 Introduction

Electromagnetic fields (EMF) represent one of the most common and fastest growing environmental influences in our lives. The so called "electromagnetic pollution" is referred to the potential health effects of EMF [18]. In the last years, the attention of the public community on this phoenomenon has developed, especially because of growing use of hand made sources such as cellular phones, which have become an essential part of business, commerce and society. Moreover the advent of third generation systems will extend the use of most forms of communication technologies, including fax, e-mail and Internet access. Geographic Information Systems (GIS) seem to be a promising means to support organizations in the monitoring activities. Indeed, GIS technology integrates common database operations such as query and statistical analysis of data coming from measurement tools with the unique visualization and geographic analysis benefits offered by maps. Scientific organizations involved in the evaluation of biological effects of EMF would greatly benefit from a uniform and structured information base, giving details of all EMF sources in a given area, in activities like siting-planning of base stations or sources like power lines. In such activities, special attention is to be put on the so-called " sensitive sites", i.e. schools, hospitals, residential areas, for which a complete, continuous, ongoing monitoring of the electromagnetic field generated by given sources is needed.

The research carried out in this paper derives from the requirements made by a group of physicians, who have studied electromagnetic pollution in an area of the

M. Tucci (Ed.): MDIC 2001, LNCS 2184, pp. 90-101, 2001.

Campania Italian region, to keep track of possible critical sites, where the legal threshold is exceeded. They analyzed high frequency electromagnetic fields through statistical methods of measurements, and defined a measurement protocol of the electromagnetic field produced by sources like power lines.

During their studies they realized that there is a need for an efficient and correct action of monitoring and information/formation in this domain, where the lack of information or misinformation is widespread among the population and the government system itself. GIS technology provides a solution to this issue, through the use of maps of electromagnetic fields measured in the surroundings of sources like power lines and/or telecommunication systems. Such maps can be elaborated considering sources, sensitive sites, results of experimental measurements and predictive models to estimate the electromagnetic pollution radiated by emitters deployed in given environments.

One problem with the use of GIS technology is that, in spite of the high potentiality offered, users are often faced with the implicit complexity of data and are forced to become familiar with the related concepts. The monitoring of EMF is no exception, since final users are supposed to be either domain experts and researchers, who are usually not familiar with GIS technology, or ordinary people interested in detecting the electromagnetic field values of a given area. The recent trend of developers has been to provide GIS with graphical user interfaces (GUI) based on international standards like Windows, whose design is facilitated by the availability of interactive graphical editors. Examples of products following this approach are *ARCVIEW* from Environmental System Research Institute [15], *SPANS MAP* from TYDAC [16], and *MGE Project Viewer* from Intergraph Corporation [17]. Users of a GIS provided with a GUI are allowed to focus on specific issues of the application, since however complex commands are filtered through the widgets characterizing the interface (see, e.g, [6]). Yet, when trying to retrieve and manipulate spatial data, the need arises to establish an easier and more adequate interaction between the man and the machine performing the powerful functionality of a GIS.

Visual language offer a solution. Recent studies on visual languages show that they represent a promising means for allowing unskilled users to query geographic databases, and to interpret and possibly reuse recorded queries [1, 13]. Systems like Cigales [2], GISQL [5] and the GIS Wallboard [8] are mainly based on the definition of graphical representations for the spatial properties associated with the geographic data manipulated, and for the involved spatial operators. Spatial properties are referred to the geometry of the geographic data and to their topology, which describes objects' relative positions. When trying to add user-friendliness to GIS, the association of visual descriptions to such features seems to be quite a natural step. As a matter of fact, many systems have been primarily targeted for visually querying spatial features of GIS data (see also [10, 14]).

The goal of our research has been to provide those users with further intuition about the data processed, by means of a visual query language, which also describes the semantics of those data in the real world. The visual environment *Metaphor GIS Query Language* (*MGISQL*, in the following), which can be used on top of an available GIS, was conceived to provide users with further intuition about the semantics of the spatial and the thematic components of geographic data in the real world [12]. The experimentation described in the paper shows that the combination of GIS technology and visual languages has two major benefits. On one hand it allows electromagnetism experts to perform the data analysis with a continuous reference to the involved land. On the other hand, it may bridge the gap between the complexity of the monitoring activities and the final non-expert users, who might be interested in the level of EMF pollution in a given area.

A protoype of *MGISQL* relies on a client-server architecture, and has been implemented using MapObjects [15] with the Internet Map Server extension to run files on the Internet. In particular, the server interacts with two major databases, a GIS database, where spatial and alphanumeric data are stored and managed, and a geometaphor database. The client side is realized through Java.

The paper is organized as follows. Section 2 provides some preliminary notions, needed for readers not familiar with GIS technology. In Section 3 the basic concepts are recalled that underlie the visual query formulation in MGISQL. Section 4 contains an overview of the visual environment and a description of its practical use in the given domain of interest. Section 5 concludes the paper with some final remarks.

2   Background

Geographic information is typically concerned with spatially referenced and interconnected phenomena, such as towns, roads, as well as less precisely defined regions with environmental attributes, such as woodlands. Such real world phenomena can be graphically represented by a structured set of spatial and descriptive data, which form a *geographic database*. Indeed, in a geographic database, spatial data are represented by visualizing the geometry of their elements in a map.

The basic geometric elements are points, lines and regions, which contribute to create more complex objects by applying some topological primitives. Descriptive data are instead organized as attributes of relational tables by an underlying DBMS. Thus, we can distinguish among merely *alphanumeric* data, merely *spatial* data, which are uniquely identified by their geometric representation, and *geographic* data, where spatial features are associated with alphanumeric attributes. Figure 1 illustrates the alphanumeric and the spatial components of a geographic data which refers to an environmental map.

Geographic data processing is more complex than conventional structured data processing because of both the nature of geographic information itself and the type of retrieval and analysis operations performed upon it. A lot of efforts have been devoted to the task of geographic data manipulation. As a result, in recent years the field of *geographic information systems* (*GIS*) has quickly evolved. A typical GIS provides an integrated environment including tools for the input and manipulation of geographic information, a database management system, to help store, organize, and manage data, and tools that support geographic query, analysis and visualization [9].

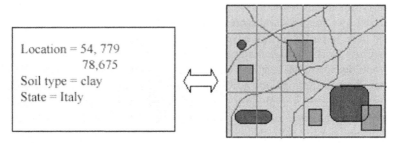

Fig. 1. Geographic Data.

Information about the world is stored in a GIS as a collection of *layers* that can be linked together by geography. In particular, layers are organizational schemes in which all data of a particular level of classification, such as roads, rivers or vegetation types, are grouped. They can be combined with each other in various ways to create new layers that are functionally related to the individual ones. Moreover, any association which relates each object of a layer to a set of attributes, is said to *realize a theme* and to *derive thematic layers*. For example, in an environmental map, built-up area, census area, and aquifer and sensitive sites represent some of its thematic layers (see Figure 2).

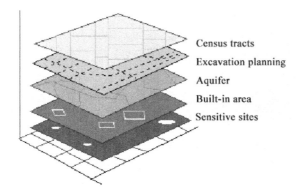

Fig. 2. The Thematic Layers Composing an Environmental Map.

Thus, GIS provide methods for representing geographic data that allow the user to adopt conceptual models closely related to the source data. This implies an emphasis on the geometry and topological primitives that characterize surveyed data. There are two categories of geographic models encountered in commercial GIS, the *vector data model* and the *raster data model*. The former represents phenomena in terms of spatial primitives, or components, consisting of points, lines, areas, surfaces and volumes (see Figure 3). The raster data model represents phenomena as occupying the cells of a predefined, grid-shaped tessellation. It is commonly used to describe continuously varying features, but the kind of information which can be derived is very limited with respect to the vector data model.

While carrying out our research, we have focused on the vector data model, which is characterized by a more natural representation of the geometry and the topology of the surveyed data. In particular, we have based the formalism underlying *MGISQL* on the *9-intersection model* by Egenhofer and Herring [7]. It is a comprehensive model for binary topological spatial relations and applies to objects of type region, line and point. It characterizes the topological relation t between two point sets, A and B, by the set of intersections of A's interior (A°), boundary (∂A), and exterior (A⁻) with the interior, boundary and exterior of B. With each of these nine intersections being empty ($\varnothing$) or non-empty ($\neg\varnothing$), the model has 512 possible topological relations between two point sets, some of which can never occur, depending on the dimensions of the objects, and the dimensions of their embedding space.

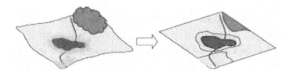

Fig. 3. A Vector Representation for a Geographic Layer.

As example, let us consider the topological relation adjacent (between two regions A and B). It can be represented as follows.

A adjacent B $\Leftrightarrow$

$$A° \cap B° = \varnothing, A° \cap \partial B = \varnothing, A° \cap B^- = \neg\varnothing,$$
$$\partial A \cap B° = \varnothing, \partial A \cap \partial B = \neg\varnothing, \partial A \cap B^- = \neg\varnothing,$$
$$A^- \cap B° = \neg\varnothing, A^- \cap \partial B = \neg\varnothing, A^- \cap B^- = \neg\varnothing.$$

Spatial relations are used as a basis in the definition of *MGISQL* spatial operators. In the next section we recall the basic concepts that underlie the visual query formulation in *MGISQL*.

3   The Metaphor GIS Query Language

Visual languages are today being widely used as a means for reproducing the user's mental model of the data manipulated [4]. In particular, in the area of database systems, several visual query languages have been proposed, which relate the computer representation of the information contained in a database to the users' understanding of the database content [3]. When dealing with the information manipulated by a GIS, the definition of appropriate visual query languages becomes an especially challenging task. A study on computational models of spatial relations has revealed that human subjects tend to draw a geographic object by providing its geometric representation, while referring to its meaning in the real world, namely to the theme that the object describes [11]. This means that the two parts of a geographic data are intrinsically related in human minds. The visual approach we proposed in [12] is based on the concept of *geometaphor*, a special type of visual description which was conceived to simultaneously capture the double nature of geographic data, namely the its geometric and its thematic components.

Figure 4 shows how geometaphors collect both aspects of a geographic data. The graphical part carries information about the underlying spatial element (its topology), while the icon recalls the descriptive part corresponding to the visual representation of the real world phenomenon which the GIS element refers to (i.e., the theme it describes). The topology of the involved GIS element is represented by associating with it the corresponding symbol. In particular, an elipse bordering its label is meant to represent regions, a line underlying its label is used to represent lines, and a bold dot near its label represents points.

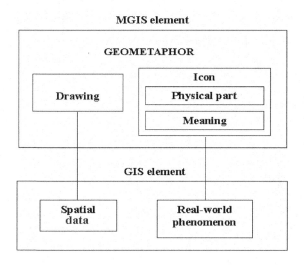

Fig. 4. The Geometaphor for a GIS Data in *MGISQL*.

For example, the geographic data Cell-phone may be described as the geometaphor

whose components are displayed in Table I.

Geometaphors underlie the definition of *MGISQL* and are used to specify all the elements featuring in a GIS domain, including, e.g, geographic data, and either topological, or directional or metric relations. The main feature of the *MGISQL* environment is the use of a *Sensitive Board*, which is an interactive drawing area, where visual queries are formulated. Its sensitivity is related to the capability of translating a visual query (expressed in terms of geometaphors) into a corresponding GIS query by taking into account the context in which the query is posed. Besides that, the Sensitive Board can be assigned one out of four different *sensitivity levels*, level 0 corresponding to the absence of spatial relations in the query formulated, and the others corresponding to the specification of topological, directional and metric relations, respectively. The higher is the level, the more meaningful become the details about the kind of spatial operators involved.

Table 1. The Components of a Geometaphor for the Geographic Data Cell-Phone.

Geometaphor		
Drawing		Point
Icon	*physical representation*	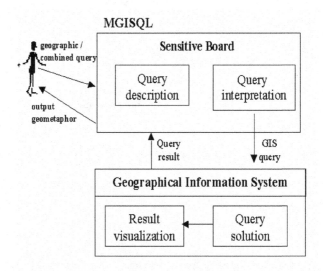
	meaning	Cell-phone

As sketched in Figure 5, the interaction of *MGISQL* with the underlying GIS ends up with the creation of appropriate geometaphors associated with the query results, which the user may decide to retain and exploit in the formulation of compound queries. The figure also shows the Query Descriptor, which can be used to visualize a textual description of the *MGISQL* query, at any time during its construction.

Fig. 5. The Interaction with the Underlying GIS.

In *MGISQL* the manipulation and retrieval of geographic data are performed by two kinds of queries, geographic queries and combined queries, respectively. A *geographic* query is an extended kind of spatial query, which involves spatial operators and *thematic functions* as a means to derive new information, while a *combined* query retrieves semantically related data from separate alphanumeric and spatial databases. In particular, in order to retrieve geographic data from a GIS by taking into account their spatial features, geographic queries are formulated explotinig *spatial operators* and *thematic functions*. As spatial operators, three categories have been identified, namely the topological, the directional and the metric ones that can be applied to geometaphors. The underlying relations characterize the definition of the corresponding operators.

Besides spatial operators, users can formulate a geographic query through the application of thematic functions. Thematic functions can be used to create new geometaphors for a given theme starting from existing ones. The resulting set of geometaphors represents a real world situation associated with the original theme and is therefore called a *context*.

More details about formal definitions can be found in [12]. In the following section we provide examples of queries formulated in *MGISQL*, by describing the case study of EMF pollution monitoring.

4   Monitoring the Electromagnetic Pollution

In the present section we show the effectiveness of the proposed visual environment in monitoring electromagnetic fields and delivering test results, by describing the experimentation carried out with *MGISQL*. Thanks to the use of geometaphors and to the expressiveness of the *MGISQL* language, users can intuitively manipulate both the spatial and the thematic components of the geographic data. Besides the Sensitive Board, which is the interactive area where queries are formulated and the resulting geometaphors are displayed, the environment displays the *Geodictionary*, which contains the geometaphors on which queries may be posed.

Figure 6 shows the formulation of a geographic query, by which user asks to retrieve all the hospitals which are within a range of a kilometer from long distance power lines. The Geodictionary (the area on the right of the interface) contains the geometaphors characterizing the application domain. These refer to cell-phones, long-distance power lines, base stations and all the sensitive sites which can be affected by these polluting sources. As illustrated, the Geodictionary only contains the iconic representation of each geometaphor, while its drawing part (i.e., the representation of its topology) is visualized only when the icon is put on the Sensitive Board to take part in the query composition.

The user formulates such a query through the spatial arrangement of spatial operators and geometaphors. During the query formulation, s/he drags the involved geometaphors and from the Geodictionary, spatially arranges them on the Sensitive Board, and specifies the spatial operator **distance**, by selecting the third sensitivity level of the Board, namely the one referring to metric operators. A pop-up menu has been displayed, from which the user might select the appropriate metric operator and possibly associate a condition with it. When the user presses the Generate button, the output geometaphor is built, with the corresponding topology as its drawing part. The icon is automatically built by bringing the dominant element to the front. Finally, the Sensitive Board displays the sites satisfying the query and, on demand, the user can visualize more details related to the required geographic data, such as images and videos.

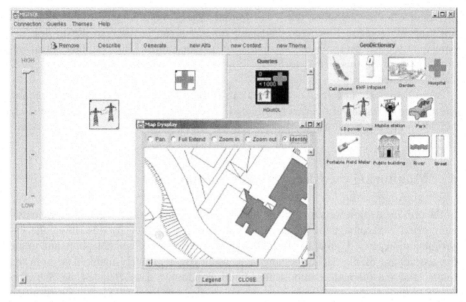

Fig. 6. The Formulation of a Visual Query.

More sophisticated queries can also be posed, which combine spatial and alphanumeric output. Figure 7 shows a new query posed on the output obtained by the query in Figure 6. It retrieves alphanumeric data and photos of all the measurements performed around the polling sources previously retrieved. The alphanumeric data are reported in a table and are visually represented by a chart. A photo of one of these portable field meters may also be displayed on demand.

As discussed in Section 3, users can formulate a geographic query through the application of thematic functions. As an example of the application of a thematic function, let us consider Figure 8 which shows a city map where the ELECTROMAGNETIC POLLUTION theme corresponds to a view which includes polluting sources, such as industries and power stations, and sensitive sites, such as hospitals, rivers, parks, gardens and schools. The thematic function **EMF_test** is applied to the geometaphors

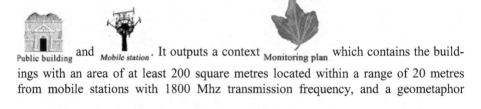

Public building and Mobile station . It outputs a context Monitoring plan which contains the buildings with an area of at least 200 square metres located within a range of 20 metres from mobile stations with 1800 Mhz transmission frequency, and a geometaphor

Laboratory which refers to the laboratories that can be set up inside those buildings. The laboratories correspond to a new geometaphor since new geometric and alphanumeric attributes characterize them (e.g, their position and range, as geometric attribute, and the the typology of measurements performed, as alphanumeric attribute).

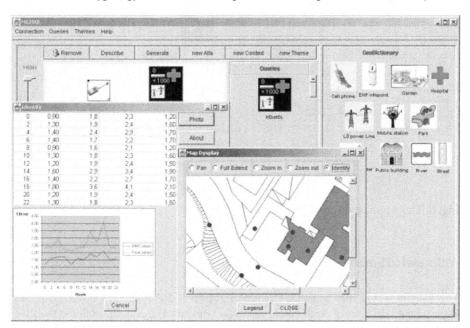

Fig. 7. The Data Resulting from the Pollution Monitoring.

5   Final Remarks

The goal of our proposal has been to encourage the exploitation of GIS technology in the organization and manipulation of electromagnetic pollution data analysis. The experimental system has been developed within the *MGISQL* visual environment in order to provide non- expert GIS users with full visual support to the manipulation of geographic data carrying information about the EMF pollution level. The concept of geometaphor has been profitably exploited to associate the visual representation of the spatial properties with an iconic component, able to resemble the described thematism. The usability evaluation of the system is an on-going process. As a matter of fact, it is being experimented by a group of physicians who recognized the need to geo-reference the data coming from their measurements. Further evaluation is planned on a sample set of non-expert users.

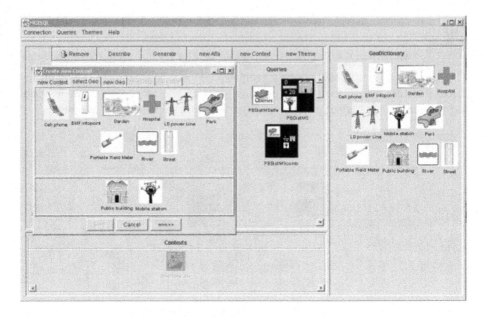

Fig. 8. The Application of a Thematic Function.

Acknowledgment

The authors would like to thank Carmine Lubritto and Antonio D'Onofrio, from the Dipartimento di Scienze Ambientali, Seconda Università di Napoli, both for the fruitful discussions held as domain experts, and for supplying us with actual data about electromagnetic pollution of an area of the Campania region.

References

1. M. A. Aufaure-Portier (1994) Definition of a Visual Language for GIS. in *Cognitive Aspects of Human-Computer Interaction for Geographic Information Systems*, Dordrecht, The Netherlands, (T. Nyerges, D. Mark, R. Laurini, and M. Egenhofer, eds.), Kluwer Academic Publisher, pp. 163-178.
2. D. Calcinelli and M. Mainguenaud, (1994) Cigales, a Visual Query Language for Geographic Information System: the User Interface. *Journal of Visual Languages and Computing* 5, pp. 113 – 132.
3. T. Catarci, M.F. Costabile, S. Levialdi, and C. Batini (1997) Visual Query Systems for Databases: A Survey. *Journal of Visual Languages and Computing* 8, pp. 215-260.
4. S.K. Chang (1990) *Visual Languages and Visual Programming*, Plenum Publishing Corporation, New York.
5. G. Costagliola, G. Tortora, and M. Tucci. (1995). GISQL - A Query Language Interpreter for Geographic Information Systems. *Procs 3rd IFIP 2.6 Working Conference on Visual Database System,* (S. Spaccapietra and R. Jain, eds.), pp. 275-286.

6. M. Egenhofer and H.T. Bruns (1997) User Interfaces for Map Algebra. *Journal of the Urban and Regional Information Systems Association* 9, n. 1, pp. 44 – 54.
7. M. Egenhofer and J. Herring (1990), "Categorizing Binary Topological Relationships Between Regions, Lines and Points in Geographic Databases", Technical Report Department of Surveying Engineering, University of Maine, Orono, ME.
8. J. Florence, K. Hornsby, and M. Egenhofer (1996) The GIS Wallboard: Interactions with Spatial Information on Large-Scale Displays. *7th International Symposium on Spatial Data Handling* (SDH'96), Delft, The Netherlands, (M.- J. Kraak and M. Molenaar eds.), pp. 8A.1-15, August 1996.
9. C. Jones (1998) *Geographic Information System and Computer Cartography,* Longman.
10. Y.C. Lee and F.L. Chi (1995). An Iconic Query Language for Topological Relationship in GIS. *International Journal on Geographical Information Systems* 9, pp. 25-46.
11. D. Mark, D. Comas, M. Egenhofer, S. Freundschuh, M. Gould, and J. Nunes (1995) Evaluating and Refining Computational Models of Spatial Relations Through Cross-Linguistic Human-Subjects Testing. *Procs. COSIT'95*, (A. Frank and W. Kuhn eds.), *LNCS* vol. 988, Springer-Verlag, pp.553-568.
12. M. Sebillo, G. Tortora, and G. Vitiello, "The Metaphor GIS Query Language", *Journal of Visual Languages & Computing*, vol. 11 n. 4, August 2000, Academic Press, pp. 439 - 454.
13. C. Traynor and M.G. Williams (2000) Usability of Visual and Textual Representations for Geographic Information Systems. *First International Conference on Geographic Information Science*, Georgia, USA
14. M. Wessel and V. Haarslev (1998). VISCO: Bringing Visual Spatial Querying to Reality. *Procs. IEEE Symposium on Visual Language*, Nova Scotia, Canada, 170-177.
15. Environmental System Research Institute, www.esri.com .
16. *SPANS MAP*, Intera Tydac Technologies Inc, www.tydac.ch.
17. *MGE Project Viewer*, Intergraph Corporation, www.intergraph.com/federal.
18. International EMF project, World Health Organization , www.who.int/peh-emf .

Part IV

Image and Visual Information Querying and Browsing

Querying and Browsing
Multimedia Presentations

Augusto Celentano and Ombretta Gaggi

Dipartimento di Informatica, Università Ca' Foscari Venezia
via Torino 155, 30172 Mestre (VE), Italy
{auce,ogaggi}@dsi.unive.it

Abstract. Querying and searching the Web is an important research field which has drawn a number of concepts from databases and information retrieval fields, but has added its own models, requirements and techniques.

Multimedia information adds another dimension to the problem, when information is globally conveyed by different media which are archived and delivered separately, and must be coordinated and synchronized.

In this paper we discuss some issues about information retrieval in synchronized multimedia presentations. We introduce a class of multimedia presentations made of independent and synchronized media, and discuss how retrieval requirements can be defined. Then we discuss the need of a model for retrieving and browsing multimedia data in a way capable of integrating atomic media objects in coherent presentations.

1   Introduction

Multimedia is entering all fields of communication, and information presentation is becoming more and more rich. The Internet technology is growing and delivery of complex multimedia presentations, made of several continuous streams and static documents, does not suffer any more of technical constraints that have characterized the early stage of the World Wide Web.

Today it is possible to build and deliver video and audio information in a Web environment for domains who demand a good quality of images and audio and information organization according to complex schemas.

As the Web size grows the traditional navigation paradigm shows unbearable limits, and querying becomes a mandatory entry point for any meaningful exploration. Querying and searching the Web is an important research field which has drawn a number of concepts from databases and information retrieval fields, but has added its own models, requirements and techniques.

Multimedia information adds another dimension to the problem, when information is globally conveyed by different media which are archived and delivered separately, and must be coordinated and synchronized.

In this paper we discuss some issues about information retrieval in synchronized multimedia presentations. We introduce a class of multimedia presentations made of independent and synchronized media, and discuss how retrieval

M. Tucci (Ed.): MDIC 2001, LNCS 2184, pp. 105–116, 2001.

requirements can be defined. Then we discuss the need of a model for retrieving continuous data in a consistent way, able to reconstruct the fragments of a presentation from the atomic components returned by the query execution.

2   Querying Synchronized Multimedia Presentations

We consider hypermedia presentations made of one or more continuous media file, such as video or audio streams, which are presented to a user in a Web-based environment. As streams play, static documents, such as images or text pages, are sent to the browser and displayed in synchrony with them. From the user point of view the documents constitute a whole presentation which is coherent in terms of time relationships among the component media item, like a single compound stream. The user can interact with the presentation by pausing and resuming it, and by moving forward or backward along its timeline in a VCR style.

In a Web environment documents can be linked to other documents, therefore the user can follow a link, possibly reaching a completely different context. From a usability point of view the presentation should in some cases be paused, or stopped, while in other cases it could continue playing. As a general requirements, after any user action media delivery and playback must be coordinated in such a way that the user always sees a coherent presentation.

News-oriented applications (e.g., news-on-demand and Web advertising) and distance education are good representative of such presentations. The latter is a quite old scenario that at different phases of technology development has been used as a test bed for multimedia applications, due not only to its interest as a strategic field (e.g. in terms of long-life learning) but also because it demands high quality in terms of usability. The former is a relatively new field in which richness of information, variety in presentation and ease of interaction can attract the Web user. Lessons are made of text, animated presentations, slides, talks, movies, and of course of linked supplemental material that a student can access during the lesson itself. News are presented through audio or a video clips, and images and texts are displayed according to the particular argument the speaker is talking about.

2.1   Multimedia Retrieval

Retrieving information in such documents is a task which presents a number of peculiarities. First, information is contained in documents of different types; i.e., querying must retrieve information from different media at the same time. Second, the user is not interested in any single document but in the part of presentation in which at least one of the documents satisfy the query; i.e., the retrieved item is only a component of a part of the presentation which is the true query result. Third, being the presentation dynamic, a coherent and understandable segment must be returned to the user; i.e., the query result extent must be identified according to a context which takes into account the presentation structure.

The first issue does not present conceptual problems with respect to information retrieval state of art. Multimedia databases encompass multiple representations of data in order to answer queries on different media types. We do not suggest that such a problem is of small concern or simple, or that all technical aspects are solved. For example, the language (textual or pictorial) used to formulate the query belongs to a specific syntactic domain against which data representation of different types must be matched (see [5] for an extensive survey of combined text, audio and video retrieval in news applications).

The second and the third issues require that the static organization of a presentation, which relates media together, and the temporal aspects of its behavior, which describe how the different segments evolve, be defined according to a structured model.

2.2   Managing Query Results

At a first glance the result of a query on a multimedia database is a set of media objects which respond to the query criteria. Each media item can be a (section of) audio or video file, but also a non continuous medium like a text page or an image. If retrieved items are also part of a composite multimedia document, such as a complex presentation, they cannot be displayed or played alone: for example, a slide of a lesson without the accompanying audio track, which is recorded separately, is scarcely useful.

For this reason, it is not possible, in general, to return to the user only an index of retrieved media items. We need to retrieve also any other items belonging to the composite original presentation, which has to be reconstructed and shown.

The correctly retrieved information must be a list (an index) of complete fragments of different multimedia documents, in which at least one medium item responds to the query criteria. The system should retrieve all media items that belong to a coherent section of the presentation, and display them to the user in a coordinated and synchronized way.

A consequence of such a behavior is that the number of media objects retrieved can be different from the number of results shown to the user. Each media item can be part of a different presentation, or some of them can belong to a same presentation. If two media objects belong to the same multimedia document, they can be part of different sections of the document, or be close in time: in the first case, they must be proposed as two different results, in the second case they must presented as a same result.

For these reasons, the retrieval system must be integrated with knowledge about the structure of the presentations in order to show the results in a complete and coherent way. Two kinds of information are needed:

- the hierarchical structure, for deciding when two items are part of a same section, and

– the temporal relationships, for displaying different results according to the author design of the presentation.

3 Related Work

3.1 Modeling Multimedia Presentation

Many research papers have presented different ways of specifying structure and temporal scenarios of a hypermedia documents.

Amsterdam Hypermedia Model [7,8] was the first serious attempt to combine media items with temporal relations into hypertext document. AHM structures document objects into atomic and composite components. Media items are played into channels while synchronization inside composite components is described by synchronization arches and offsets that establish time relationships between two components or two anchors.

SMIL, Synchronized Multimedia Integration Language[12], is a W3C recommendation defined as an XML application. It is a very simple markup language that defines tags for presenting multimedia objects in coordinated way. Synchronization is achieved through two tags: `seq` to render two or more objects sequentially and `par` to reproduce them in parallel. Using attributes it is possible to play segments inside the time span of an object.

In [1,2] we discuss the problem of authoring and navigating hypermedia documents composed of continuous and non continuous media objects delivered separately in a Web-based environment. We have introduced a model which defines a static structure and synchronization relationships among media objects of a presentation. Our model overcomes the limitations of SMIL because it considers user interaction. The user can interact separately with each single object of the presentation and the presentation is synchronized accordingly. SMIL native features allow interactions only with the whole document.

3.2 Multimedia Querying and Browsing

Problems related to querying, browsing and presenting multimedia information has been largely investigated in the literature.

In [9] the authors describe an integrated query and navigation model built upon techniques from declarative query languages and navigational paradigms. The system implemented provides facilities to help not expert user in query writing activity. Navigation hierarchies are used to present to the user summary information instead of a simple listing of query results. Differently from our approach, the authors never consider timing relations between objects, while they manage to hide querying of heterogeneous data on distributed repositories with an unified user interface.

Delaunay^{MM}[4] is a framework for querying and presenting multimedia data stored in distributed data repositories. The user specifies a multimedia presentation spatial layout by arranging graphical icons. Then, each icon is assigned

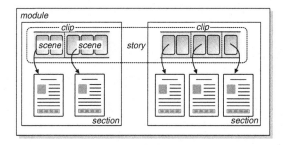

Fig. 1. Hierarchical Structure of Multimedia Presentation.

to a query, thus combining data selection with presentation. Delaunay^{MM} uses ad hoc querying capabilities to search each type of media item in distributed database and on the Web. Also in this proposed paper, the authors did not address any solution for the specification of temporal synchronization among the objects.

In [10,11] the authors present TVQL, a multimedia visual query language for temporal analysis of video data. They consider a video of a teacher's lesson in classroom and annotate the video to identify interesting events, such as a student question or the teacher talk. TVQL (for temporal visual query language) enables user to browse for temporal relationships between two objects subsets. For example the user can search for which student speaks frequently after a teacher talk. The authors do not approach complex presentations with heterogeneous synchronized objects, but only a single video stream at a time.

In [3] a model is presented that fully integrate browsing and querying of hypermedia data capabilities. The model gives particular emphasis to structured information and combines two components: the hypermedia component and the Information Retrieval (IR) component. The hypermedia component contain information about both structure and content of a document. This integrated system allow users to compose queries which contain both kind of information in their formulation. The IR component contains information about the model and the resolution of the queries. Although it deals with composite documents, this paper doesn't consider time relationships among atomic objects of a structured documents.

4   A Model for Describing Hypermedia Dynamics

The model we have proposed in [1,2] describes the hierarchical structure of the document's components. A hypermedia presentation contains different kinds of media objects: static objects are referred to as *pages*; dynamic objects, video and audio clips, are hierarchically structured.

A multimedia presentation is composed of a set of *modules*, which the user can access in a completely independent way. The continuous media, an audio, or a video stream, which constitutes the main module content, is called a *story*. A

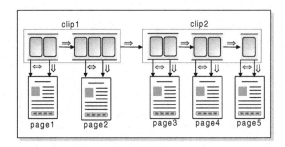

Fig. 2. Synchronization Relationships between Media Items

story is composed by a sequence of *clips*, each of which correspond to an audio or a video file. Clips are divided into *scenes*, each of which is associated to a static document, a *page*. A clip, with its scenes and associated pages, build up a *section*. Figure 1 pictorially shows this structure.

For example, in a distance education application, the video of a lesson can be divided into different *stories* according to the lesson topics. Stories are divided into *clips* according to the video segmentation into files and clips are divided into *scenes* according to the time a slide remains on the user screen. The slides of the lesson are the *pages* of the presentation which are displayed in turn as the lesson goes on. Media objects use *channels* (e.g., windows for displayable media) for their playback.

Synchronization is achieved with a set of primitives which define objects behavior during presentation's playback and channels' utilization. We have defined five synchronization relationships which describe the reaction of media objects to events. The events can be *internal*, like the beginning or termination of an object playback, or *external*, like a user action.

The synchronization primitives are:

- *A* plays with *B*, denoted by $A \Leftrightarrow B$, to play two objects in parallel in a way such that object *A* controls the time extent of object *B*;
- *A* activates *B*, denoted by $A \Rightarrow B$, to play two objects in sequence;
- *A* is terminated with *B*, denoted by $A \Downarrow B$, to terminate two objects at the same time as a consequence of an user interaction or of the forced termination of object *A*;
- *A* is replaced by *B*, denoted by $A \rightleftharpoons B$, to force the termination of object *A* so that object *B* can use its channel;
- *A* has priority over *B* with behavior α, denoted by $A \overset{\alpha}{>} B$, to stop (if $\alpha = s$) or pause (if $\alpha = p$) object *B* when the user activates object *A*.

Figure 2 shows an example of such relationships for the module depicted in Figure 1. Each scene starts and ends a text page to which is associated. The whole document uses two channels, one for the clips and one for the pages. The reader is referred to [1,2] for a complete discussion of the model.

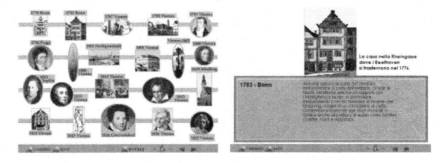

Fig. 3. Screenshots from a Presentation about Beethoven's Life.

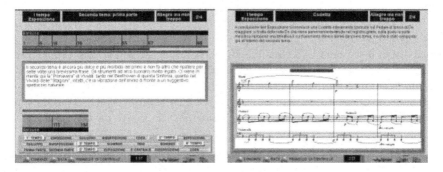

Fig. 4. The Guide to Listening and Score Analysis of the *Pastoral* Symphony.

5   An Example from a Music Masterworks Collection

As a working example for the remainder of this paper we illustrate briefly the overall structure of a collection of multimedia CD-ROMs[1] featuring masterworks of famous musicians, published in Italy a few years ago[6]. Each CD-ROM follows a constant structure and contains a wide set of information about the musician's life, the historical period, the masterwork itself (as an audio file), a description of its musical structure in form of graphical score and text comments, a criticism, in form of written text, which accompanies the music play, and a set of audio files of related works. The CD-ROM collection could be viewed as a multimedia data repository for queries about biographies, musical structure and critical analysis, historical references and other kinds of information. Figures 3 and 4 show some screen shots from the CD-ROM on Beethoven Symphony no. 6 "Pastorale".

In Figure 3 a description of the life of Beethoven is illustrated. It is an animated presentation (the left image shows the final state) stepping through selected years in Beethoven's life. Each year is described by a short animation

---

[1] We use a CD-ROM based example because it is a complete product featuring a complex multimedia presentation, even if our target is the World Wide Web. In Section 6 we'll discuss the main differences between the two environments.

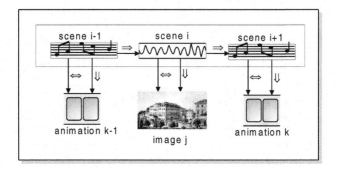

Fig. 5. The Synchronization Schema for the Presentation about Beethoven's Life.

which draws a segment of a timeline, displays an image and starts a spoken comment. A background music plays during the whole animation. As the narration goes on, a complete timeline is built. At the end of the presentation the user can click over an image to display a text page which reproduces the comment that was given by voice about that year, as shown in the image on the right.

The speaker's voice and the background music are integrated in the same audio file. According to our model, the audio track is a *clip*, which is divided into a sequence of *scenes* which interleave the speaker's voice and the background music. The animations which draw the timeline, between two events in Beethoven's life, are also *clips*, while the images displayed during the spoken comments can be considered *pages* since they are static media objects. Since the presentation starts with an animation, even numbered scenes correspond to voice comments and images, while odd numbered scenes correspond to the transitions from one year to the next.

Figure 5 shows the synchronization schema of this part of the presentation. The scenes play in sequence, hence $scene_i \Rightarrow scene_{i+1}$. Each scene which draws a timeline segment begins and ends with the related animation, and is described by the relationship $scene_{2i-1} \Leftrightarrow animation_i$. Similarly, each spoken comment goes in parallel with an image, as described the relationship $scene_{2i} \Leftrightarrow image_i$.

The user can stop the presentation by clicking over a "bypass" button. The audio track is terminated, and also the animation or the image displayed are terminated. This behavior is described by the relationships $scene_{2i-1} \Downarrow animation_i$ and $scene_{2i} \Downarrow image_i$.

Figure 4 shows two different but similar sections of this multimedia presentation: the analysis of the music work from the points of view of the artistic quality and the musical structure. In the left image the overall structure of the work is shown, and as the music play a bar moves showing the position in the score length. Text comments help the user to interpret the execution. In the right image the musical score is drawn and updated as the music plays. Also in this case some text comments are displayed. The regular structure of these two sections can be described, in terms of synchronization relationships, in a way similar to the example shown above.

6   Presentation in Multimedia Document Retrieval

We may notice that in several contexts the information which is presented to the user is composed of several media which are to be coherently harmonized in order to be meaningful. This is evident in the CD-ROM sections illustrated in Figure 4, where a text comment without the music and the context given by the visual interface is meaningless.

If we want to query or browse a multimedia database based on such an information structure we need to identify, retrieve and integrate all the components of the presentation segment which contains the relevant information.

In this paper we do not consider models and technologies for retrieving multimedia contents. Our concern is the reconstruction of a coherent multimedia document fragment given one or more of its components media objects. Therefore we assume (maybe with some imagination effort) that a system for retrieving multimedia information such as texts, voice talks, musical fragments, scores and images by content analysis is available, even if information other than text still exhibits a high degree of uncertainty in existing products or prototypes.

Let us suppose that we want to retrieve all the musicians in the data repository which have been living in Leipzig, and for each of them we want a description of such periods, or in general the information about their life in that town. We could find a set of voice comments, taken from the presentation of the musician's life, and the texts associated of them, as in Figure 3, plus other information chunks taken from different sections of the repository.

If we want to retrieve all the music passages where strings play in a *crescendo* style we could ask for such a text description in the guide to listening and in the score analysis, or perform a content analysis on the score itself in order to identify such annotations.

In both cases the retrieval system will return a set of (pointers to) multimedia data instances, but the user should receive composite parts of the original presentation in order to understand the result of the query. Browsing has similar problems: once identified a relevant information, the user needs to enlarge the scope and access a more complex information in order to understand it.

A model, such the one presented in Section 4 allows the system to fill the gap between the retrieval of separate components and the presentation of the composite document. One could argue that in many cases the presentation is built as a single file or a set of tightly coupled files, i.e. a set of *tracks*, therefore a reference from the components to the time interval in which they are played is all is needed to identify the relevant context. Even if the presentation is made of separate files integrated by a player, the execution proceeds linearly in time, therefore something similar to a time stamp could solve the problem.

In many cases this is true, but we have assumed as the enclosing scenario of our discussion the World Wide Web, and there are at least two issues that make this simplification not realistic:

- the media are delivered by a server according to a composite document structure which can be distributed in several files, and is known as they are delivered to the client;
- a WWW document usually has links that allow the user to explore its structure in a non linear way, and the user can also interact by backtracking or reloading the documents as they are displayed.

6.1   Building a Multimedia Query Answer

Presentation of multimedia information can rely on the static structure and the dynamic synchronization relationships defined by a model like the one described in Section 4, in order to build a query answer which contains all the presentation elements related to the media objects retrieved as results of the query execution.

Answer building is performed in two steps:

- the static structure of the presentation is used to collect all the media items that complete the fragment in which the retrieved object is located;
- the dynamic relationships are used to select the presentation unit to be delivered to the user as the query answer.

With a reference to Figure 5, if the query retrieves a passage of the voice comment in $scene_i$, the answer to be reported to the user is at least that scene, which is dynamically linked to an image j, which should also be displayed according to the presentation behavior.

In the same way, after retrieving a text in which a *crescendo* of strings is described it is easy to identify the corresponding part of the audio track in the guide to listening because a relationship links that segment of the audio track to the comment that describes it. In the score analysis, the text comment is related to the same segment of audio track, but also the image of the pertaining score page is related, and the whole presentation fragment made of the music, the score and the text can be delivered and displayed.

If more than one object is selected as a retrieved item, it is easy to check if they are part of a same section or of different sections of a same presentation, or of different presentation, avoiding duplicates. The hierarchical structure of a multimedia document helps to identify the scope of a module, of a clip or of a scene.

Thanks to the same hierarchical structure, it is possible to give the user different levels of access to the resulting presentation. A first attempt is to index the scenes, which are the finest level of access in our model. The user can quickly browse them without being compelled to browse longer sections. In our example, if the user is interested in a particular moment of a musician's life, he or she wants to listen only the scene regarding that year. This level of indexing gives thus the user the possibility to evaluate the accuracy of the retrieve in terms of precision.

The user could then select, according to a relevance analysis, some responses which appear more appropriate than others, and gain access to the higher level of hierarchy, which give a broader context for the retrieved items. In our example, the user could be interested in the whole life of one musician, say Beethoven, identified through a specific information about one of the narrated episodes. The higher level is in this case the whole presentation of a specific instance in the retrieved set, together with animations and images.

In all cases the presence of a synchronization model guarantees that the sections of the presentation which are displayed are coherent.

7 Conclusion

Information retrieval in distributed multimedia presentations requires modeling of the relationships among the media objects which build the presentations. We have illustrated a synchronization model which makes a step further, with respect to other models defined in the literature, in considering also user actions such as pausing or stopping when reading such a presentation in a hypermedia context.

In this paper we have analyzed the model in the perspective of information retrieval and browsing, showing how such model can help in building coherent answers to information retrieval queries to multimedia data repositories where complex presentations are stored. Technical issues concerning retrieval of multimedia data and index construction for complex composite documents deserve of course great attention and investigation in order to move from a modeling approach like the one described here to a prototype implementation.

References

1. A. Celentano, O.Gaggi. Synchronization Model for Hypermedia Document Navigation. *Proceedings of the 2000 ACM Symposium on Applied Computing*, pages 585–591, Como, 2000.
2. A. Celentano, O. Gaggi. Modeling Synchronized Hypermedia Documents. *Technical Report n. 1/2001*, Department of Computer Science, Università Ca' Foscari di Venezia, Italy, January 2001, submitted for publication.
3. Y. Chiaramella. Browsing and Querying: Two Complementary Approaches for Multimedia Information Retrieval. *Proceedings of Hypertext - Information Retrieval - Multimedia'97*, pages 9–26, Dortmund, WA, USA, 1997.
4. I.F. Cruz, W.T. Lucas. A Visual Approach to Multimedia Querying and Presentation. *Proceedings of the Fifth ACM International Conference on Multimedia'97*, pages 109–120, Seattle, WA, USA November 9-13, 1997.
5. A. Del Bimbo. *Visual Information Retrieval*. Morgan Kauffmann,1999
6. Enda Multimedia. *CD-ROM Musica*. Enda Srl Milano, Italy, 1996.
7. L. Hardman. Using the Amsterdam Hypermedia Model for Abstracting Presentation Behavior. In *Electronic Proceedings of the ACM Workshop on Effective Abstractions in Multimedia*. San Francisco, CA, 4 November 1995.

8. L. Hardman, D.C.A. Bulterman and G. van Rossum. The Amsterdam Hypermedia Model: adding time and context to the Dexter Model. *Comm. of the ACM*, 37(2), pages 50–62, 1994.

9. R. J. Miller, O. G. Tsatalos and J. H. Williams. Integrating Hierarchical Navigation and Quering: A User Customizable Solution. In *Electronic Proceedings of the ACM Workshop on Effective Abstractions in Multimedia*. San Francisco, CA, 4 November 1995.

10. S. Hibino, E. A. Rundensteiner. A Visual Multimedia Query Language for Temporal Analysis of Video Data. *Multimedia Database Systems: Design and Implementation Strategies*, Kluwer Academic Publishers, ISBN 0-7923-9712-6, pages 123–159, 1996.

11. S. Hibino, E. A. Rundensteiner. User Interface Evaluation of a Direct Manipulation Temporal Visual Query Language. *Proceedings of the Fifth ACM International Conference on Multimedia'97*, pages 99–107, Seattle, WA, USA November 9-13, 1997.

12. Synchronized Multimedia Working Group of W3C. Synchronized Multimedia Integration Language (SMIL) 1.0 Specification. *W3C Recommendation*, 15 June 1998. http://www.w3.org/TR/REC-smil.

Content Image Retrieval: A New Query Paradigm Toward Analogy Based Indexing

Maurizio Cibelli[1], Michele Nappi[2], and Maurizio Tucci[2]

[1]Microsoft Corporation, US Mobility Division
One Microsoft Way Redmond, Seattle WA 98052
mcibelli@microsoft.com
[2]University of Salerno
Dipartimento di Matematica e Informatica
via S.Allende, I-840841 Baronissi, Salerno (Italy)
{mnappi,mtucci}@unisa.it

Abstract. In this paper, we address the visual analogies recognition problem. Often morphogeometric-based metrics are not sufficient to express high-level relations as well as complex queries. The model we are proposing extends the original virtual image formalism[2], into a hierarchical list of attributes. The lowest level is composed of spatial relations, whereas the highest level model relations between groups in terms of homogeneity and cardinality. The information stored in each layer is the basis for the new similarity metric, that models the query by analogy paradigm (QBA for short) we present in this work. This new analogy-based index, allows users to express complex relations as well as search for pictures expressing similar relations, such as functional association or group membership between objects.

1 Introduction

High-level perceptual processes synthesize low-level object features into high-level structures. People recognize basic categories[13], but changes in internal configuration and individual variations are irrelevant. We recognize group of humans regardless of whether they are sitting or standing, they are driving or walking. Grouping is a necessary precursor to object recognition[6].

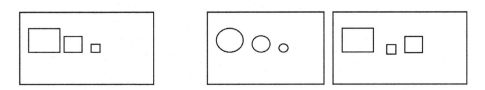

Fig. 1. The Three Boxes Express a Strong "Dimension" Relation.

M. Tucci (Ed.): MDIC 2001, LNCS 2184, pp. 117-129, 2001.

Often physical attributes are insufficient to describe complex relations. The example depicted in figure 1 shows that similarity is not only limited to morphologic object attributes.

The three boxes in the left image communicate to our perceptual system a strong group relation in terms of dimension, the same attributes expressed by the picture containing circles. The rightmost image even if contains boxes does not capture the underlying relations expressed by the leftmost image. Moreover organizing object in high-level structure simplifies the search problem. As shown by Grimson[7], the expected complexity of recognizing objects in an un-segmented, cluttered environment is exponential in the size of the correct interpretation.

Different approaches for high-level objects descriptions have been presented in the last decade. According to Feldman[5] group interpretations are caste into a formal language with its own rules of construction and interpretation. The problem of image recognition is projected in the context of logic programming, which considers how logical structures can be computed. Feldman also uses a dot world[6] to build a prolog prototype that recognized similarity between pictures composed of points. The system recognizes geometric properties such as collinearity, coincidenty between dots and builds the so called qualitative parse tree that represents the group interpretation. Successively the system uses this structure to perform similarity matching among the other parse tree.

A different approach is presented by Goldstone[8], where similarity means establishing alignments (e.g. distances) between the parts of compared entities. A localist connectionist model is used to compute correspondence between scene parts, and these units mutually influence each other according to their compatibility.

Jacobs[10] presents a method of grouping edges. The system, called GROPER, uses groups to index into libraries of objects. More precisely, it begins by locating edges in an image using an edge detector algorithm. Successively, it finds connected or nearly connected lines that form convex curves. Convex groups come from a single object with a high probability, and provide useful hints for further grouping. However this information can not be distinctive. Thus, GROPER calculates a measure of likelihood for any pair of convex contours to estimate the probability they come from the same object. Finally, it extends these pair of contours when necessary, by adding additional convex contours.

A similarity measure based on the isomorphism between represented similarity and corresponding shape similarity is presented by Eldeman[3,4] et al. The proposed model is trained (using a distributed network) to recognize relevant object components belonging to the same shape space. Such training is also useful to respond equally to different views of the same object. An object prototype corresponds to a high-level description and overcome variability in the object's appearance caused by different factors such as pose and illumination. Thus, a shape is represented by its similarity to a number of reference shapes, measured in a high-dimensional space of elementary features.

To elaborate a hierarchical image representation, Schlüter[14] proposes a contour grouping based on a subset of Gestalt principle such as proximity, symmetry, closure, and good continuation. The bottom level is represented by object segments, where contour segments are approximated by parametric models like lines or elliptical arcs, provided by an initial segmentation process. Each segment is analyzed and grouped according to symmetry and parallel attributes. Moreover, the concept of areas of perceptual attentiveness is introduced to model spatial attributes such as orientation differences, gap length etc.

The surveyed works represents a valid answer for the object recognition problem. However, they do not provide a method to integrate high-level image descriptions into a pictorial index. On the contrary, our work focuses on the combination of high and low level image decomposition in order to provide a framework where users can express complex relations like functional relationships as well as low-level query constraints like spatial relations. As basis of our work, we adopted the Virtual Image[2] formalism and we extended the original similarity metrics. In the current implementation, a picture description is fragmented in three different layers. The lowest level contains spatial relation information, while in the highest layer we describe an image in terms of group relationship. It is important to note that the presented framework is not heavily coupled with respect to the adopted metric. In theory, different measures can replace the current implemented framework.

The new proposed index supports a more efficient pictorial search, improving the underlying query mechanism providing a query-by-analogy paradigm (QBA for short). The QBA framework can support any iconic indexing method that is based on spatial relations and in general based on morpho-geometrical information. In fact, we provided operational metrics definition that can encapsulate different iconic indexing formalisms. Moreover, we designed an iconic language to easily express searching criteria as well as simplify the annotation process. The paper is organized as follow: in section 2 we illustrate the hierarchical structure and the new similarity metrics we introduced to model a image; section 3 concludes and presents our future works.

2   Image Description Layer

To quote Riesenhuber[12] "The classical model of visual processing in cortex is a hierarchical of increasingly representation". We defined three object description layers corresponding to a different image index (see figure 2).

- Meta-group Layer

The Meta-group layer index is composed of a *second level virtual image*. A group it is an object itself. It has a dimension and can be identified with spatial coordinates. We consider the minimum-bounding rectangle containing all the elements and introduce an additional virtual image, named the second level virtual image, to describe group physical information. This index also stores group homogeneity and cardinality.

- Group-layer

The Group Layer index captures relations between the elements of a group. Different factors determine the association of an object to a group: morph-geometric similarity, functional association (for example a locker and a key), and spatial proximity etc[9].

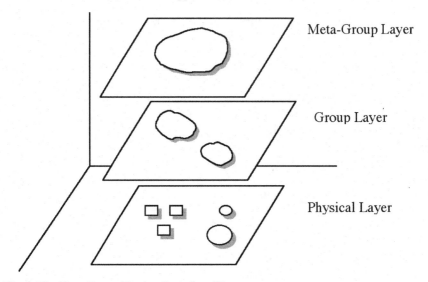

Fig. 2. The Three Layers Used to Describe a Picture.

• Physical Layer

The last layer, named the Physical layer, contains spatial information, and is modeled using the original VI approach.

This hierarchical image description allows users to compose high-level queries. For example, suppose we are browsing a database containing pictures of animals. We can search for pictures with a group of *preys* and *predators*. The answer set can be refined, for example, specifying what kind of predator we are interested. Note that the above layers do not depend on the underlying similarity metric. This means that we can easily replace the virtual image description with another formalism that integrates spatial and/or morpho-geometrical information. In the following sections, we presents a detailed descriptions for each layer we introduced.

2.1   Meta Group Layer

The meta group layer models groups relations rather than object features. To capture these relations, we introduced a second level Virtual Image. An example is depicted in figure 3.

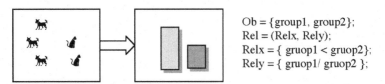

Fig. 3. An Example of Second Level Virtual Image.

A group is considered a meta-object with its own spatial information. Thus, the original VI formalism is well suitable. However, groups can be also compared in terms of homogeneity and cardinality. More precisely, we define

Group Cardinality - A group cardinality *GCard (r)* for a given group r is the number of elements composing the group

Group Homogeneity - A group homogeinity *GHom (r)* for a given group r is

$$GHom\ (r) = 1/\ \#different\ objects\ in\ r$$

The meta-group similarity metric is calculated in two different steps:

Meta-Group Similarity Metric - Let *img^q* and *img^r* be two distinct images. The group similarity distance is defined by the following steps:

- Collects the pictures that have the same number of groups and calculates the distance in terms of cardinality and homogeneity for each group in *img^q* and *img^r*. More precisely, compute the following

$$\frac{1}{1+ \min \sum_{i,j} |\ GCard_i - GCard_j\ | + |\ GHom_i - GHom_j\ |}$$

where i,j are two groups in *img^q* and *img^r*.
In this layer each group is considered a generic object (for example, we do not recognize groups of dogs and cats, but only groups of elements). We are interested in generic collections of objects that are similar in terms of number of elements they are composed of as well as their class homogeneity. In fact, given a group *i* from the image *img^q* what we want to do is to find the corresponded group *j* in *img^r* that minimize this distance regardless of its identity.

- Sort all pictures having the same rank, using a similarity metric. In our case, we calculate that by using the original sim_deg.

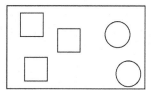

Fig. 4. Two Groups of Geometric Figures.

$$
Sim\_deg\ (Q,\ im_{vi}\ ) = \begin{cases}
\begin{aligned}
&\text{if } (F \subseteq Ob_{im}) \text{ and } (Rel\ x_F \subseteq R_{x\ im}\ \text{ and } (Rel\ y_F \subseteq R_{y\ im}) \text{ then} \\[2pt]
&\dfrac{|F| + |Rel\ x_F| + |Rel\ y_F| + |G \cap Ob_{im}| + \displaystyle\sum_{(q\,\gamma\,q',\,s)\,\in X} s + \sum_{(q\,\gamma\,q',\,s)\,\in Y} s}{|F| + |G| + |Rel\ x| + |Rel\ y|}
\end{aligned} \\[20pt]
\text{otherwise } 0
\end{cases}
$$

It is important to note that, this operative definition allows us to use any spatial metric we want. As an example, suppose we are interested in images analogue to figure 4. For simplicity, the database is composed of few sample images as shown in figure 5.

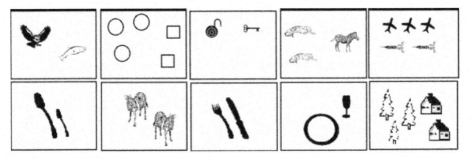

Fig. 5. A Subset of Images Extracted form the QBA Database.

We now compute the similarity degree step-by-step.

1.   *Collects the pictures that have the same number of groups.* Let us limit our discussion to the first 5 retrieved image for simplicity. (see figure 6)

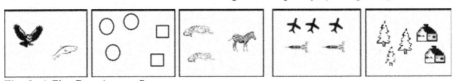

Fig. 6. A First Raw Answer Set.

2.   Calculate the meta-group distance

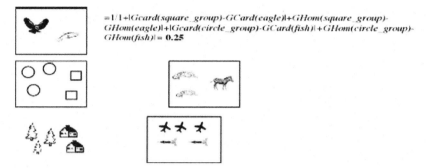

$=1/1+|Gcard(square\_group)-GCard(eagle)|+GHom(square\_group)-GHom(eagle)|+|Gcard(circle\_group)-GCard(fish)|+GHom(circle\_group)-GHom(fish)|=$ **0.25**

Fig. 7. The Meta-group Formula Results.

According to this distance, the pictures are sorted as depicted in figure 8.

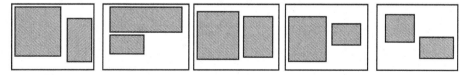

Fig. 8. The New Answer Set, Sorted According to First Step of the Meta-group Similarity Measure.

3.   Sort all pictures having the same rank, using a spatial metric

Note that the notion of object in this layer is projected into the notion of meta-object (e.g. a group). In fact, the previous answer set is synthesized as shown in figure   9.

Fig. 9. Objects Are Grouped into Generic Elements.

In this case, we have three different images with rank 1. The *sim_deg* provides a new answer set (see figure 10).

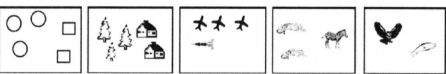

Fig. 10. An Example of Meta-group Answer Set.

2.2   Group Layer

Physical attributes are often insufficient to recognize and classify objects. In fact, grouping is a necessary precursor to object recognition[6]. A group expresses relation between two or more entities as shown in figure 11.

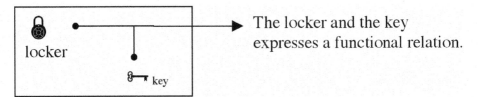

The locker and the key expresses a functional relation.

Fig. 11. An Example of Functional Relation.

While the meta-group layer describes relation among groups, in this layer information between elements of the same group are stored.

Different factors promote an element to be part of a group: morpho-geometric similarity, functional association, spatial proximity etc[9].

However, it is not a goal of this work to focus on the description of all possible attributes that influence our perception when we visually group elements. The QBA prototype we present uses basic relations according to the target domain. However new relations can be easily introduced and customized.

Table 1. A Subset of Iconic Relation.

	A and B express a functional relation
	A and B are generically in the same group
	A and B are in the same group, but expresses opposite concepts
	A and B are not in the same group
	A and B are partially in the same group
	A is bigger than B
	A is as big as B
	Predator- prey relation

The model we propose is domain-oriented system. That is, the relations will be used to match pictures depends on the target domain. This not limits the application of this new image index, but simplify the description of our work.

For each object, we annotate a set attributes (according to the modeled domain) during the segmentation process (this annotation can be substituted with supervised algorithms). In the implemented prototype, we introduced an iconic language that simplifies both the annotation and the query process. In particular let A and B be two objects. The iconic relations we modeled are summarized in table 1. Note that he last three icons are an example of customized relation according to domain we will introduce in our examples.

The annotation process and the query composition as well, are done by using the so-called relation palette. (see figure 12)

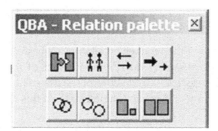

Fig. 12. The Relation Palette in the QBA Prototype.

The annotation process is done by using the same set of iconic relations. In the QBA prototype a user can specify different details for a picture. In fact, each relation can be enriched by introducing quantitative information. In the implemented prototype a when a relation icon displays a yellow background means that quantitative information are specified (see figure 13).

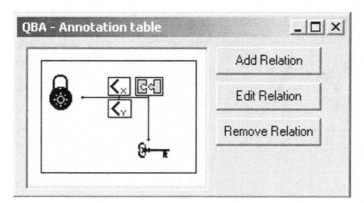

Fig. 13. An Example of Annotation Process in QBA.

These relation are captured using the following metrics.

Group Similarity Metric - Let q and img be two distinct images (respectively the query image and a generic picture). The group similarity distance is defined as follow:

- Find all the pictures that have one or more relations as specified in the query. Sort the answer set (in a increasing order) according to the following formula

$$Group\_similarity = \frac{\#Satisfied(img)}{\#Relation(q)}$$

where *#satisfied(img)* is the number or relation requested in the query and present in the image, whereas *#requested(q)* is the number of the requested relations. To check if a relation is satisfied, we can control the associated annotation (an extended VI annotation containing also group relation IDs). In this example the extendVI is

$$VI= \{locker<key; \ locker \ funcAss \ key;\}$$

- Sort all pictures having the same rank, using a similarity metric. Also in this step, we use the virtual image formalism.

Following the previous example, we can compose a query specifying that we are interested in all the analogue pictures that matches meta-group and group relations as shown in figure 14.

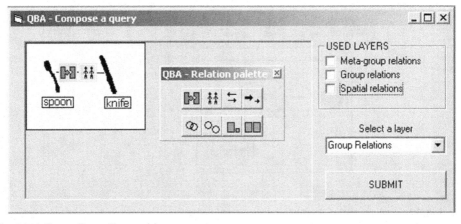

Fig. 14. A Group Query Composition.

We now compute the similarity degree step-by-step.

1. Find all the pictures that have one or more relations as specified in the query

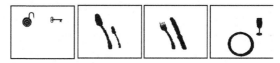

Fig. 15. A First Raw Answer set.

2. Calculate the group similarity

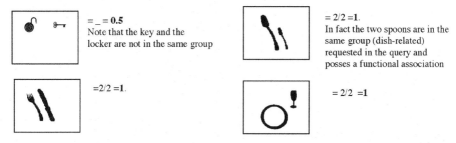

Fig. 16. The Group Formula Results.

The new answer set is the following

Fig. 17. The New Answer Set, Sorted According to First Step of the Group Similarity Measure.

3. Sort all pictures having the same rank, using a similarity metric. Similar to the previous layer, the image are synthesized as follow

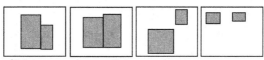

Fig. 18. An Example of Meta-group Answer Set.

The final answer set, provided by using the sim_deg, is depicted in figure 19.

Fig. 19. An Example of Meta-group Answer Set.

In the current QBA prototype we included some customized relations, such as the prey-predator attribute. This relation allows a user to retrieve picture analogue to figure 20.

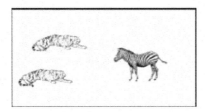

Fig. 20. A Group of Preys and Predators.

As a result, the system provides the following images

Fig. 21. Two Images that Expresses a Prey-Predator Relation.

2.3   Physical Layer

The spatial information embedded in a real image is represented in a relational format and the spatial relations among its objects are explicitly expressed. The interest of using virtual images as an iconic index is essentially motivated by the possibility of exploiting traditional database techniques for the solution of pictorial queries. Moreover, virtual images are well-suited for defining a similarity measure between images, used for the similarity retrieval with inexact matching that is flexible and easy to compute efficiently[2]

Essentially, we can query the system using only physical information. This case is similar to a classic interrogation using the VI.

3   Conclusions and Future Works

The hierarchical scene description supports a more efficient pictorial search. Users can compose high-level queries and retrieves images that shares group and functional relations. In particular, we enriched the original virtual image index introducing new similarity measures combining both low and high-level picture features.

Our future works, will address the query by analogy paradigm in multimedia. More precisely, we will extend our methodology to video interrogation.

In the current prototype, images are manually annotated. However, the introduction of a supervised algorithm can simplify this process. Part of our future work will be the definition of a semi-automatic methodology to mine high-level relations.

Finally, we will improve our current prototype, in order to provide a more detailed evaluation of its precision in retrieving analogue images as well as evaluate its usability.

References

1. James F. Allen "Maintaining knowledge about temporal intervals" Communications of the ACM,11(26):832-843, November 1983
2. M. Cibelli, M. Nappi, M. Tucci "Content-based Access in Image Database by Quantitative Relationships", Journal of Visual Languages and Computing (2000) 11, 573-589
3. S. Edelman, S. Duvdevani-Bar "A model of visual recognition and categorization", Phil. Trans. Royal Soc. (B), 352:1191-1202 (1997)
4. S. Edelman, S. Duvdevani-Bar "Similarity, connectionism, and the problem of representqtion in vision" Neural Computation 9:701-720 (1997)
5. Jacob Feldman, "Regularity-based perceptual grouping" Computational Intelligence, 13(4), 582-623, 1997
6. Jacob Feldman, "The role of objects in perceptual grouping", Acta Psycholoica, 102, 137-163, 1999
7. W. Grimson "The Combinatorics of Objects Recognition in Cluttered Environments using Constrained Search", Artificial Intelligence, Vol 44, No. 1--2 pp 121--166, 1990.
8. Robert L. Goldstone "Hanging Together: A Connectionist Model of Similarity" In J. Grainger and A. M. Jacobs (Eds.) *Localist Connectionist Approaches to Human Cognition.* (pp. 283 - 325). Mahwah, NJ: Lawrence Erlbaum Associates, 1998
9. Douglas R. Hofstadter "Fluid Concept and Creative Analogies" Adelphi 1996, ISBN: 88-459-1252-3
10. D. Jacobs, ``GROPER: A Grouping Based Object Recognition System for Two-Dimensional Objects", *IEEE Workshop on Computer Vision. pp.164--169, 1987*
11. David Prewer, "Connectionist Pyramid Powered Perceptual Organization: Visual Grouping with Hierarchical Structures of Neural Networks", Honours Thesis, Department of Computer Science, University of Melbourne, Nov 1995.
12. M. Riesenhuber, T. Poggio "Hierarchical models of object recognition in cortex" *Nature Neuroscience, 2(11)*:1019-1025, 1999
13. E. Rosh, "Principles of categorisation" A.M. Collins and E.E. Smith, editors, Reading in cognitive science: A perspective from psychology and artificial intelligence, 312-332- Morgan Kauffman, 1998
14. Daniel Schlüter and Stefan Posh "Combining Contour and Region Information for Perceptual Grouping" in proceeding of DAGM-Symposium, Springer, 1998, 393-401

Robust Image Retrieval Based on Texture Information

Riccardo Distasi[1] and Sergio Vitulano[2]

[1] Dipartimento di Matematica e Informatica, Università di Salerno
84084 Baronissi, Italy
ricdis@unisa.it
[2] Dipartimento di Scienze Mediche, Facoltà di Medicina
Via S. Giorgio 12, 09124 Cagliari, Italy
vitulano@vaxca1.unica.it

Abstract. This paper illustrates a method for image indexing based on texture information. The texture's partitioning element is first put into 1-d form and then its Hierarchical Entropy-based Representation (HER) is obtained. This representation is used to index the texture in the space of features. The experiments performed show that the proposed method works very well for retrieval in image databases; furthermore, it has invariance and robustness properties that make it attractive for incorporation into larger systems.

1 Introduction

Multimedia database management is one of the hottest research topics of the day. Indeed, multimedia computing systems are widely used, even among the general public, who was quick in recognizing their usefulness for everyday tasks.

In particular, image databases are widespread—image data is the most common type of multimedia—and they surface in many applications. Searching for an image in a database is a complex issue. If we are willing to restrict the queries to exact matches, then there are several effective solutions, which generally include some form of hashing. However, searching for approximate or similarity matches is quite another story. A definitive solution to this problem has not been found yet, and the best solution for the case at hands depends on several factors.

As a broad distinction, homogeneous databases—such as those utilized by applications in a specific field—e.g., medicine or astronomy—are characterized by having very small differences among the objects (think of an archive of astronomical photographs); the most effective approaches to date are based on object contour shapes and spatial relationships among them. In this case, the most frequently used tools are Attributed Relational Graphs [11] and 2-D Strings [3,4,10], but several approaches are possible [9].

Images in heterogeneous databases, on the other hand, present a much wider range of variability and therefore can usually be represented by coarser global features, such as texture or color percentage [7,8]. Some systems combine the two approaches to restrict the query answer set. Reference [5] presents a survey

M. Tucci (Ed.): MDIC 2001, LNCS 2184, pp. 130–139, 2001.

of content-based image indexing systems. Most of them work by extracting a number of selected features from the images, thus realizing a mapping from the set of all possible images (*image space*) to some, usually smaller, set of all possible feature values (*feature space*). The whole database is then indexed on those features, which are used as the search key when the user submits a query.

The effectiveness of these systems depends on how well the selected features capture the aspects that the user feels to be most significant in describing the content of an image; their efficiency depends heavily on how the low level features extracted from the images are organized into indices. The techniques available to avoid a linear search of the database include spatial access methods such as K-d-trees, R*-trees and others [1,12,13] as well as general-purpose methods such as hash tables.

It is often desirable to have an indexing system that is invariant—or at least robust—to several image transformations: geometrical transformations such as changes in the viewpoint or in the orientation of the object; pixel intensity transformations such as those produced by a change in the illumination or in the sensitivity of the medium; transformations due to transmission, such as added noise, and so on. The proposed method is indeed invariant to some such transformations.

Additionally, desirable 'performance' characteristics of an ideal indexing system include precise retrieval, small index size and easy computability.

The paper is organized as follows: Section 2 describes how our method works and some of its properties; Section 3 shows the results obtained from experimentation, and finally Section 4 makes a few concluding remarks.

2   The Method

The Hierarchical Entropy-based Representation (HER) has been shown to work well whenever the data, no matter what their origin, could be meaningfully made into a time series by some kind of transformation [6].

How do we generate a time series—that is, a sequence—from intrinsically 2-d texture data? Our solution is that of following a spiral path in the texture element, as shown in Fig. 1.

Supposing we have a time series $x(\cdot)$ with N points, let us define the energy of the i-th sample as $E(i) = |x(i)|^2$. The total energy of $x(\cdot)$ is simply $E = \sum_{i=0}^{N-1} E(i)$, while the relative energy of $x(i)$ is $E_r(i) = E(i)^2/(E - E(i))$.

Here is how the HER representation vector $\widehat{\mathbf{y}}$ of the sequence $x(\cdot)$ is obtained.

H1. [Initialize counter and output vector. Compute the total energy.]
  $k \leftarrow 0;\ \widehat{\mathbf{y}} = (\ );\ E = \sum_{i=0}^{N-1} |x(i)|^2$

H2. [Find the m signal maxima and put them in a queue Q in decreasing magnitude order, along with their x-axis position and their 4-distance from the first (largest) maximum.]
  $Q \leftarrow \Big(\big(i_1, 0, x(i_1) \big), \ldots, \big(i_m, d_m, x(i_m) \big) \Big);$

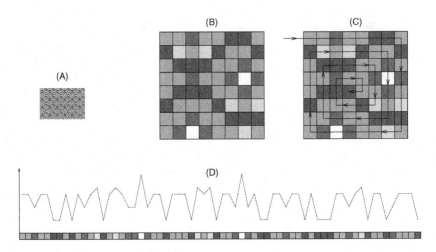

Fig. 1. Converting a 2-d texture into a 1-d time series. (A): what the texture looks like; (B): the partition element (texture tile); (C): the spiral; (D): the resulting 1-d signal.

H3. [Pop the largest maximum from Q.]
$(t, x(t)) \leftarrow \text{pop}(Q)$;
[Compute its relative energy $E_r(t)$.]
$E(t) = |x(t)|^2$; $E_r(t) = E^2/(E - E(t))$;
H4. [Compute the standard deviation relative to the current maximum.]
$$\sigma(t) = \frac{1}{\sqrt{2\pi \left(E_r(t)\right)^2}};$$
[In other words, we are considering $x(t)$ to be the midpoint of a Gaussian distribution. Compute its relative entropy.]
$$S(t) = \frac{1}{x(t)} \sum_{i=-\sigma(t)}^{\sigma(t)} |x(t+i)|;$$
H5. [Append the newly found values to the HER output vector $\widehat{\mathbf{y}}$.]
$\widehat{\mathbf{y}} = \widehat{\mathbf{y}} \otimes \left(x(t), S(t), d_t\right)$;

H6. [Go back to Step H3 until we have used a predefined number M of maxima.]
$k \leftarrow k + 1$;
If $k < M$ go to Step H3 , else output $\widehat{\mathbf{y}}$.

An alternate form for Step H6 stops iterating when the fraction of the total energy remaining in the signal $x(\cdot)$ falls below a given threshold. In most cases, the alternate test offers more control on index accuracy at the expense of unpredictable index size. In order to perform our tests with preset index sizes, the simpler 'number of maxima' test has been preferred.

A cursory analysis of the algorithm shows that its time complexity is basically linear in the number of points N. More precisely, let us consider an N-pixel signal. Assuming that the number of relevant maxima is m (typically $m \ll N$), Step H1 requires constant time, while Step H2 can be carried out by performing one sequential scan of the N-pixel input and sorting the local maxima—that is, time $c_1 N + c_2 m \log m$. The loop including Steps H3 through H6 is executed m times. Steps H3, H5 and H6 require constant time, while Step H4 takes a time proportional to $\sigma(t)$, which has N as a tight upper bound—for all practical purposes, however, $\sigma(t)$ can be considered as a constant. This yields a running time of $c_3 + c_4 \sigma(t)$ for one iteration. Therefore, the total running time for the algorithm is $O(N + m \log m + Nm)$. Since m is usually fixed to some low value such as 5 or 6, the whole expression reduces to $O(n)$.

Once the index data is extracted as shown above, it is organized into a spatial data access structure for subsequent searching. The structure of choice in this case is a k-d-tree.

As stated earlier, this method is invariant to some types of image transformations. Here are a few more details about the existing invariances.

Let us consider pixel transformations first. Contrast scaling—that is, multiplying all image pixel values by some constant—does not change the relative energy of any pixel. For this reason, none of the data generated by the algorithm undergoes any change. Similarly, luminance shifting–that is, summing a constant to all the pixel values–does not change the relative order of the maxima and therefore does not modify the index.

As for geometric transformations, translation is not even 'seen' by our method, since it only deals with data coming from a segmentation phase [14]. Image rotation/reflection and zooming, however, do change the partition element (texture tile) and in general yield different index data. Consider the theoretical partition element shown in Fig. 2 as an example. The local maxima in the sequence are marked by asterisks. As a clockwise rotation of $\pi/2$ is applied, the maxima reported by the spiral method change. However, it can be seen that 'real' 2-d maxima (i.e., the value 9) are always reported; what happens for different rotated versions of the element is that 'spurious' 1-d maxima appear. A similar line of reasoning comes into play with mirror reflections and zoom.

Summing up, it is possible to make the method invariant to both rotations and zoom if the maxima are located with a true 2-d algorithm and if the computation of relative energy (Step H3 in the algorithm) is done with a 2-d, rather than 1-d, Gaussian.

Table 1 summarizes the invariance properties. The asterisks denote issues that the method can be made invariant to, provided some caution is exercised (e.g., the 4-distance in Step H2 should be normalized with respect to the size of the element). Even as it is now, however, the method appears to be robust with respect to transformations—such as rotation—for which there is no theoretical (that is, absolute) invariance. This is illustrated in more detail in Section 3, which deals with the results obtained by experimenting with the method.

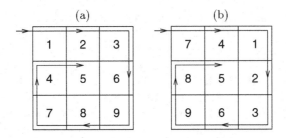

Fig. 2. Rotating the Partition Element Yields Different Local Maxima.

Table 1. Invariance Properties.

Contrast Scaling	YES
Luminance Shifting	YES
Rotation	NO*
Reflection	NO*
Translation	YES
Zoom	NO*

3 Experimental Results

Several experiments have been performed in order to assess the validity of the proposed method. For these tests, the main database used was the Brodatz set of textures [2].

The original Brodatz dataset included 167 textures, as shown in Fig. 3, but we added several transformed versions in order to test the robustness of retrieval. Furthermore, we have scaled the textures down to 32×32 pixels from the original 128×128. There are several reasons for this choice, the main one being that in most practical applications applications the texture element is usually limited to sizes in the range of 16×16 to 64×64.

The experiments were mainly aimed at assessing the robustness to pixel transformations and geometric transformations. For this reason, the database was augmented with variations of the original textures including the following:

- Luminance-shifted versions (made brighter and darker by different amounts);
- Color-reduced versions where the colors were reduced in number from the original 256 to 16;
- Contrast-scaled versions, with different amounts of scaling;
- Noisy versions, with different amounts of Gaussian noise added—10%, 20% or 50% of the total dynamic range (that is, since we are dealing with 8-bit images, average 25.5, average 50 and average 128);
- Mirror-reflected versions;
- Rotated versions (only integer multiples of $\pi/2$ were considered).

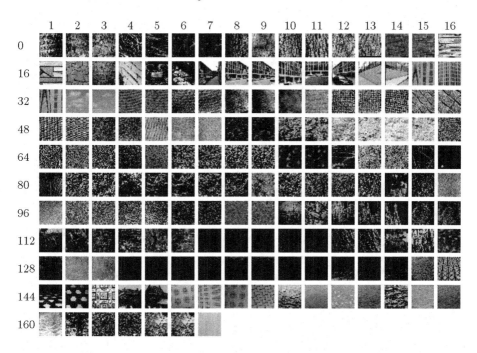

Fig. 3. The Original Brodatz Texture Dataset.

A part of the augmented database can be seen in Fig. 4. As an example, Element #1 is *Bark.0000* (it is #1 also in Fig. 3) and its transformed versions are in positions 3–16 inclusive; Element #2 (#96 in Fig. 3) is *Metal.000* and its transformed versions are in positions 172–185.

In the first set of experiments, we used one of the original textures as the query and looked at the returned results to see which transformed versions came up highest (closest) in the answer set. In all cases, there were several matches at distance 0 in feature space from the query texture. In particular, color reduction, contrast scaling and luminance shifting do not change the value of the index and therefore come out at distance 0. Other transformations do change the index, but the change is small enough for the transformed image to be returned in the top positions of the answer set, just after the images at distance 0.

The results of a sample query are depicted in Fig. 5. As can be seen, the first 8 matches consist entirely of transformed versions of the query image. The following 8 matches (that is, those in the second row) contain several spurious elements, including *Fabric.0005* and some of its transformed versions. Similar results were obtained for all the 15 query tiles that were used in our full-database retrieval experiments.

Another example is shown in Fig. 6. In this case the query image is *Bark.0000*; as before, the first row consists entirely of transformations of the query image. Some spurious results such as *Food.0000* and *Fabric.0000* appear in the second and third rows, along with other representatives of the *Bark* family.

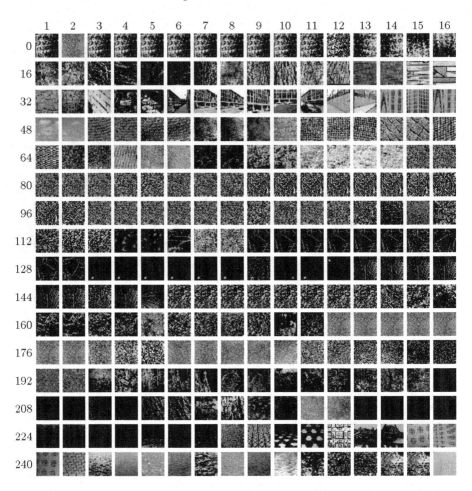

Fig. 4. A selection of 256 tiles from the complete texture database utilized for the experiments.

A nice side effect of any query is that of partitioning the database into bins (clusters) which are plainly visible by graphing the distances. As an example, Fig. 7 shows the 250 smallest distances from the images in the database to the query image—in this case, *Fabric.0001* (Element #36 in Fig. 4). The distances are sorted in increasing order. The apparent plateaus or quasi-plateaus in the graph point to clusters of similar (or index-identical) images in the database.

Another set of experiments was performed on restricted versions of the database, containing the full set of original textures and only the transformations of a single tile. In these cases the query tile was one of the transformed versions. We found that in most cases the original and all transformed versions of the query image were retrieved in the very first positions of the answer set, the one exception being the versions with added Gaussian noise. This was to be expected,

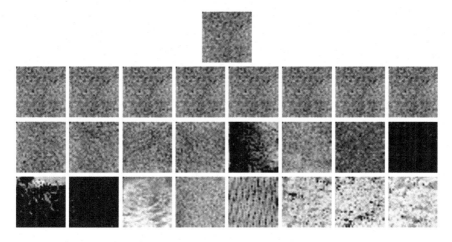

Fig. 5. Results of a Sample Query: *Metal.0000* (Element #2 in Fig. 4).

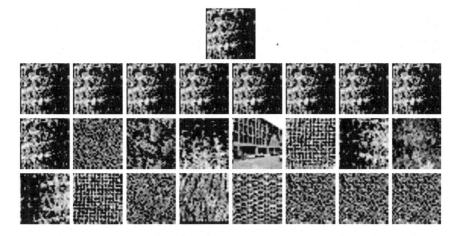

Fig. 6. Results of a Sample Query: *Bark.0000* (Element #1 in Fig. 4).

since the addition of substantial amounts of noise tends to distort the textures significantly, especially considering the small size of the tiles (32 × 32 pixels).

4   Conclusion

This paper presented a method for texture indexing based on a hierarchical entropy-based representation (HER). The 2-d texture data are first converted to a time series (1-d) and then the HER representation is obtained by means of a lightweight algorithm. As currently implemented, the metod has several invariance properties and is empirically robust with respect to more transformations.

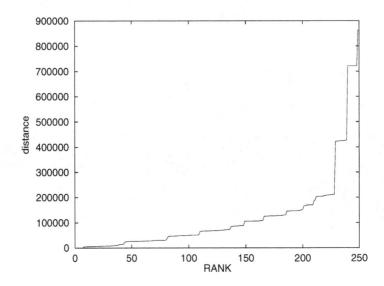

Fig. 7. Distances from *Fabric.0001* (#36 in Fig. 4) to the Closest 250 Matches in the Database.

The experiments performed show that the method is highly effective for texture-based image retrieval. As a nice side effect, we get a sort of clustering for next to nothing.

There is more work in progress on this project; most research efforts are aimed at modifying the method in order to achieve wider invariance properties.

References

1. N. Beckmann, H. P. Kriegel, R. Schneider, B. Seeger. "The R*-tree: An efficient and robust access method for points and rectangles." *Proc. ACM SIGMOD'90*, pp. 322–331, May 1990.
2. P. Brodatz, *Textures, A Photographic Album for Artists and Designers*, Dover Publications, New York, 1966. Avalaible (128 × 128) in a single `tar` file: `ftp://ftp.cps.msu.edu/pub/prip/textures/`
3. S.K. Chang, Q.Y. Shi, C.W. Yan. "Iconic indexing by 2D-strings." *IEEE Trans. Pattern Analysis Mach. Intell.*, **9**(3), pp. 413–427, 1987.
4. A. Del Bimbo, M. Campanai, P. Nesi. "A 3-dimensional iconic environment for image database querying." *IEEE Trans. Soft. Eng.* **19**(10), pp. 997–1011, March 1993.
5. M. De Marsico, L. Cinque, S. Levialdi. "Indexing pictorial document by their content: A survey of current techniques." *Image and Vision Computing* Vol. 15, p. 119–141, 1997.
6. R. Distasi, D. Vitulano, S. Vitulano, "A hierarchical representation for content based image retrieval," *Journal of Visual Languages and Computing*, Special Issue on Multimedia Databases and Image Communication, Vol. 5, n. 8, Aug. 2000.

7. C. Faloutsos, W. Equitz, M. Flickner, W. Niblack, D. Petkovic, R. Barber. "Efficient and effective querying by image content." *Journal of Intelligent Inf. Systems*, **3**(3/4), pp. 231–262, July 1994.

8. M. Flickner et al. "Query by image and video content: The QBIC system." *IEEE Computer*. "Finding the right image." Special Issue on Content Based Image Retrieval Systems, **28**(9), pp. 23–32, Sep. 1995.

9. H. V. Jagadish, "Linear clustering of objects with multiple attributes," *Proc. ACM SIGMOD*, pp. 332–342, Atlantic City, May 1990.

10. S. Y. Lee, F. J. Hsu. "Spatial reasoning and similarity retrieval of image using 2D C-String knowledge representation." *Pattern Recognition*, **25**(3), pp. 305–318, 1992.

11. E. G. M. Petrakis, C. Faloutsos. "Similarity searching in medical image databases." *IEEE Trans. Knowledge and Data Eng.* **9**(3), pp. 435–447, May/June 1997.

12. J. D. Ullman. *Principles of Database and Knowledge-Based Systems*. Computer Science Press, Rockville, MD, USA, 1988.

13. H. Samet, *The Design and Analysis of Spatial Data Structures*, Addison Wesley, 1989.

14. S. Vitulano, C. Di Ruberto, M. Nappi "Different methods to segment biomedical images," *Pattern Recognition Letters* 18, pp. 1125–1131, 1997.

Symbolic Tile Categories for Spatial Reasoning on Objects Represented in Multiple-Resolution

Erland Jungert and Fredrik Lantz

FOI, (Swedish Defence Research Agency)
Box 1165, S-581 11 Linköping, Sweden
{jungert,flantz}@foi.se

Abstract. Methods for symbolic spatial reasoning requires quite often a representation of the objects in multiple resolutions. The traditional methods are in such cases less useful since the objects are either represented in a resolution of an order that is too low or they are based on a structure that does not easily allow the representation of the object in a symbolic or a qualitative way. The approach taken here has been to develop an approach that shares some of the characteristics found in resolution pyramids and quad-trees resulting in a structure represented in terms of symbolic tiles. This symbolic structure can be used for spatial reasoning in applications where, among other things, the purpose is to reason about object shape and relationships where the objects need to be represented in multiple resolutions.

1 Introduction

Spatial objects need, in a large number of applications to be represented in different resolution. Basically, there exist two different structures that are suitable for this. The first type is the quad-tree [1] and the second type is the resolution pyramid [2]. The quad-tree structure is quite popular in geographical applications while the resolution pyramids mainly are used in applications concerned with image processing. The two methods are related in some ways but differ in others. A quad-tree represents a spatial object completely and is for this reason used as a storage structure as well. The resolution pyramid corresponds to a set of images where the first image is represented in full resolution and the following images are represented in lower and lower resolutions where the reduction in resolution follows a set of basic reduction rules. The resolution pyramid can also be as an index technique in image processing. Both methods have their advantages and disadvantages. A disadvantage with the quad-tree is that the reduction in resolution deteriorates too quickly when lower and lower resolution levels are applied. In the resolution pyramid, for instance, long, thin objects *may* disappear in an unacceptable way when the resolution decreases between two steps in the pyramid. This is due to the fact that the pyramid works in a bottom up approach where the resolution decreases in each step. The quad-tree works the other way around and gives in each step a higher resolution, i.e. a top down approach. However, neither of these two structures are particularly useful in spatial reasoning, new approaches are therefore needed. The approach proposed here is not only intended for the traditional applications of the quad-trees and the resolution pyramids but for spatial reasoning as well. For this reason, the structure has also been provided with a symbolic characteristic to support the latter type of operations. It also turns out that this approach allows generation of object descriptions in more or less arbitrary resolution in an efficient way. Furthermore, it will also be shown that the method either can be viewed as a tree structure or alternatively as a pyramid. The fundamental

M. Tucci (Ed.): MDIC 2001, LNCS 2184, pp. 140–151, 2001.

aspects of this structure are due to both the symbolic description technique and the way the underlying points of the spatial object are chosen for the representation of the objects. In short, the proposed method can be described as made up by a set of symbolic square shaped tiles primarily used to describe spatial objects in two dimensions. However, it is also possible to view the method as a set of points positioned on the edge of the object and along consecutive lines in both x- and y-directions of the coordinate system. Thus the method can be considered as a surface model with dual properties, i.e. both symbolic and quantitative.

Another variation of the method intended for description of and reasoning on terrain objects can be found in [3]. Some related work has also been found which is based on Symbolic Projection [4] and among these the following can be mentioned [5], [6] and [7]. The drawback in these approaches is that they cannot represent the object in a sufficiently high resolution and are besides too complex. In image processing work on multi-scale object representation for shape determination has been made since the eighties, an example on this is a semi-symbolic approach proposed by Crowley [8].

The main purpose of the symbolic multi-resolution structure described in this work has been to design a structure that efficiently can be used for spatial reasoning. More specifically the purpose is to determine and recognize spatial objects or parts of objects, as well as to determine relations between objects either in a matching process or in a spatial query language for multiple data sources [9]. The latter application is of particular interest since a multi-resolution structure can be used as an index to a spatial database. Beside these applications a multi-resolution structure of the type described here can also be considered as a generalization technique.

2   The Symbolic Tile Structure

A symbolic tile can be defined as a square shaped area that may be combined with a small set of irregular data points positioned at the edge of the area; there are no points internal to the square available. A set of symbolic tiles are then part of the description of an object and subsequently such a description is called the symbolic tile description of the object. A tile represents a part of an object i.e. either the edge of the object (a *partially filled tile*) or the inside of the object (a *filled tile*) or in some cases it may represent an area outside the object (an *empty tile*). The symbolic tile structure differ from the quad-tree and the resolution pyramid in that a tile even on the lowest resolution level is allowed to cover the object just partly. However, the symbolic tile structure differs from the other two in that it will allow the user to arbitrarily set the resolution that may from the full resolution of the image. More precisely, the symbolic tile structure need at least three by three pixels and even that may in the end be ill suited for most applications. Another aspect that need be pointed out is that here all the terminal nodes of the resulting tree structure always are represented at the same resolution level. This is, of course, not a necessary condition but it is chosen here since it simplifies the use of the structure, as it becomes completely regular in this way and it is for this reason possible to keep the duality to both the quad-tree and the resolution pyramid.

Two types of symbolic tiles can be identified of which both are invariant with respect to the resolution. The first type is here called atomic since it is allowed to contain only a single line segment (or point) of the object to be represented. Each single atomic tile type is called a category. The second type may include multiple line segments and will be called a compound tile. It turns out that all compound tiles can be split up into a set of atomic tile categories.

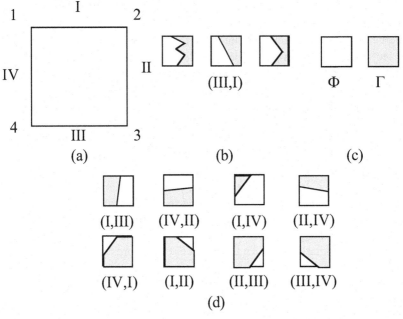

Figure 1   The coding elements of the atomic symbolic tiles (a), three equivalent atomic tiles (b), the empty and filled tiles, Φ and Γ (c). A subset of atomic tiles where the edges are running between two sides of the tiles (d).

2.1   Atomic Tiles

To accomplish the description of the atomic symbolic tile categories, their basic descriptive elements must first be determined. The approach taken here uses the four corners and the four sides of the square as descriptive elements, i.e. for indication of the object points corresponding to the start and end of the segment(s) of the edge of the object occurring inside the square. Starting from the upper left corner, the corners are numbered from 1 through 4. The sides are numbered as well but here Roman numerals are used starting with the upper side (I) ending with the left side (IV). The description method is illustrated in figure 1a. An atomic symbolic tile is an approximation of a part of the edge of a spatial object described in terms of a line segment between a start and an end point on the edge of the square constituting the tile. When moving from the start point to the end point the inside of the object is always to the right. Figure 1b shows three tiles corresponding to the same category that differs internally; basically with respect to the internal points of the tiles. What happens to the edge of the object between these two points is of no importance at this resolution level and can besides remain unknown if the tile corresponds to the highest resolution level. Consequently the three alternatives categories in figure 1b are interpreted in the same way, i.e. (III, I). An empty tile is indicated with (Φ) and a filled tile, i.e. a tile entirely inside an object is indicated with (Γ), see figure 1c. Furthermore in figure 1d a set of different tiles are shown.

Figure 2 shows a set of tiles that are not that frequently used but nevertheless they have to be accepted. The first row shows eight different tiles where the edge of the objects coincide with an edge of the tiles. In the first four tiles the remaining part of the tile is outside the object while the following four tiles are entirely inside the object. All these tiles have a start and end point in a corner of the object; this does not always have to be the case, a side of an object may start and end along a part of a tile-side. The last row shows tiles with an object corner along the edge of a tile side or tile corner. In all these particular cases the remaining part of the tiles are outside the object; although not demonstrated here filled tiles with a corner point exist as well.

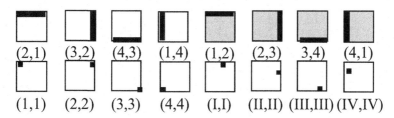

| (2,1) | (3,2) | (4,3) | (1,4) | (1,2) | (2,3) | 3,4) | (4,1) |
| (1,1) | (2,2) | (3,3) | (4,4) | (I,I) | (II,II) | (III,III) | (IV,IV) |

Figure 2   Four tiles outside the object edge and four tiles inside the object at the edge (first row); tiles at a corner of the object (second row).

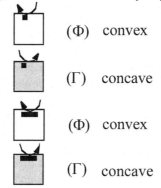

(Φ)   convex

(Γ)   concave

(Φ)   convex

(Γ)   concave

Figure 3   Extreme points possible to identify in filled and empty tiles with their traversal directions.

In figure 3 some cases where single points and short segments follow the same side of a tile. It is easy to see that depending on whether the remaining part of the object is inside or outside the tile there is either a *concavity* or a *convexity* present in the object. The arrows in the figure demonstrate the direction of the movement when traversing the object. Thus when the remaining part of the tile is empty, there is a convexity while for a filled object there is a concavity. In figure 3 there are just some illustrations to this given while in reality a number of further cases can be found.

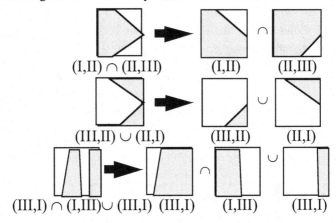

Figure 4   Three examples of compound tiles and their split up into atomic tiles.

2.2   Compound Tiles

A compound tile is a combination of two or more atomic tiles. Basically, there are two main types that may be combined with each other as well; this is illustrated in figure 4. Generally a compound tile includes a multiple set of line segments each with a start and an end point. Again each such segment determines a part of the edge of the spatial object. An end point of a segment may coincide with the start point of a consecutive segment thus corresponding either to a convex or concave point of the object. These two cases are illustrated with the two top cases in figure 4. The convex case can be separated into two atomic tiles where the object description corresponds to the *intersection* of the atomic tiles. The concave case corresponds to the *union* between the atomic tiles. The third case in the figure is more complicated since here there are no points common to any pair of segments. Nevertheless, in this case a pair of the tiles forms a part of the object that either is convex or concave and again the former corresponds to an intersection whereas the latter corresponds to a union. A consequence of the multiple occurrences of points in the square that eventually is described by the combined atomic tiles is that the order of the points and their internal connections must be kept. Otherwise the structure of the objects will be lost and at the same time the knowledge of the shape will be lost as well.

2.3   Generation of the Tile Structure

The algorithm for generation of the tile structure of a spatial object is fairly simple. The first point is to let the user determine the max resolution of the structure. The max resolution could also set to a default level. For practical reasons the max level should correspond to a 2^k by 2^k split up. Once the maximum resolution is set the points positioned at the edge of each square are determined by traversing their edges horizontally and vertically. This is a straight forward process and the only extra operation that need to be performed while doing this is to determine which points are connected to each other along the edge of the objects. These two steps are efficient, since they are both linear. The next step in the generation process is to generate the symbolic tile descriptions row by row for each square; this is also a linear process.

2.4   Multi-resolution Structure

No matter whether the symbolic tile structure is regarded as a resolution pyramid or as a tree structure the basic representation is still hierarchical. As a consequence of the twofold view the structure can be viewed either as a bottom up or as a top down structure where the bottom up structure is related to the resolution pyramid and the top down approach is more related to the quad-tree representation.

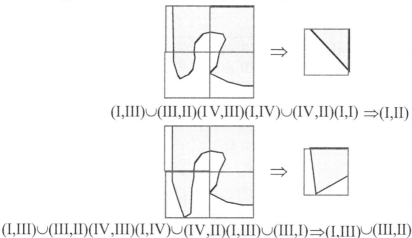

$$(I,III)\cup(III,II)(IV,III)(I,IV)\cup(IV,II)(I,I) \Rightarrow(I,II)$$

$$(I,III)\cup(III,II)(IV,III)(I,IV)\cup(IV,II)(I,III)\cup(III,I)\Rightarrow(I,III)\cup(III,II)$$

Figure 5   Two examples of the transformation from one resolution level to the next lower resolution in the symbolic resolution pyramid.

2.4.1   The Pyramid View

The pyramid approach uses the same strategy as the traditional resolution pyramid, i.e. 2 by 2 squares are taken row by row and transformed, according to some rules [2], into a single square on the next higher resolution level which can be interpreted as a new symbolic tile. The new tile can be either of atomic or of compound type; this is illustrated in figure 5 where the first example shows an atomic tile while the second example shows a compound tile with a convex corner point. The rule used here can basically be expressed as:

Through away all points internal to the set of 2 by 2 tiles and keep the points at the edge, identify the connections between the new edge points and determine the new tile type, proceed to the next 2 by 2 tile set if any, otherwise terminate.

The pyramid approach is demonstrated by the example in figure 6. Observe however, that the pyramids always have a "cut off top", contrary to the traditional pyramid that always ends with a single pixel.

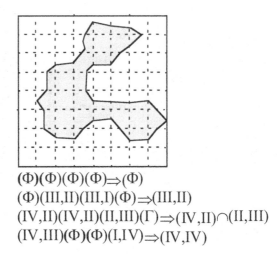

$(\Phi)(\Phi)(\Phi)(\Phi)\Rightarrow(\Phi)$

$(\Phi)(III,II)(III,I)(\Phi)\Rightarrow(III,II)$

$(IV,II)(IV,II)(II,III)(\Gamma)\Rightarrow(IV,II)\cap(II,III)$

$(IV,III)(\Phi)(\Phi)(I,IV)\Rightarrow(IV,IV)$

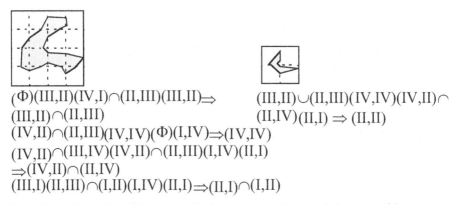

$(\Phi)(III,II)(IV,I)\cap(II,III)(III,II)\Rightarrow$ $(III,II)\cup(II,III)(IV,IV)(IV,II)\cap$

$(III,II)\cap(II,III)$ $(II,IV)(II,I)\Rightarrow(II,II)$

$(IV,II)\cap(II,III)(IV,IV)(\Phi)(I,IV)\Rightarrow(IV,IV)$

$(IV,II)\cap(III,IV)(IV,II)\cap(II,III)(I,IV)(II,I)$

$\Rightarrow(IV,II)\cap(II,IV)$

$(III,I)(II,III)\cap(I,II)(I,IV)(II,I)\Rightarrow(II,I)\cap(I,II)$

Figure 6 An illustration of the symbolic tile structure to the resolution pyramid concept.

2.4.2 The Tree Structure

The tree structure correspond to a top down approach, i.e. like in the quad tree the whole object is split horizontally and vertically into four subparts for which the corresponding tiles are identified. This approach is identical to the quad-tree structure. The difference between this and the pyramid approach is that the empty tiles are not enclosed here although in the given example there are no empty tiles. The result of the approach taken here, given the object in figure 8a, can be seen in figure 7. The traversing directions when building the tree are illustrated with the arrows in 8b. The long arrow corresponds to the lowest resolution while the short ones to the next lower resolution.

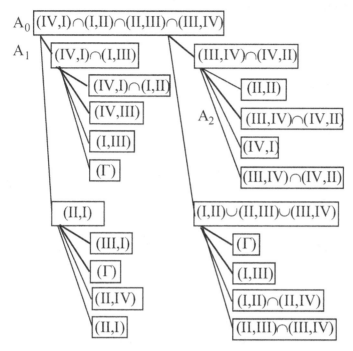

Figure 7 The quad-tree like representation of the hierarchical tile structure of the object in figure 8a.

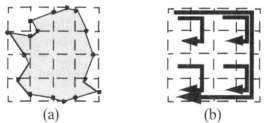

(a)   (b)

Figure 8 The splits of an object, A, down to its A_2-representation including the cutting points (a) and its traversal orders (b).

2.5   Elementary Functions

To transform a spatial object, for instance, to its next lower or higher resolution level a number of elementary functions need to be developed. Other examples of necessary functions are to change the interpretation order of the object tiles. For this reason, the following convention has been chosen to identify the object on the different resolution levels; A_0 represents the object on the top level of the hierarchical structure, i.e. the lowest resolution. The next resolution level is A_1 and so forth, as can be seen in figure 7. In certain cases the objects need to be traversed in different ways at any resolution, to accommodate this the order of the traversal must be possible to change; this means indirectly that there must be a way of telling in which direction the next tile will appear. Clearly, there must also be a way of traversing the object along its edge, i.e. a structure related to chain-code is therefore required. The top representation of object A_0 in figure 8a (see also figure 7) is:

$$A_0 = ((IV, I) \cap (I, II) \cap (II, III) \cap (III, IV)$$

This can be transformed into the chain-code representation $(\overline{A_0})$. On the next lower level $(\overline{A_1})$, this becomes (starting with upper left tile):

$$\overline{A_1} = (III, IV) \cap (IV, II)(IV, I) \cap (I, III)(I, II) \cap (II, III) \cap (III, IV)(II, I)$$

This description is clearly cyclic since the object here is of extended type. On this level only four tiles exists and the chain code becomes in this particular case equal to the tree structure. However, generally this is not the case and on higher resolution levels the difference becomes clear and for instance all the empty and filled tiles disappears as well as those tiles that are empty beside just a single point. Thus A_2 becomes:

$$\overline{A_2} = (III,IV) \cap (IV,II)(IV,I) \cap (I,II)$$
$$(IV,III)(I,III)(I,III)(I,II) \cap (II,IV)(II,III) \cap (III,IV)(II,IV)(II,I)$$
$$(III,I)(III,IV) \cap (IV,II)(IV,I)$$

No delimiters between the tiles in the chain-coded description are required beside the union and the intersection operators. The reason for this is that both the exit position of a tile and the enter position of the next forthcoming tile are known. Rules that determines the crossing between two tiles in the traditional way can, for instance, be described as $(X, II)(IV, X) \Rightarrow 0$ and $(X, 2)(4, X) \Rightarrow 1$ etc. However, for the purpose of illustrating the directions of a chain code it can sometimes be practical to include the directional delimiter as well.

To transform one of these representations into the another we can identify the functions:

$$A_i = \text{tree-structure}(\overline{A_i})$$
$$\overline{A_i} = \text{chain-code}(A_i)$$

For which the following is true:

$$A_2 = \text{tree-structure}(\text{chain-code}(A_2))$$

Functions for transformation of the chain-code structure into a pyramid structure can be determined although their behavior is evident and need not be discussed here. Functions that allow the change of resolution level are also required. Here *up* means a change into lower resolution while *down* means a change to higher resolution.

$$A_1 = Up(A_2)$$
$$A_{i-1} = Up(A_i)$$
$$A_{i+1} = Down\ (A_i)$$

Clearly these functions satisfies the following conditions:

$$A_i = Up(Down\ (A_i))$$
$$A_i = Down(Up(A_i))$$

3   Visualization

The power of the visualization of an object represented in the symbolic tile structure is illustrated in three different resolution levels in figure 9, see the lower row. As a comparison, the same object is also represented by a quad-tree at the same resolution levels in the upper row. As can be seen, when going from the highest resolution to the lowest, the quad-tree deteriorates much quicker than the tile structure does. Basically, this is due to the triple value set of the latter, which also allows a partly filled square.

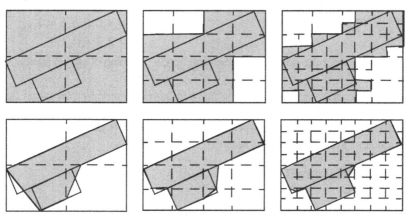

Figure 9   The traditional quad-tree (above) and the symbolic tile tree (below).

4   Matching

An operation of importance that, however, needs to be studied further, concerns matching. This operation will be useful in applications. An object described in terms of chain-code made up by symbolic tiles maybe useful for queries of type query-by-example, since a user can draw a query describing an object or a part of it. An alternative to this is to use predefined filters of sets of symbolic tiles. These two alternatives can be transformed in to the same type of chain-code structure, which in a second step can be matched against a single object, or a set of objects to determine the particular shape of interest. This matching can be performed on different resolution levels as well. A method for matching chain-code is described in [10] and is also illustrated to a part in figure 10. This approach to chain-code matching is, contrary to here, concerned with the matching of object trajectories in video clips. The approach described by Yoshitaka et al. is not concerned with the problem of representing the trajectories in multiple resolution, which would be possible, by using the symbolic tile structure demonstrated here.

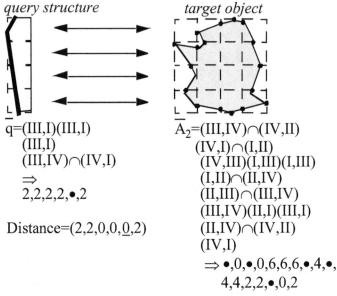

Figure 10   A simple illustration to the chain-code matching of spatial objects.

The query structure can step by step be mapped onto an interval of the target object by calculation of the distance vector between the two structures. The distance is in itself a chain code. The matching process performed over all possible combinations of the parameters, for further details, see [10].

5   Future Research

A number of reasoning problems that require representation of the objects in multiple resolution and where the symbolic tile structure can be applied can be thought of; this will, however, require further research efforts. For this reason, they will not be discussed further here. However, among these problems can the following be mentioned:

- object rotation,
- trajectories of objects in motion,
- spatial object relations,
- shape of spatial objects,
- similarities between spatial objects (globally as well as between pairs of objects),
- similarity retrieval.

6   Conclusion

The symbolic tile structure is primarily determined to represent spatial objects in multiple resolution and for spatial reasoning. A few observations can be made in accordance with this. First the structure can only be applied to linear and extended object types and second the symbolic tile structure has a triple value set, i.e. {empty, full, partial} instead of the binary value set of the quad-tree and of the resolution pyramid.

The symbolic tile structure is more related to the resolution pyramid rather than to the quad-tree structure. This is because the pyramid and the symbolic tile structure both inherit a bottom-up approach rather than the top-down split and test technique of the quad-tree. A number of further aspects that characterize the symbolic tile structure can be mentioned as well. A characteristic of the symbolic tile structure is that no points internal to the squares are allowed only cut points on the edge of the squares are accepted independent of the resolution level. This can also be expressed in another way: *the vertices of an object polygon do not necessarily have to be preserved by the structure.*

References

1.   H. Samet, "*The Design and Analysis of Spatial Data Structures*", Addison-Wesley, Reading, Mass., 1990.

2.   D. H. Ballard, Ch. M. Brown, "*Computer Vision*", Prentice-Hall, Englewoods Cliffs, New Jersey, 1982, pp 106-110.

3.   F. Lantz, E. Jungert, "*Dual aspects of multi-resolution grid-based terrain data model with supplementary irregular data points*", Proceedings of The 3rd Int. Conf. on Information Fusion (FUSION'2000), Paris, France, July 10-13

4.   S.-K. Chang, E. Jungert, "*Symbolic Projection for Image Retrieval and Spatial Reasoning*", Academic Press, London, 1996.

5.   F.-J. Hsu, S.-Y. Lee, B.-S. Lin, "*Video Data Indexing by 2D C-Trees*", Journal of Visual Languages and Computing, 1998, Vol 9, pp 375-397.

6.   E. Jungert and S.-K. Chang, "*An Image Algebra for Pictorial Data Manipulation*", Journal of Computer Vision, Graphics and Image Processing (CVGIP): Image Understanding edition, Vol. 58, No 2, September 1993, pp 147-160.

7.   S.-K. Chang, Y. Li, "Representation of multi-resolution symbolic and binary pictures using 2D H-strings", Proceedings of the 1988 IEEE Workshop on Language for Automation, College Park, MD, Aug. 29-31, 1988, pp 190-195.

8.   J. L. Crowley, "*A Multi-Resolution Representation for Shape*", Proceedings of the IEEE Computer Society Conference on Computer Vision and Pattern Recognition, Washington DC, June 19-23, 1983, pp 326-335.

9.   S.-K. Chang, G. Costagliola, E. Jungert, "*Spatial/Temporal Query Processing for Information Fusion Applications*", In Advances in Visual Information Systems, R. Laurini (Ed.), Springer Verlag, Berlin, 2000, pp 127-139.

10.   A. Yoshitaka, Y.-I. Hosoda, M. Yoshimitsu, M. Hirakawa, T. Ichikawa, "*VIOLONE, Video Retrieval by Motion Example*", Journal of Visual Languages and Computing, 1996, Vol 7, pp 423-443.

Content-Based Indexing and Retrieval Supported by Mobile Agent Technology

Harald Kosch, Mario Döller, and László Böszörményi

Institute of Information Technology
University Klagenfurt, Austria
{harald.kosch,mdoeller,laszlo.boeszoermenyi}@itec.uni-klu.ac.at

Abstract. In this paper we present the MultiMedia Database Mobile
agent technology (M^3) which supports personalized content-retrieval and
indexing in a distributed Oracle 8i DB. We implemented an agency on
top of the Oracle 8i JServer and realized mobility with the embedded
Visbroker Corba ORB. A performance comparison of our mobile agent
technology with a client-server solution for a nearest-neighbor search in
an image database shows the efficiency of the proposed solution.
Keywords: Mobile Agents, Multimedia Database System, Content-based
Indexing and Retrieval.

1   Introduction

The increasing development of indexing and retrieval tools in distributed multimedia database systems (MMDBMS), as well as the growing quantity of multimedia data, require efficient technologies to ensure the access and the management of the network and client resources [1].

In this context, we take advantage of mobile agent technology as an enhancement of distributed multimedia database indexing and retrieval. Mobile agents
allow the execution of the retrieval tasks in an automated way, with minimal
human interaction [2]. This allows the user to concentrate on other client activities, like the preparation of the client's buffer/cache for the expected multimedia
delivery. Furthermore, it fits well with the requirement of efficient multimedia indexing and retrieval based on user's preferences by offering personalized processing of multimedia data through the access and pre-processing of the multimedia
raw data where they are stored. For instance, a user is interested in retrieving
the nearest images to a reference image in a multimedia database, however the
database proposes only a simple range-search. Using the mobile agent technology the agent can contain a method, provided by the user, for processing the
nearest-neighbor search directly in the database management system.

Internet applications, actually using effectively the mobile agent technology
are for instance electronic commerce [3], telecommunication [4], information retrieval [5], and management of distributed resources [6]. This paper introduces
a mobile agents technology in the scope of content-based indexing and retrieval
in a distributed Oracle8i MMDBMS. We will demonstrate that these problems

M. Tucci (Ed.): MDIC 2001, LNCS 2184, pp. 152–166, 2001.

are well suited to mobile agent technology (see section 3). Yet, astonishing, that few related work considered mobile agent technology in this context (see section 2), although applications running on top of a MMDBMS have the very similar features to the applications mentioned beforehand : they are characterized by asynchronous transactions, high latency, complex information processing and distributed task processing features.

2   Related Work

One key functionality in a multimedia database (MMDMBS) is how to index and then to retrieve continuous and non-continuous multimedia information efficiently. One broadly used method, the *Content-Based Retrieval (CBR)* of multimedia objects relies on extraction properties of a multimedia object [7,8]. CBR in distributed MMDBMS involve the retrieval of multimedia data from various, possibly heterogenous database sites, and to compute the result in mutual agreement.

A typical approach to CBR is the similarity search between extracted multimedia features [7]. Here, the query is actually posed against the low-level feature vectors extracted from the multimedia object. A broadly used Image CBR system is QBIC (Query By Image Context, see http://wwwqbic.almaden.ibm.com), another popular system for videos is Virage (http://www.virage.com). Features described for CBR include measures expressing the color/texture/shape distribution of an image plus motion for a video. A CBR query is translated into a point query in a multi-dimensional feature space. The similarity between a query- and a database-object is estimated using a distance function.

CBR in a distributed MMDBMS is broadly supported by a client/server architecture. It includes (1) user interfaces to submit requests, their transfer to the DB server; (2) the retrieval operations at the DB server; and (3) the results return. A broadly used protocol for the client (written in Java) and server is JDBC (Java Database Connection; see java.sun.com/products/jdbc/index.html). If several sites are involved, multiple client-server connections are spawned and the different results are compared and merged at the client-side. An example is MetaSEEk (http://www.ctr.columbia.edu/MetaSEEk/). It is a meta-search engine for images based on the content of CBIRs located at IBM, Virage and Columbia University servers.

Our previously developed SMOOTH system [9] provides besides CBR also means for high-level annotation and querying, works in a client-server environment as well. A recent system enhancement (introduction of 'Domain Transparency' meaning that the client interface automatically adapts to extensions made by a new application domain to the base annotation classes) revealed serious performance bottlenecks of the JDBC connection (thin driver) to an Oracle 8i DB. The repeated JDBC calls to build the client interface dynamically combined with a high volume of requested data worsened the response time considerably. A first-aid solution was the integration of a JDBC client cache for query results.

However, the use of a mobile agent solution might improve the situation more efficiently. We address such a solution in the near future.

Many mobile agent systems have been established. Some of these are Aglets [10], Mole [11] and Grasshoper [12]. They are well-suited to a wide range of Internet applications, to mention only WWW mining [13], or telecommunication [14]. However, to the best of our knowledge, there are few works which deal with the use of mobile agents in a distributed database system. Some related work concentrated on the use of mobile agents in distributed Web databases [15,16]. Others dealt with distributed data warehousing. For instance Weippl et al. [17] propose a mobile AgentDB technology, based on the JServer capabilities of the Oracle 8i DBMS which is tailored to the inserting process in a data warehouse. These related work rely mainly only on simple access functions and do not address the problem of handling multimedia data. In the context of distributed multimedia systems, mobile agents are successfully utilized for Quality of Service (QoS) negotiations [18,19]. For instance, Manvi et al. [19] propose a mobile agent based QoS management system which provides means for efficient agent based bandwidth negotiation. However, the issue of CBR is not yet treated in this context.

3   Mobile Agent Technology in a Distributed MM-System

3.1   General Considerations

A mobile agent is defined as a self-contained software element that acts autonomously on behalf of a user (e.g. person or organization, or a multimedia content customer) and in addition, has the unique ability to migrate from one host in a network to another [16].

The definition of a mobile agent contains at least three issues which deserve special interest when developing mobile agent systems in a distributed multimedia database systems. The first issue refers to the autonomy of a mobile agent. This is a feature that allows the agent to act on its own by using the data (e.g. the feature vector of an image whose nearest-neighbors have to be searched), and the mobile logic which it incorporates (e.g. the similarity search code), and requires only little human intervention (e.g. provide the iterinary) or guidance (e.g. error handling). Further, the time needed to fulfill the tasks is reduced because interaction with the user is avoided. For instance, a similar image to the reference one found in the first database is used as input for the search in a second image database. Obviously, the agent has to be designed to deal with any situation that may occur during execution, such as the violation of the private information associated to the agent's owner [20], or a resource violation at the remote agency which let return the agent immediately.

The second issue in the definition refers to the mobility of an agent. The mobility feature enables the agent to travel to the host where the data are physically stored. In this way the transfer of a large amount of data in the network is prevented. This is obviously of great interest in a distributed multimedia database system. For instance reconsider a distributed nearest-neighbor search. Instead of downloading the best matches from all involved databases, as required in a client/server solution, the mobile agent incorporates the result of the first visit as internal state and uses it for the further search.

The final argument for using mobile agent technology is the personalization of the indexing and retrieval process. The effectiveness of automatic multimedia indexing is conditioned to a great extent by the amount of a priori information available in the application domain [21]. An elegant solution is the integration of this information as mobile logic. For instance, in an surveillance application a mobile agent might include detailed information on the intruder objects to the video server which allows the selective coding of video clips (e.g. as MPEG-4 Video Objects) [22].

3.2   Architecture of our M^3 Agency

In the following we describe a set of concepts upon which our mobile agents M^3 system relies. Principally, it is a Java-based mobile agent system which uses CORBA services to implement mobility. Its main characteristics are the agent execution in the core of the database, i.e. the agency and the agent are database objects, and the possible use of direct access and retrieval methods of multimedia data through server-sided JDBC and *inter*Media Java classes (see section 3.2).

Every Oracle 8i MMDBMS server which wants to host an M^3 agent must provide an agent *run-time environment*. This environment is responsible for execution and migration of the agents. Furthermore, an *agent dispatcher* is needed to initially start up the run-time environment. The role of the agent dispatcher in an Oracle DB is played by the JServer. The JServer offers an encapsulated environment, sessions, which are independent from each other, as well the CORBA advanced services. Our run-time environment relies on the offered CORBA services, as well as on the Java language features, to implement mobility. The advantages of this approach are manifold, e.g. use of security mechanism offered by CORBA services, use of the advanced naming service to locate the MMDBMS servers, as well as use of object serialization for conversion and reconstruction of java classes and instances, in connection with the Java networking support. Similar strategies have been successfully employed in related systems (see [23] for CORBA services, and [24] for Java-based mobile agents).

Introduction to Oracle JServer. The architecture of the JVM in Oracle 8i is based on a session model. Sessions are private address spaces that clients have exclusive access to. They are not shared with any other client, although they may be serially re-used between clients. This means that the actions of one client can not interfere with any other client. All interactions between clients is done through the database itself, using transactional semantics. Each session has its own JVM. It is a 'thin' JVM which uses the shared memory architecture. This means that all clients share the read only static portion of their own JVM.

Java classes and its sources in Oracle 8i are not stored in the file system, but in the database system the same way that PL/SQL packages are stored.

Java classes, sources and resources are therefore database objects. Java Threads running in the Oracle 8i session are scheduled non-preemptively, i.e. a thread must yield control explicitly in order that the JVM runs another thread.

The whole environment is called JServer. Furthermore, the JServer consists of a Java Accelerator, an integrated CORBA 2.0 ORB (Visibroker), an embedded SQLJ translator and an Enterprise JavaBeans 1.0 compliant container for EJB components. The CORBA environment provides an user with the ability to call into and out of the database server by using the CORBA IIOP protocol. CORBA servers can be invoked from clients using IIOP. In this scenario the database then behaves as a CORBA server.

Session Architecture in the M^3 Agency. The JServer is responsible for the session management (creation, destruction etc.). Each session possesses a 'thin' JVM (~40 KB), a session memory, which is used for static variables, and a call memory for the instance variables of the currently executed class. The session's memory is limited to secure the system and to offer some kind of equality between all sessions. Figure 1 shows the session architecture. Before a database object can be invoked (e.g. a java CORBA Server), all class files and all help files have to be loaded and to be "published". Agency and agent run in the same session. However, only the agency is published and activated via the Java Naming and Directory Interface (JNDI). The arriving mobile agent is received by the agency and loaded with a Class Loader provided by the JServer. The agency obtains then a reference to the agent and can interfere so at any time with it (stop, resume etc.). For the publishing of the agency, one needs to know the valid username and password of the user which hosts the mobile agents (agency publishing can only be done by an agency administrator). However, the agent itself needs not to know user/password, as the session is already spawn by the agency. Furthermore, the agent accesses the stored multimedia data via server-sided JDBC directly, without supplemental authentification (see subsection 3.2). Therefore, it is the task of the agency to provide the necessary security level for the agent execution (see next subsection).

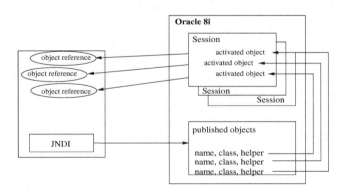

Fig. 1. *Session Architecture.*

Run-Time Environment. The M^3 Agent system is not an always running server, but is activated on demand. It reminds therefore of the servlet technology where for each call a new servlet instance will be created. In the following, we will give a short description of the necessary classes, database tables and database users:

- *AgencyServant*: This class is the published object in the database. Oracle's JServer will return a reference to a newly created AgencyServant in a new session to the calling client. Furthermore, the AgencyServant accepts the incoming agents and starts them in an AgencyThread. When an agent terminates, it will be sent to the next host in the itinerary. The AgencyServant is also responsible for keeping track of the currently running agents. If a new agent arrives, the agency has first to test with the help of the `Agencyinfo` table whether the maximal number of running agents is reached.
- *AgencyThread*: Every agent is started in such a thread. The agency is able to start and stop this thread whenever it wants.
- *Migrateable*: Each agent has to implement this interface.
- *Agent_Sec database user*: This is the security user of the agency. This user has system privileges and can grant or revoke rights to our agency user. Every access to the file system or tables of other users have to be granted by this user. Only the agency can contact the security user.
- *Itinerary*: This interface defines the methods of an itinerary. The agency, where the agent resides at the moment, can get the next target host name and is able to send the agent to the new agency.
- *XNotified*: This interface is used to communicate with the original client. Its implementation is usually on the original client side.
- *Agency database user*: This is the database user account where the agency is published. It has to be a user who only has access to his own database space. No further rights are necessary. We use SCOTT in our current test environment.
- `Agencyinfo` database table: The `Agencyinfo` table contains information of the agency and the currently running agents. The table consists of the following entries:
  - ACTIVE: contains the number of currently running agents in the database.
  - MAX: maximal number of simultaneously running agents.
  - SERVERNAME: The DNS-name of the database server.
  - DATABASENAME: The SID of the database.
  - USERNAME: Name of the agency user. In this way the agency is able to run in different user spaces on different databases. However, the security user needs to know whom to grant and restrict rights.

Migration in the M^3 Agency. The migration of an agent occurs through the following steps:

1. The client creates an agent for his/her needs, serializes it and creates a jar-file with the class files.

2. The client creates instances of the implementations of the XNotified and the Itinerary interface and connects them to the ORB. The Itinerary contains a list of the servers which the agent intend to visit.

3. The reference of the first agency is returned by the Oracle's JServer handling the client call. The client sends then a message, containing the byte-code of the agent (as a jar-file-type byte array), the serialized state of the agent, the Itinerary and a handle (remote reference) to the Xnotified.

4. The agency receives the message and tries to create the agent. An agent can only be created iff the number of currently running agents is lower than the maximal number of running agents specified in the `Agencyinfo` table. If there is a free slot for the new agent, then the value of the ACTIVE column in the `Agencyinfo` table is increased by one. If the maximal number of agents is currently reached, then the agency makes three more attempts to get a free slot. If these attempts fail again, the agent is sent to the next host.

5. The agency loads the agent's classes into the database.

6. The agency creates an AgentThread and transfers the serialized data of the agent to the thread.

7. The thread deserializes the agent and calls its execute method.

8. When the agent and the AgentThread terminates (no more host in the Itinerary), the agent's result will be sent back to the Xnotified object of the client.

9. The agency serializes the agent, "gzips" the resulting stream and contact the next host in the itinerary in order to prepare the sending process. If the next host is accessible, the agent is sent to the next host and the procedure pursues through step 4.

10. After having sent the agent, the agency cleans up the system and decreases the value of the ACTIVE column in the `Agencyinfo` table.

If an exception occurs during the execution of the agent, and it is not caught by the agent, the thread saves the exception. The agency gets then this exception and returns it to the Xnotified object.

Support for CBR in the the M^3 Agency. A mobile agent in M^3 may build up personalized and efficient CBR through two mechanisms, which are related strongly to each other. First, through the possibility of server-sided JDBC for a direct access to database objects and second through the use of *inter*Media Java classes for the access, retrieval and streaming of multimedia data (for more information on *inter*Media see technet.oracle.com). The use of both mechanisms are enabled by the implementation of the agency as database objects and the execution of the agent inside a database session.

The Oracle JDBC server-side internal driver (KPRB) is built into the Oracle JServer and is intrinsically tied to the Oracle8i database and to the JVM. The driver runs within the default session–the same session in which the JVM was invoked. It is optimized to provide direct access to SQL data and PL/SQL subprograms on the local database, through native function call (no Net8 call involved). Running the mobile agent inside a database session has the advantage

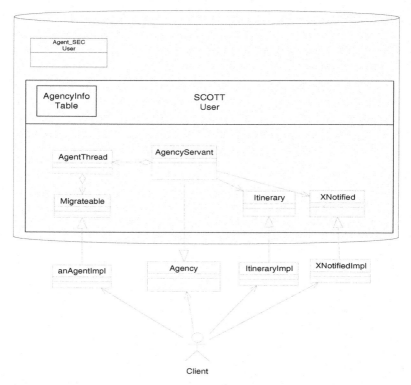

Fig. 2. *Architecture of the M^3 Agency System.*

that the mobile agent needs not to provide the database name, the agency user and password for obtaining a database connection through server-side internal driver. It is the task of the agency to spawn the session which hosts the agent and to load its byte-code, as well as its instance directly into the database. Therefore the same agent code can be executed without no adaptation on any host participating in the distributed MMDBMS system.

The server-sided internal driver is one prerequisite for the support of CBR, the other one are the *inter*Media Java classes provided by Oracle 8i. Oracle8i *inter*Media supports multimedia domain-specific types, methods, and interfaces. The following multimedia object types are supported: ORDAudio for audio, ORDImage and ORDVir for images, and ORDVideo for videos. For all of these data types, special *inter*Media Java classes are provided which enables the user to create own Java applications to use, manipulate, and modify multimedia data stored in an Oracle 8i database.

The multimedia retrieval part of the mobile agents has to be designed in the following way, first make a server-sided connection from the Java application to the Oracle database through JDBC's `defaultConnection()` method (no user/password needs to be provided). Second, execute a SELECT statement on the database table containing multimedia data and store the results in the Java application (based on the *inter*Media Java classes). Third, move the results into an *inter*Media object with the `getCustomDatum()` method. Perform operations on the Java multimedia application object to obtain the desired functionality (possibly through repeated SELECT statements).

Example: The following statements show how to retrieve the first stamp of an *image table* `stamps` (1), how to move the results into an *inter*Media object `imgObjj` (2), and finally how to produce an *MemoryImageSource* `mis` for further processing. This *MemoryImageSource* can e.g. be used for the computation of a color histogram (see the mobile agents in the experimenal section 4).

```
...
(1) Statement stmt = conn.createStatement();
(1) OracleResultSet rs  = (OracleResultSet)stmt.executeQuery
            ("SELECT image1 FROM stamps WHERE id=1");
(2) OrdVir imgObjj = (OrdVir)rs.getCustomDatum(1, OrdVir.getFactory());
(3) int width  = imgObjj.getWidth();
(3) int height = imgObjj.getHeight();
(3) MemoryImageSource mis =
            new MemoryImageSource(width, height,ColorModel.getRGBdefault(),
            imgObjj.getDataInByteArray(), 0, width);
...
```

4   Performance Evaluation

The performance evaluation is given in two parts. In a first part we show how our agent system might enhance the server capabilities for the example scenario of a nearest-neighbor search in a stamp database. In a second part, we compare for the same problem, but for a larger face database, the response time of our agent system to a solution based on a client-server architecture.

4.1   Evaluation of the Enhancement Capabilities

One of the main advantages of using our mobile agent systems concerns its capacity to enhance the database functionality by injecting personalized programs in the database system.

The example image database contains 59 US stamps in jpeg format, each with 24 bits per pixel (16 Million colors). The example problem to be solved within this part is that of a nearest-neighbor search (NN-search). That means we detect the most similar stamp to a reference one, in the stamp image database. Such a search is useful for many applications, for instance a user finds an interesting stamp in a newspaper, scans it and likes to retrieve more information (e.g. price, where to obtain, etc.) about this stamp from a stamp database. Therefore, he/she intends first, to find the most similar stamp in the database and second, retrieve information as provided by it.

The indexing and retrieval task is solved by two agents, the first one (indexing agent) computes a color histogram feature vector of length 256 from the image

Fig. 3. *Reference Image of the NN-Search.*

database and stores it in a separate table. This table has two attributes, the feature vector of type **VARRAY(256) OF NUMBER**, and the id of the respective image. We suppose that the images are stored in an object-relational image table with one attribute of type **ORDVir** referencing the images and one attribute of type **NUMBER** containing the id of the image stored. The second mobile agent (retrieval agent) performs the NN-search of the reference stamp (Aircraft 'Staggerwing') shown in figure 3. This stamp is not contained directly in the database, however appears as a thumbnail in a collection of images showing classic American Aircrafts (this collection is shown to the left of figure 4).

Fig. 4. *Left : Closest Image found by the Mobile Agent. Right : Images found by the* OrdVir *System for a Threshold Value of 26.*

Let us now compare our mobile agent to the build-in capacities of the Oracle8i *inter*Media Visual Information Retrieval system **ORDVir**. Please refer to technet.oracle.com for more technical information on **ORDVir**.

The ORDVir system provides CBR functionality through the object type ORDVir and associated methods and functions. CBR functionality is provided by the ability to extract an image feature vector from four different visual attributes : global and local color[1], texture and shape. The image comparison mechanism is provided by a similarity function ORDSYS.VIRSimilar() which takes two elements of the ORDVir type as input. Furthermore, the user must define a threshold similarity value governing the difference of the respective feature vectors, i.e. if the weighted sum of the distances for the visual attributes is less than or equal to the threshold, the function returns true, otherwise it returns false. Note that the same principle is also applied in other systems, e.g. the Informix Excalibur Image DataBlade module (see examples.informix.com and then goto Using DataBlade modules).

Experimental Protocol

a) M^3 Agent System: The mobile agent incorporates the feature vector of the reference image. After the complete scan of the stamps database it returned the closest image to the reference one, as shown to the left of figure 4.

b) ORDVir System: In order to implement the NN-search with the ORDVir system, one has to know exactly the threshold value. We started to use a value (10) of the reference examples provided in Oradoc[2]. Furthermore, in order to compare the two algorithms on the same feature extraction base, we specified that the globalcolor visual attribute has to be used exclusively. With this first threshold value (10), the ORDVir system didn't find any matching image. We augmented then the value to 30, and then the system found 5 matching images. For the values 29 and 28 we found three matching images and for a value of 26 we found 2 matching images (they are shown in the middle and to the right of figure 4). Then for a value 25 we found the closest image, as shown to the left of figure 4. Finally, beyond the threshold value of 25 no match can be returned.

Obviously, such a search for an adequate threshold value is not acceptable for a NN-search (multiple scans of the image table are required) and our mobile agent represents therefore a useful enhancement to the ORDVir functionality for the retrieval tasks to be solved.

4.2 Response Time Evaluation

Here, the NN-search of the qualitative first part is adapted for a response time evaluation through considering a larger face database of size 4000. We are interested in computing the nearest-neighbor image of a reference image in the face database. Thereby, we merged the functionality of the former index- and retrieval agent into one NN-search agent. The sample database used was the AR Face Database created by Aleix Martinez and Robert Benavente at the Computer Vision Center (CVC) at Purdue University. It contains 4000 images corresponding to 126 people's faces (70 men and 56 women) [25].

---

[1] Global color represents the distribution of colors within the entire image. Local color represents color distributions and where they occur in an image.

[2] http://www.oradoc.com/ora817/inter.817/a85333/virj_ref.htm.

The testing environment consisted of two similar agent hosting machines with the following parameters, CPU : AMD 800 MHz CPU, OS : Win NT 40 SP6 and Program Environment : JDK 1.3. Both machines communicated over a 100 MBit/sec Ethernet segment. Furthermore on each machine the Oracle 8.1.7 database was installed.

Our mobile agent computes on the database server for each face first a feature vector with 256 values. Second, it compares the difference of this vector and the reference vector to the difference of the yet best match to the reference one (either found on a previous host or on the same host). If the difference is smaller than the previously found best one, it retains it for further processing. The client-server solution has to download each image to the client, and performs the image comparison locally.

The metric, we examine here, is the response time for computing the nearest-neighbor for the client-server solution and the mobile agent solutions. The performance of the mobile agent solution depends on the database load, which depends itself to a great extent on the available free main memory. To account for this, we limited the available server java pool memory space for each session, once to 20 MB, 60 MB and once to 100 MB. The number of faces in the databases was varied from 400 to 10400 (database size). For a size n smaller than 4000, the first n images of the available ones are retained, for a size greater than 4000, the images are replicated. We performed two experiments: in the first we used one host and in the second two hosts.

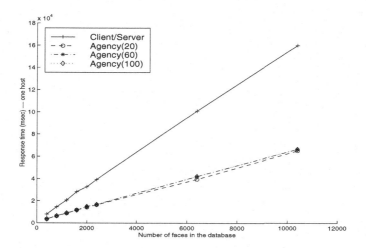

Fig. 5. *Response Time of the Client/Server Solution vs. Our Mobile Agent for One Host.*

Figure 5 shows the response time of a first experiment using one host depending on the available java pool size and the database size. The figure clearly shows that our mobile agent solution outperforms the client-server case. The

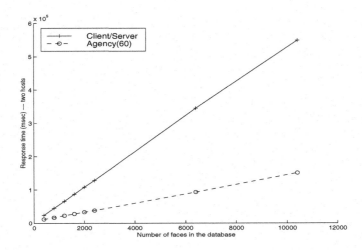

Fig. 6. *Response Time of the Client/Server Solution vs. Our Mobile Agent for 2 Hosts.*

response time of the client-server solution is on average 2.38 times higher than that of the mobile agent one. The response time of the mobile agent solution is almost invariable to the size of the available java pool size per session and varies only minimally between the different values, e.g. the highest variance of 2.5% occurs between 20MB and 100MB.

Figure 6 shows the response time of a second experiment using two hosts depending on the available java pool size and the database size. Once again, the response time of the mobile agent solution is clearly smaller than that of the client-server solution. Moreover the performance gain (3.08 times less response time of the mobile agent) is higher than in the first experiment (2.38 less response time). The response time is again invariable with respect to the java pool size and therefore not shown in figure 6. If one compares now the results using two hosts to the results using one host, it can be noticed that the response time of the mobile agent solutions doubles approximately compared to the first experiment, as the response time of the client-server solution is more than two and half times higher than that of the first experiment. This is due to the intermediate processing on the client machine in the client-server solution. Therefore, the mobile agent solution scales better with respect to the number of hosts involved in the search.

5   Conclusion

One of the main advantages of the mobile agent technique is the ability of migration and mobility, that means to bring the problem solver directly to the problem which results in processing cost and time benefits. This paper shows that it is possible and profitable to establish an agency system inside a distributed Oracle 8i multimedia database.

In this context, we implemented the M^3 -MultiMedia Database Mobile agents- which supports personalized content-indexing and retrieval (CBR) in a distributed Oracle 8i multimedia database system. Support for CBR follows directly from the implementation of the agency system inside the Oracle 8i database (i.e. both agency, as well as agent are database object) and by using server-sided JDBC combined with the *inter*Media Java Class libraries. Our agent system proposes an advanced security concept, through session management and an own security user which grants and revoke database and resource access rights for the agent. A final performance comparison of our mobile agent technology with a client-server solution for a nearest-neighbor search in an image database shows the efficiency of the proposed solution.

In the near future we will rely the implementation of our multimedia database SMOOTH [9] on the M^3 mobile agency, in order to overcome the communication bottleneck of a client/server JDBC (see section 2).

References

1. Guojun Lu. *Multimedia Database Management Systems*. Artech House, 1999.
2. N.M. Karnik and A.R. Tripathi. Design issues in mobile-agent programming systems. *IEEE Concurrency*, 6(3):52–61, July/September 1998.
3. P. Dasgupta, L. E. Moser, and P. M. Melliar-Smith. The security architecture for MAgNET: A mobile agent E-commerce system. In *Third International Conference on Telecommunications and E-commerce*, Dallas, TX, USA, 2000.
4. H-Jeon, C. Petrie, and M.R. Cutkosky. JATLite: A Java agent infrastructure with message routing. *IEEE Internet Computing*, 4(2), March/April 2000.
5. B. Brewington, R. Gray, K. Moizumi, D. Kotz, G. Cybenko, and D. Rus. Mobile agents in distributed information retrieval. In *Intelligent Information Agents*, chapter 12. Springer Verlag, 1999.
6. P. Bellavista, A. Corradi, and C. Stefanelli. Mobile agent middleware for mobile computing. *IEEE Computer*, 34(3):73–81, March 2001.
7. Y. Rui, T. S. Huang, and S.-F. Chang. Image retrieval: Past, present and future. *Journal of Visual Communication and Image Representation*, 10:1–23, 1999.
8. A. Yoshitaka and T. Ichikawa. A survey on content-based retrieval for multimedia databases. *IEEE Transactions on Knowledge and Data Engineering*, 11(1):81–93, 1999.
9. H. Kosch, R. Tusch, L. Böszörményi, A. Bachlechner, B. Dörflinger, C. Hofbauer, C. Riedler, M. Lang, and C. Hanin. SMOOTH - A distributed multimedia database system. In *Proceedings of the International VLDB Conference*, Rome, Italy, September 2001. Accepted for Publication as Demonstration Paper.
10. D.B. Lange and M. Oshima. *Programming and deploying Java mobile agents with Aglets*. Addison-Wesley, Reading, MA, USA, 1999.
11. J. Baumann, F. Hohl, K. Rothermel, and M. Strasser. Mole - Concepts of a mobile agent system. *World Wide Web*, 1(3):123–137, 1998.
12. C. Bäumer, M. Breugst, S. Choy, and T. Magedanz. Grasshopper — A universal agent platform based on OMG MASIF and FIPA standards. In *First International Workshop on Mobile Agents for Telecommunication Applications (MATA'99)*, pages 1–18, Ottawa, Canada, October 1999. World Scientific.

13. H. Ouahid and A. Karmouch. An XML based web mining agent. In *First International Workshop on Mobile Agents for Telecommunication Applications (MATA'99)*, pages 393–404, Ottawa, Canada, October 1999. World Scientific.

14. C. Bäumer and T. Magedanz. Grasshopper : A mobile agent platform for active telecommunication networks. In *Proceedings of the 3rd International Workshop on Intelligent Agents for Telecommunication Applications (IATA-99)*, pages 19–32, Berlin, Germany, August 9–10 1999. LNCS 1699, Springer Verlag.

15. S. Papastavrou, G. Samaras, and E. Pitoura. Mobile agents for WWW distributed database access. In *Proceedings of the International Conference on Data Engineering (ICDE)*, pages 228–237, Sydney, Australia, March 1999.

16. Dejan Milojicic. Mobile agent applications. *IEEE Concurrency*, 7(3):80–90, July/September 1999.

17. E. Weippl, J. Altmann, and W. Essmayr. QoS management by mobile agents in multimedia communication. In *Proceedings of the International DEXA'2000 Workshops*, pages 477–481, Greenwich, UK, September 2000.

18. L.A. Guedes, P.G. Oliveres, L.F. Paina, and E. Cordozo. An agent based approach for supporting quality of service. *Computer Communications*, 21:1269–1278, 1998.

19. S. Manvi and P. Venkataram. QoS management by mobile agents in multimedia communication. In IEEE CS Press, editor, *Proceedings of the International DEXA 2000 Workshops*, pages 407–411, Greenwich, London, UK, September 2000.

20. C. Tschudin. Mobile agent security. In *Intelligent Information Agents: Cooperative, Rational and Adaptive Information Gathering on the Internet*, pages 431–445. Springer Verlag, 1999.

21. S.-C. Chen, R.L. Kashyap, and A. Ghafoor. *Semantic Models for Multimedia Database Searching and Browsing*. Kluwer, 2000.

22. P. Correia and F. Pereira. The role of analysis in content based video coding and indexing. *Signal Processing*, 66(2):125–142, 1998.

23. M. Amer, A. Karmouch, and T. Gray. Adding mobility to CORBA. In *First International Workshop on Mobile Agents for Telecommunication Applications (MATA'99)*, pages 143–160, Ottawa, Canada, October 1999. World Scientific.

24. D. Wong, N. Paciorek, and D. Moore. Java-based mobile agents. *Communications of the ACM*, 42(3):92–102, February 1999.

25. A.M. Martinez and R. Benavente. The AR face database. Technical Report CVC Technical Report Number 24, 1998, Computer Vision Center (CVC) at Purdue University, 1998.

Display Optimization For Image Browsing

Qi Tian[1], Baback Moghaddam[2], and Thomas S. Huang[1]

[1]Beckman Institute, University of Illinois, Urbana-Champaign IL, USA 61801
{qitian,huang}@ifp.uiuc.edu
[2]Mitsubishi Electric Research Laboratories, Cambridge MA, USA 02139
baback@merl.com

Abstract. [1]In this paper, we propose a technique to visualize a multitude of images on a 2-D screen based on their visual features (color, texture, structure, etc.). The resulting layout will automatically display the mutual similarities of the viewed images. Furthermore, audio features, semantic features, or any combination of the above can be used in such a visualization. The original high dimensional feature space is projected on the 2-D screen based on Principle Component Analysis (PCA). PCA has the desired property of being simple, fast and unique (i.e. repeatable) and the only linear transformation that achieves maximum distance preservation in projecting to lower dimensions. Furthermore, we have developed a novel technique for solving the problem of overlapping (obscured) images shown in the proposed 2-D display. Given the original PCA-based visualization, a constrained nonlinear optimization strategy is used to adjust the position and size of the images in order to minimize overlap (maximize visibility) while maintaining fidelity to the original positions which are indicative of mutual similarities. A significantly improved visualization of large image sets is achieved when the proposed technique is applied.

1   Introduction

Traditional browsing and navigating in a large image database is often disorienting unless the user can form a mental picture of the entire database. Content-based visualization can provide an efficient approach for image browsing and navigation for large image databases.

In this paper, we proposed a content-based visualization technique for image browsing and navigation. The visual features used for content-based visualization are discussed in Section 2 and the proposed visualization technique is presented in Section 3.

In Section 4, a novel optimization technique for solving the overlapping problem is introduced. Example visualizations, showing maximally visible layouts, are shown in Section 5.

---

[1] The figures in this paper are best viewed in color and at higher resolution at http://www.ifp.uiuc.edu/~qitian/mdic01/.

M. Tucci (Ed.): MDIC 2001, LNCS 2184, pp. 167-176, 2001.

2   Visual Features

There are three visual features used in our system: color moments, wavelet-based texture, and the water-filling structural features.

Color is one of the most widely used visual features for content-based image analysis. It is relatively robust to background complication and independent of image size and orientation [1]. To represent color, we choose the HSV color space due to its de-correlated and uniform coordinates. Color histograms are the most commonly used color feature representation. While histograms are useful because they are relatively insensitive to position and orientation changes, they do not capture spatial relationship of color regions and thus, they have limited discriminating power. Stricker and Orengo [2] showed that characterizing a 1-D color distribution with the first three moments is more robust and more efficient than working with color histograms. The mathematical foundation of this representation is that if we interpret the color distribution of an image as a probability distribution, then the color distribution can be uniquely characterized by its moments. Therefore, a 9-dimensional color feature vector (3 moments for each color channel, HSV) is extracted and stored from every image in the database.

Texture refers to the visual pattern with properties of homogeneity that do not result from the presence of a single color or intensity [3]. It contains important information about the structural arrangement of surfaces and their relationship to the surrounding environment. To represent texture, we used the wavelet texture representation proposed by Smith and Chang in [4]. Specifically, we feed an image into a wavelet filter bank and decompose the image into three wavelet levels, thus having 10 subbands. Each subband captures the feature of some scale and orientation of the original image. For each subband, the standard deviation of the wavelet coefficient is extracted. Therefore, a 10-dimensional texture feature vector is extracted for each image in the database.

Structure is a feature between texture and shape. It is more general than texture or shape in that it requires neither uniform texture region nor a closed shape contour. In this paper, we used so-called *water-filling* structural feature [5]. For water-filling structural feature, we use a suitable edge detector and extract eighteen (18) elements from the edge maps, including *max fill time, max fork count, etc.* For a complete description of this structural feature vector, interested readers are referred to [5].

3   Content-Based Visualization

One of our central focuses is augmenting a user's perception in order to grasp a large information space that cannot be perceived by traditional image browsing methods, e.g., images are either randomly displayed or tile-based displayed. In this section, we propose a technique that visualizes the mutual similarities of a set of images on the 2-D screen based on visual features. We believe having an idea of the "context" of the current query can suggest where to go next in image browsing and navigation because the user can form a mental picture of the entire database [6].

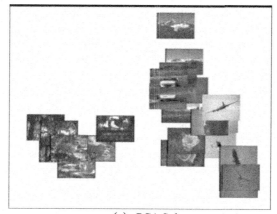

(a) PCA Splat.

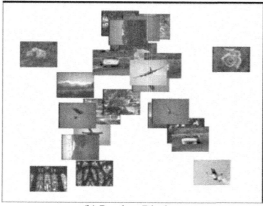

(b) Random Display.

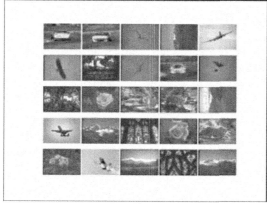

(c) Tile-Based Display.

Figure 1. Different Display Schemes.

In our experiments, the 37 visual features (9 color moments, 10 wavelet moments and 18 water-filling features) are pre-extracted from the image databases and stored off-line. The 37 visual features are formed into a single feature vector and projected to the 2D space based on Principle Component Analysis (PCA) [7]. PCA is a very fast linear transformation that achieves the maximum distance preservation when projecting from high to low dimensional feature spaces. The PCA layout is denoted as a "PCA Splat". The mutual distance between image locations respects their visual similarity, thus forming visual groupings of image clusters.

Figure 1 (a) shows an example of PCA Splat for 25 images from a natural image database. Traditional displays, e.g., random display and tile-based display are shown Figure 1(b) and (c), respectively. Clearly similar images are close to each other in a PCA Splat. PCA Splat also conveys information about all $\binom{n}{2}$ similarities between images while traditional displays (like tile-based rank-ordered browsers) cannot provide such 2nd-order information.

We can also project images onto a 3-D space for more advanced visualization. The features used can be individual visual features, audio features, semantic features (keyword annotations) or any combination of the above, which we are currently experimenting with.

Multidimensional Scaling (MDS) is an alternative approach to perform dimensionality reduction for visualization. MDS [8] is a nonlinear transformation that minimizes the stress between high dimensional feature space and low dimensional space. However, MDS is rotation invariant, non-repeatable, and is about 3 order slower than PCA on the average to implement due to its iterative computational nature. These drawbacks make MDS inappropriate for real time browsing or visualization of images.

4   Minimizing Window Overlap

One drawback of a PCA Splat is that similar images are most often partially overlapped which makes the visualization difficult to digest. This problem can be regarded as an optimization of window size and location in order to minimize overlap and hence maximize visibility. The following is the description of the proposed approach.

4.1   Problem Formulation

Given a set of windows, the number of windows is N. The center coordinates of the windows are denoted as (x_i, y_i), $i = 1, \square, N$ and the initial window positions are denoted as (x_i^o, y_i^o), $i = 1, \square, N$. The maximum and minimum coordinates of the 2-D screen are $[x_{min}, x_{max}, y_{min}, y_{max}]$. The window size is represented by its radius r_i, $i = 1, \square$, N for simplicity and the maximum and minimum window size is r_{max} and r_{min} in radius. The initial window size is r_i^o, $i = 1, \square$, N.

We wish to find a solution that modifies the image windows slightly without deviating too much from the initial locations (which convey mutual similarities). Two factors are taken into account for cost function design. The first is to keep the total area of window overlap as small as possible. The second is to keep the overall deviation from the initial positions on the screen as small as possible.

This represents a trade-off between minimizing overlap and minimizing deviation. To minimize the overlap, one could simply move the windows away from each other but this would simply increase the deviation of the window from the original position. Large deviations are certainly undesirable since the initial positions are important. Without increasing the overall deviation, another way to minimize the overlap is to shrink the window size. Of course, the window size cannot be arbitrary small. Since increasing the window size risks increasing overlap it is disallowed in the optimization process. For this reason the initial window size r_i^o is assumed to be r_{max}, $i = 1, \square$, N.

The total cost function is designed as a linear combination of the individual cost function, taking into account each factor mentioned above.

$$J = F(p) + \lambda \cdot S \cdot G(p) \tag{1}$$

where $F(p)$ is the cost function of total overlap and $G(p)$ is the cost function of the total deviation from the original positions and S is a scaling factor set to *(N-1)/2* in order to equalize the range of $G(p)$ and $F(p)$. λ is a weight with $\lambda \geq 0$. When λ is zero, the total deviation is ignored in overlap minimization. When λ is less than one, minimizing total overlap is more important than minimizing total deviation, and vice versa for λ is greater than one.

4.2   Cost Function Design

The cost function of overall overlap is designed as

$$F(p) = \sum_{i=1}^{N} \sum_{j=i+1}^{N} f(p) \tag{2}$$

$$f(p) = \begin{cases} 1 - e^{-\frac{u^2}{\sigma_f}} & u > 0 \\ 0 & u \leq 0 \end{cases} \tag{3}$$

where $u = r_i + r_j - \sqrt{(x_i - x_j)^2 + (y_i - y_j)^2}$, u is a measure of overlapping. When $u \leq 0$, there is no overlap between the ith window and the jth window, thus the cost is 0. When $u > 0$, there is partial overlap between the ith window and the jth window.

When $u = 2 \cdot r_{max}$, the ith window and the jth window are totally overlapped. σ_f is curvature-controlling factor.

Figure 2 shows the plot of $f(p)$. Note that with an increasing value of u $(u > 0)$, the cost also increases.

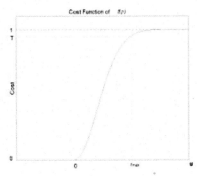

Figure 2. Cost Function of Overlap Function $f(p)$.

From Fig. 2, σ_f in Eq. (3) is calculated by setting $T=0.95$ when $u = r_{max}$.

$$\sigma_f = \frac{-u^2}{\ln(1-T)} \big|_{u=r_{max}} \tag{4}$$

The cost function of overall deviation is designed as

$$G(p) = \sum_{i=1}^{N} g(p) \tag{5}$$

$$g(p) = 1 - e^{-\frac{v^2}{\sigma_g}} \tag{6}$$

where $v = \sqrt{(x_i - x_i^o)^2 + (y_i - y_i^o)^2}$, v is the deviation of the ith window from its initial position. σ_g is curvature-controlling factor. (x_i, y_i) and (x_i^o, y_i^o) are the optimized and initial center coordinates of the ith window, respectively, $i = 1, \square, N$.
Figure 3 shows the plot of $g(p)$. With an increasing value of v, the cost of deviation is also increasing.

From Fig. 3, σ_g in Eq. (6) is calculated by setting $T=0.95$ when $v = maxsep$. In our work, $maxsep$ is set to be $2 \cdot r_{max}$.

$$\sigma_g = \frac{-v^2}{\ln(1-T)} \big|_{v=maxsep} \tag{7}$$

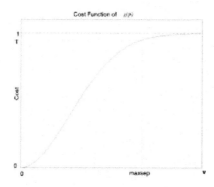

Figure 3. Cost Function of Function $g(p)$.

The optimization technique we used was to minimize the total cost J by adjusting the size and positions of the windows until a local minimum is found. It was implemented by an iterative gradient descent procedure. The images are then positioned and sized according to their windows' optimal parameters.

5   Experimental Results

The above technique is a general approach and can be applied to avoid overlapping of various kinds of windows, frames, boxes, images or multimedia icons. When this technique is applied to the PCA Splat, a better content-based visualization can be achieved.

Figure 4 (a) shows the optimized PCA Splat for Fig. 1(a). Clearly, the overlap and crowding is minimized and at the same time the similar images are still close to each other. An improved visualization can even be achieved when this technique is applied to the random layout of Fig. 1(b) (see Figure 4(b)) simply because the overlap is minimized.

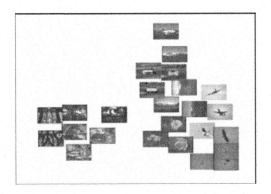

(a)   Optimized PCA Splat.

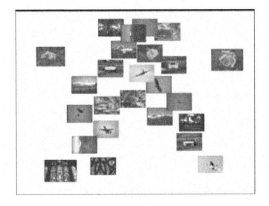

(b)   Optimized Random Display.

Fig. 4. Optimized Displays.

When the proposed optimized technique is applied for content-based image retrieval, a better visualization of the retrieval results can be made, since in addition to rank information (1st-order) one can also see 2nd-order relations (mutual similarities). This would not only provide a better understanding of the query results but also aid the user in forming a new query or provide relevance feedback. An example is shown in Figure 5.

(a) The top 20 retrieved images in our system (ranked from left to right, from top to bottom, the top left 1 is the query).

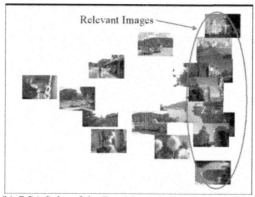

(b) PCA Splat of the Top 20 Retrieved Images in (a).

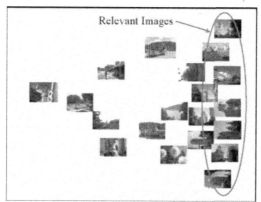

(c)   Optimized PCA Splat of (b).

Fig. 5. An Example for Content-Based Image Retrieval.

Acknowledgement

This work was supported in part by Mitsubishi Electronic Research Laboratory, Cambridge, MA 02139 and NSF grant CDA 96-24396 and EIA 99-75019.

References

1. C. S. McCamy, H. Marcus, and J. G. Davidson, " A Color-Rendition Chart", *J. Applied Photographic Eng.*, Vol. 2, pp. 95-99, Summer 1976.
2. M. Stricker and M. Orengo, "Similarity o Color Images", *Proc. SPIE Storage and Retrieval for Image and Video Databases*, 1995.
3. J. R. Smith and S. F. Chang, "Automated Binary Texture Feature Sets for Image Retrieval", *Proc. IEEE Intl. Conf. Acoust., Speech, and Signal Proc.*, Atlanta, GA, 1996.
4. J. R. Smith and S. F. Chang, "Transform Features for Texture Classification and Discrimination in Large Image Database", *Proc. IEEE Intl. Conf. on Image Proc.*, 1994.
5. S. X. Zhou, Y. Rui and T. S. Huang, "Water-filling algorithm: A novel way for image feature extraction based on edge maps", in *Proc. IEEE Intl. Conf. On Image Proc.*, Japan, 1999.
6. Y. Rubner, "Perceptual metrics for image database navigation", Ph.D. dissertation, Stanford University, 1999.
7. Jolliffe, I.T., *Principal Component Analysis*, Springer-Verlag, New-York, 1986.
8. W. S. Torgeson, *Theory and methods of scaling*, John Wiley and Sons, New York, NY, 1958.

Part V

Video Indexing and Communication

Semantic Characterization of Visual Content for Sports Videos Annotation

Jürgen Assfalg, Marco Bertini, Carlo Colombo, and Alberto Del Bimbo

Dipartimento di Sistemi e Informatica
Via S.Marta 3, 50139 Firenze, Italy
{assfalg,bertini,colombo,delbimbo}@dsi.unifi.it

Abstract. This paper illustrates an approach to semantic video annotation in the specific context of sports videos. Videos are automatically annotated according to elements of visual content at different layers of semantic significance. Unlike previous approaches, videos can include several different sports and can also be interleaved with non sport shots. Each shot is decomposed into its visual and graphic content elements, including foreground and background, objects, text captions, etc. Several different low-level visual primitives are combined together by domain-specific rules in order to capture semantic content at a higher level of significance. Results of experiments on typical sports videos are presented and discussed.
Keywords: Content-Based Video Retrieval; Video Annotation; Video Semantics; Sports Videos.

1   Introduction

The dramatic quantity of videos generated by digital technologies has originated the need for automatic annotation of these videos, and the consequent need for techniques supporting their retrieval. Content-based video annotation and retrieval is therefore an active research topic. While many of the results in content-based image retrieval can be successfully applied to videos, additional techniques have to be developed to address their peculiarity. In fact, videos add the temporal dimension, thus requiring to represent object dynamics. Furthermore, while we often think of video just as of a sequence of images, it actually is a compound medium, integrating such elementary media as realistic images, graphics and audio. Finally, application contexts for videos are different than those for images, and therefore call for different approaches in the way in which users may annotate, query for, and exploit archived video data.

The huge amount of data delivered by a video stream requires development of techniques supporting an effective description of the content of a video. This necessarily results in higher levels of abstraction in the annotation of the content, and therefore requires investigation and modeling of video semantics. This further points out that general purpose approaches are likely to fail, as semantics inherently depends on the specific application context. Semantic modeling of content of multimedia databases has been addressed by many researchers. From

M. Tucci (Ed.): MDIC 2001, LNCS 2184, pp. 179–191, 2001.

a theoretical viewpoint, the semantic treatment of a video requires the construction of a hierarchical data model including, at increasing levels of abstraction, four main layers: raw data, feature, object, and knowledge [1]. For each layer, the model must specify both the elements of representation (*what*) and the algorithms used to compute them (*how*). Upper layers are typically constructed by combining the elements of the lower layers according to a set of rules (however they are implemented). Concrete video retrieval applications by high-level semantics have been reported on in specific contexts such as movies [7], news [6], and commercials [4].

Due to its enormous commercial appeal, sports video represent another important application domain, where most of the research efforts have been devoted so far on the characterization of single, specific sports. Miyamori et al. [11] proposed a method to annotate the videos with human behavior. Ariki et al. [2] proposed a method for classification of TV sports news videos using DCT features. Sahouria et al. [14] proposed a method for the analysis of videos based on principal components analysis, and applied their method to sports scene classification. Zhou et al. [16] classified nine basketball events using color features, edges and MPEG motion vectors.

This paper illustrates an approach to semantic video annotation in the specific context of sports videos. Videos are automatically annotated according to elements of visual content at different layers of semantic significance. Unlike previous approaches, videos can include several different sports and can also be interleaved with non sport shots. In fact, studio/interview shots are primarily recognized and distinguished from sports action shots; the latter are then further decomposed into their main visual and graphic content elements, including sport type, foreground vs background, text captions, and so on. Relevant semantic elements are extracted from videos by suitably combining together several low level visual primitives such as image edges, corners, color histograms, etc. according to context-specific aggregation rules. Results of experiments on representative sports videos are presented and discussed.

2   The Application Context

The actual architecture of a system supporting video annotation and retrieval depends on the application context, and in particular on end users and their tasks. While all of these different application contexts demand for a reliable annotation of the video stream to effectively support selection of relevant video segments, it is evident that, for instance, service providers (e.g. broadcasters, editors) or consumers accessing a Video-On-Demand service have different needs [5].

In the field of supporting technologies for the editorial process, for both the old and new media, automatic annotation of video material opens the way to the economic exploitation of valuable assets. In particular, in the specific context of sports videos, two possible scenarios can be devised for the reuse of archived material within broadcasting companies: *i*) *posterity logging*, which is known as one key method of improving production quality by bringing added depth, and historical context, to recent events; *ii*) *production logging*, where broadcasters use footage registered few hours before, that may be even recorded by a different broadcaster, and thus is not indexed, to annotate it in order to edit and produce a sports news program. An example of posterity logging is the reuse of shots that show the best actions of a famous athlete: they can be reused later to provide an historical context. An example of production logging is the reuse of sport highlights, such as soccer goals or tennis match points, to produce programs that contain the best sport actions of the day.

In both scenarios, video material, which typically originates "live," should be annotated automatically, as detailed manual annotation is mostly impractical. The level of annotation should be sufficient to enable simple text-based queries. The annotation process includes such activities as segmentation of the material into shots, grouping and classification of the shots into semantic categories (e.g. type of sport), supporting query formulation and retrieval of events that are significant to the particular sport.

In order to achieve an effective annotation, it is important to have a clear insight into current standards of professional sports videos, particularly concerning the nature and structure of their content. Videos comprising the data set used in the experiments reported on in the following include a wide variety of typologies. Most of the videos where drawn from the BBC Sports Library, which in turn collected them from other departments of the BBC or from other broadcasters. The data set comprises over 15 video tapes, each lasting from 30 to 120 minutes. Videos were mostly captured from Digital Video (DV) tapes, and in some cases from S-VHS tapes. DV is the lowest acceptable standard for broadcasting professionals, and provides digital quality at full PAL resolution. To speed up processing, and to lower storage requirements, videos have then been shrinked to half PAL resolution (360×288 pixels).

Many of the videos in the set cover the Barcelona Olympics of 1992, and some other contain soccer games. Thus, a variety of sports types is available to perform experiments. Videos differ from each other in terms of sports types (outdoor and indoor sports) and number of athletes (single or teams). Also, videos differ in terms of editing, as some of the them represent so called *live feeds* of a single camera for a complete event, some include different feeds of a specific event edited into a single stream, and some others only feature highlights of minor sports assembled in a summary. Very few assumptions can be made on the presence of a spoken commentary or super-imposed text, as their availability depends on a number of factors, including technical facilities available on location, and on the agreements between the hosting broadcaster and the other broadcasters. As shown in Fig. 1, the typical structure of a sports video includes sport sequences interleaved with studio scenes, possibly complemented with superimposed graphics (captions, logos, etc.).

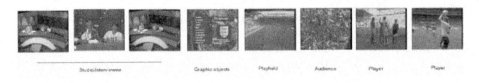

Studio/interview-anee   Graphic objects   Playfield   Audience   Player   Player

Fig. 1. Typical Sports Video Structure.

3 The Computational Approach

According to the above description of a typical sports video, the annotation task is organized into three distinct subtasks: *i*) shot preclassification (aimed at extracting from the video the actual sports actions); *ii*) classification of graphic features (which, in sports videos, are mainly text captions which are not synchronized with shot changes); and *iii*) classification of visual shot features.

This Section describes separately the computational model for each of these subtasks. Model specification is decomposed into model theory (analysis of the type and role of the features characterizing the subtask) and model implementation (how to compute the features, how the feature combination rules are implemented). For each subtask, an experimental results subsection completes the discussion.

3.1 Sports Shots Preclassification

Model Theory. The anchorman/interview shot classification module provides a simple preliminary classification of shot content, that can be further exploited and enhanced by subsequent modules. The need for this type of classification stems from the fact that some video feeds contain interviews and studio scenes featuring anchorman and athletes. An example is that of Olympic Games, where the material that must be logged is often pre-edited by the hosting broadcaster, and may contain such kinds of shots. The purpose of this module is to roughly separate shots that contain possible sport scenes from shots that do not contain sport scenes. To this end, a statistical approach can be followed to analyzes visual content similarity and motion features of the anchorman shots, without requiring any predefined shot content model to be used as a reference. In fact, this latter constraint is required in order to be able to correctly manage interviews, which do not feature a standard studio set-up, as athletes are usually interviewed near the playfield, and each interview has a different background and location. Also the detection of studio scenes requires such independence of a shot content model, since the "style" changes often, and each program has its unique style, that would require the creation and maintenance of database of shot content models.

Studio scenes show a well defined syntax: shot location is consistent within the video, the number of cameras and their view field is limited, the sequence of shot content can be represented by a repeating pattern. An example of such a structure is shown in Fig 2, where the first frames of the five successive shots comprising a studio sequence are shown.

Fig. 2. Studio Scene Containing Anchorman Shots.

Model Implementation. Shots of the studio/interviewee are repeated at intervals of variable length throughout the sequence. The first step for the classification of these shots stems from this assumption and is based on the computation, for each video shot S_k, of its shot lifetime $L(S_k)$. The shot lifetime measures the shortest temporal interval that includes all the occurrences of shots with similar visual content, within the video. Given a generic shot S_k, its lifetime is computed by considering the set:

$$T_k = \{t_i | \sigma(S_k, S_i) < \tau_s\}$$

where $\sigma(S_k, S_i)$ is a similarity measure applied to keyframes of shots S_k and S_i, τ_s a similarity threshold and t_i is the value of the time variable corresponding to the occurrence of the keyframe of shot S_i. The lifetime of shot S_k is defined as $L(S_k) = max(T_k) - min(T_k)$. Shot classification is based on fitting values of $L(S_k)$ for all the video shots in a bimodal distribution. This allows for the determination of a threshold value t_l that is used to classify shots into the *sport* and *studio/interviewee* categories. Particularly, all the shots S_k such that $L(S_k) > t_l$ are classified as studio/interview shots, where t_l was determined according to the statistics of the test database, and set to 5 sec. Remaining shots are classified as *sport* shots. Typical videos in the target domain do not contain complete studio shows, and, in feeds produced on location, interviews have a limited time and shot length. This allows for the reduction of false detections caused by the repetition of similar sport scenes (e.g. as in the case of edited magazine programs or summaries) by limiting the search of similar shots to a window of shots, whose width has been set experimentally to 6 shots. The adopted similarity metric is histogram intersection of the mean color histogram of shots (H and S components of the HSI color space). Usage of the mean histogram takes into account the dynamics of sport scenes. In fact even if some scenes take place in the same location, and thus the color histogram of their first frame may be similar, the following actions yield a different color histogram. When applied to studio/interviewee shots, where the dynamics of changes of lighting of the scene are much more compressed, and the reduced camera and objects movement do not introduce new objects, we get a stable histogram.

Although the mean color histogram accounts for minor variations due to camera and objects movement, it does not take into account spatial information.

Results of the first classification step are therefore refined by considering motion features of the studio/interviewee shots. This develops on the assumption that in an anchorman shot, both the camera and the anchorman are almost steady. In contrast, for sport shots, background objects and camera movements—persons, free-hand shots, camera panning and zooming, changes in scene lighting—cause relevant motion components throughout the shot. Classification refinement is performed by computing an index of the quantity of motion Q_M, for each possible anchorman shot. The algorithm for the analysis of this index takes into account the frame to frame difference between the shot key-frame f_1 and subsequent frames f_i in the shot according to pixel-wise comparison. To enhance sensitivity to motion the shot is sub-sampled in time, and the frames are compared to the first key-frame f_1. Only those shots whose Q_M doesn't exceed a threshold τ_M are definitely classified as studio/interviewee shots.

Experimental Results. A subset of 3 videos was used to test the algorithm. There were 28 shots comprising short interviews to athletes and studio scenes. The algorithm identified 30 studio/interviewee shots, with 3 false detections and 2 missed detection. The use of the movement feature reduces the number of false detections from 5 to 3. The remaining false detections were due to the replay of slow motion shots.

3.2   Classification of Graphic Features

Model Theory. In sports videos, graphic objects (GO) may appear everywhere within the frame, even if most of the time they are placed in the lower third or quarter of the image. Also the vertical and horizontal ratio of the GO zones varies, e.g. the roster of a team occupies a vertical box, while usually the name of a single athlete occupies a horizontal box (see Fig. 3). For text graphics, character fonts may vary in size and typeface, and may be super-imposed on opaque background as well as directly on the video. GOs often appear and disappear gradually, through dissolve or fade effects. These properties call for automatic GO localization algorithms with the least amount of heuristics and possibly no training.

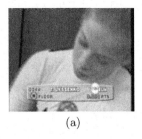   

(a)   (b)

Fig. 3. Examples of Superimposed Graphic Objects.

Several features such as edges ([10], [12], [15], [17]) and textures ([18], [19]) have been used in past research as cues of super-imposed GOs. Such features represent global properties of images, and require the analysis of large frame patches. Moreover also natural objects such as woods and leafs, or man-made objects such as buildings and cars may present a local combination of such features that can be wrongly classified as a GO [9].

In order both to reduce the visual information to a minimum and to preserve local saliency, we have elected to work with image corners, extracted from luminance information of images. Corners are computed from luminance information only; this is very appealing for the purpose of GO detection and localization in that prevents from many of misclassification problems arising with color-based approaches. This fact is particularly important when considering the characteristics of television standards, that require a spatial sub-sampling of the chromatic information; thus the borders of captions are affected by color aliasing. Therefore, to enhance readability of characters the producers typically exploit luminance contrast, since luminance is not spatially sub-sampled and human vision is more sensitive to it than to color contrast. Another distinguishing feature of our approach is that it does not require any knowledge or training on super-imposed captions features.

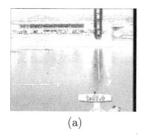
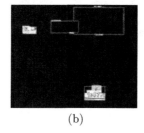

(a)   (b)

Fig. 4. a) Source Frame; b) Detected Captions with Noise Removal.

Model Implementation. The salient points of the frames, that are to be analyzed in the following steps, are extracted using the Harris algorithm [13], from the luminance map I, extracted from each frame, that is stored in $YCbCr$ color space. Corner extraction greatly reduces the number of spatial data to be processed by the GO detection and localization system.

The most basic property of GOs is the fact that they must remain stable for a certain amount of time, in order to let people read and understand them. This property is used in the first step of GO detection. Each corner is checked to determine if it is still present in the same position in at least 2 more frames within a sliding window of 4 frames.

Each corner that complies with this property is marked as *persistent*, and is kept for further analysis, while all the others are discarded. Every 8-th frame is processed to extract its corners, thus further reducing the computational resources needed to process a whole video. This choice develops on the assumption that, in order to be perceived and understood by the viewer, a GO must be stable on the screen for 1 second.

The patch surrounding each corner (20×14 pixels) is inspected, and if there are not enough neighboring corners (i.e. corners whose patches do not intersect), the corner is not considered in further processing. This process, which is repeated a second time in order to eliminate corners that get isolated after the first processing, avoids that isolated high contrast background objects contained within static scenes are recognized as possible GO zones.

An unsupervised clustering is performed on the corners that comply with the temporal and spatial features described above. This is aimed at determining bounding boxes for GOs (Figs. 4 and 5). For each bounding box the percentage of pixels that belong to the corner patches is calculated, and if it is below a predefined threshold the corners are discarded. This strategy reduces the noise due to high contrast background during static scenes, that typically produce small scattered zones of corners that can not be eliminated by the spatial feature analysis. This strategy is the only heuristics used in our method.

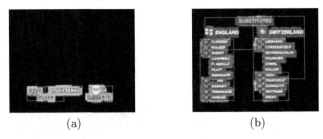

(a)   (b)

Fig. 5. Detection Results for the Frames in Fig. 3.

Experimental Results. The test set used was composed of 19 sports videos acquired from PAL DV tapes at full PAL resolution and frame rate (720x576 pixels, 25 fps) resulting in 47014 frames (31'20").

An example of GO detection is provided in Fig. 5. To test the robustness with respect to text size and video resolution, two S-VHS videos were also digitized. One video was acquired at full PAL resolution (720x576 pixels, 25 fps) resulting in 4853 frames (3'14") and 257 MB, while the second one was acquired at half PAL resolution (368x288, 25 fps), and contained 425 frames (totaling 17"). It is worth pointing out that, with this latter resolution, some text captions in videos become only 9 pixels high. Since the spatial resolution of S-VHS is about half that of the DV source, and the analog source introduced stability noise, when analyzing the video digitized from S-VHS source a corner was considered persistent if it was present within a 3x3 pixels box.

Evaluation of results takes into account GO detection (whether the appearance of a GO is correctly detected) and correct detection of the GO's bounding box (Table 1). GO detection has a precision of 80.6%, and recall of 92%. These figures are due to missed detections in the VHS video, and to only one missed detection in the DV videos. The GO bounding box miss rate is 5%. Results also included 6 false detections, which are due to scene text.

Table 1. Text Event Detection and Text Boxes Localization.

	Occurrences	Misdetection	False detection
GO event	63	5	9
GO boxes	100	5	37

3.3   Classification of Visual Shot Features

Model Theory. To support classification of sports videos in terms of the type of sports event being reported on in the video, we can observe that: *i*) most sports events take place in a playfield, with each sport having its own playfield; *ii*) each playfield has a number of distinguishing features, the most relevant of which is color; *iii*) the playfield appears in a large number of frames of a video shots, and often covers a large part of the camera windows (i.e. a large area of frames in the video).

Color features (e.g. color histograms) seem to be good candidates for supporting identification of sport types in sports videos. In fact, as outlined above, each sport takes place on a peculiar playfield, which typically features a dominant color. This is particularly the case in long and mid-range camera takes, where the frame area occupied by players is only a fraction of the whole area. Further, for each sport type, the color of the playfield is fixed, or varies in a very small set of possibilities. For example, for soccer the playfield is always green, while for swimming it is blue.

However, a straightforward classification based on the above considerations to each shot in a video is likely to fail, as some of the shots may not include a significant part of the playfield. This is particularly the case for those shots where the playfield covers only a small part of the camera window, or is not framed at all (e.g. close-ups). In fact, an analysis of the data set revealed that, along with shots framing the playfield, a number of shots appear featuring a close-up of a player, or the audience. In particular, we analyzed 32 minutes of video, totaling 211 shots. Of these shots, 138 include the playfield. Other 61 have been labeled as *player* shots, as they feature one or more players covering a large part of the camera window. The remaining 12 shots were labeled as *audience* shots, as they featured the audience at the stand. For example, in soccer, when a player shoots a goal, *audience* shots are often shown after the goal.

Therefore, to rely on the identity of the playfield for the purpose of classification, we discard shots which do not include the play field. This is achieved through a preliminary classification of video shots, aimed at assessing whether the video shot contains the playfield or not. We therefore define two classes, *player* and *audience*, along with the *playfield* class, to classify sport shots. It is worth pointing out that models for *player* and *audience* shots do not vary significantly in the data set we inspected.

A preliminary investigation on the usage of color to detect *player* and *audience* shots did not yield promising results. This required a further inspection of sports videos, which revealed that: *i*) in *player* shots, the shape of the player appears distinctly, and the background of the image tends to be blurred, either because of camera motion or lens effects (see Fig. 6); *ii*) in *audience* shots, individuals in the crowd do not appear clearly, but the crowd as a whole appears as fine texture (see Fig. 7). These observations suggest that edge features could significantly help in detecting *player* and *audience* shots in the video.

 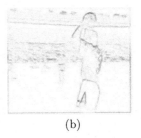

(a)   (b)

Fig. 6. a) Player Scene; b) Edge Image of the Player Scene.

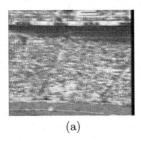 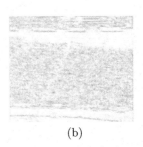

(a)   (b)

Fig. 7. a) Audience Scene; b) Edge Image of the Audience Scene.

Model Implementation. To set up a training data set, several frames were extracted from selected video shots. Both color and edge features were computed for these frames. Then, a principal component analysis was carried out, and a canonical discriminant analysis was performed to obtain the discriminant space.

Later, to classify raw data, the same feature extraction and translation procedures were applied to frames extracted from the validation data set. Resulting data, which can be represented as points in the discriminant space, were classified by evaluating the Mahalanobis generalized distance from the center of each previously defined class. Frames were then classified according to the minimum distance criteria.

To describe color content of video frames color histograms are used. These may differ in terms of the color space on which they are computed, and the number of bins into which this space is quantized. We selected the HSI color space and histograms with 64 bins for each of the three components were used to describe content of video frames.

To describe the content of video frames in terms of edges, the High Order Local Autocorrelation (HOLA, [8]) was chosen. This is a well known technique for shape or texture analysis and description, which features shift-invariance and additive properties. Further, as it can be represented with a fixed dimension vector, the same data structures as for color histograms could be used.

The HOLA is evaluated on an edge map obtained through a Canny filtering of the source video frames. The second degree HOLA is calculated as follows:

$$\text{HOLA}(2) = \sum_{r \in image} I(r)I(r + a_1)I(r + a_2)$$

where a_1 and a_2 are the offsets from the reference point r. The offsets within (3×3) pixels were used, and duplicated patterns were ignored. There are 29 kinds of offsets for a second degree HOLA, 5 kinds for the first degree and 1 for the zero degree.

Experimental Results. Table 2-a reports composition of the training and data sets used in our experiments, and shows the number of keyframes for each sport category in the data sets.

Table 2. a) Number of keyframes for each sport comprising the training and validation data sets; b) Classification results considering only color information for the playfield, or using the *player* and *audience* classes for pre-filtering.

sport	number of keyframes	
	training set	validation set
high diving	22	135
floor	35	380
field hockey	36	300
long horse	33	436
javelin	26	160
judo	27	382
soccer	61	600
swimming	36	289
tennis	32	236
track	45	719
TOTAL	353	3637

(a)

sport	color only	color and edge
high diving	57.8%	82.3%
floor	79.7%	99.0%
field hockey	89.3%	96.1%
long horse	55.0%	63.2%
javelin	36.9%	56.7%
judo	81.2%	100.0%
soccer	84.0%	92.3%
swimming	78.9%	96.1%
tennis	70.8%	93.1%
track	88.2%	91.7%
TOTAL	76.7%	89.9%

(b)

Results for the identification of sports types carried out on a data set including also player and audience scenes is shown in the first column of Table 2-b.

As expected, in this case we obtained lower rates of correct identification with respect to the case where only playfield scenes were considered.

In the following experiment, usage of edge features to identify *player* and *audience* scenes was examined. A set of shots featuring such scenes was added to the training and validating data sets of Table 2-a. In particular, 27 frames for audience and 88 frames for player shots were added to the training set, while 176 frames for audience and 692 frames for player shots were added to the validation set. Using both color and edge features, each frame is classified into one of the 10 sports or *player* or *audience* classes.

Results for this classification are shown in the second column of Table 2-b. The table reports identification rates for the different sports types. Identification rates for *player* and *audience* classes are not reported, as their identification is instrumental to improve classification results for playfield shots. By comparing results in the two columns, we can observe that introduction of the *player* and *audience* classes significantly improves the sports type identification rates. On average, these improve by 13%, with a maximum of 24%. The highest improvement rates are observed for those sports where the playfield is shown only for small time intervals (e.g. high diving), or in sports where only one athlete takes part in the competition, videos of which frequently show close-ups of the athlete (e.g. javelin).

4   Conclusions and Future Work

In this paper we have illustrated an approach to semantic video annotation in the specific context of sports videos, at different layers of semantic significance, using different elements of visual content.

Besides refining the techniques described in this paper, our ongoing work includes: *i*) the introduction of new semantic elements for a given semantic layer, such as framing terms (e.g. close-up) and motion; *ii*) increasing the overall level of semantic description (e.g. adding descriptors for events and relevant highlights); *iii*) the transition from elements of visual content to relationships among elements (spatio-temporal relations).

Acknowledgments

This work was partially supported by the ASSAVID EU Project, under contract IST-13082. The consortium comprises ACS SpA (I), BBC R&D (UK), Institut Dalle Molle D'Intelligence Artificielle Perceptive (CH), Sony BPE (UK), University of Florence (I), University of Surrey (UK).

We would also like to acknowledge the valuable contribution of Masayuki Mukunoki in developing the algorithms for sport type identification.

References

1. W. Al-Khatib, Y. F. Day, A. Ghafoor, P. B. Berra, "Semantic Modeling and Knowledge Representation in Multimedia Databases", *IEEE Transactions on Knowledge and Data Engineering*, Vol. 11, No. 1, January/February 1999.
2. Y.Ariki, and Y.Sugiyama, "Classification of TV Sports News by DCT Features using Multiple Subspace Method", in *Proc. of 14th Int. Conf. on Pattern Recognition (ICPR'98)*, pp.1488–1491, 1998.
3. Automatic Segmentation and Semantic Annotation of Sports Videos (ASSAVID), EU Project # IST-13082, http://www.bpe-rnd.co.uk/assavid/
4. Colombo C., Del Bimbo A., and Pala P., "Semantics in Visual Information Retrieval," *IEEE MultiMedia*, 6(3), pp. 38–53, 1999.
5. N. Dimitrova et al., "Entry into the Content Forest: The Role of Multimedia Portals", *IEEE MultiMedia*, July-September 2000.
6. S. Eickeler and S. Muller, "Content-Based Video Indexing of TV Broadcast News Using Hidden Markov Models", in *Proc. IEEE Int. Conf. on Acoustics, Speech, and Signal Processing (ICASSP)*, pp.2997–3000, 1999.
7. S. Fischer, R. Lienhart, W. Effelsberg, "Automatic Recognition of Film Genres", in *Proc. ACM Multimedia'95*, pp. 295-304, 1995.
8. T. Kurita, N. Otsu, and T. Sato, "A Face Recognition Method Using Higher Order Local Autocorrelation And Multivariate Analysis", in *Proc. 11th Int. Conf. on Pattern Recognition(ICPR'92)*, pp. 213-216, 1992.
9. H. Li, D. Doermann, "Automatic Identification of Text in Digital Video Key Frames", in *Proc. of ICPR'98*, 1998.
10. R. Lienhart, "Indexing and Retrieval of Digital Video Sequences Based On Automatic Text Recognition", in *Proc. of 4-th ACM International Multimedia Conference*, 1996.
11. H. Miyamori, S.-I. Iisaku, "Video annotation for content-based retrieval using human behavior analysis and domain knowledge", in *Proc. of Automatic Face and Gesture Recognition 2000*, 2000.
12. Y. Nakamura, T. Kanade, "Semantic Analysis for Video Contents Extraction – Spotting by Association in News Video", in *Proc. of ACM Multimedia'97*, 1997.
13. J. M. Pike, C. G. Harris, "A Combined corner and edge detector", in *Proc. of the 4-th Alvey Vision Conference*, 1988.
14. E. Sahouria, A. Zakhor "Content analysis of video using principal components", *IEEE Trans. on Circuits and Systems for Video Technology*, Vol. 9, No. 8, 1999.
15. T. Sato, T. Kanade, E. K. Hughes, M. A. Smith, "Video OCR for Digital News Archive", in *Proc. of IEEE International Workshop on Content–Based Access of Image and Video Databases CAIVD'98*, pp.52-60, 1998.
16. W. Zhou, A. Vellaikal, and C.C.J. Kuo, "Rule-based video classification system for basketball video indexing", in *Proceedings on ACM Multimedia 2000 Workshops*, pp. 213–216, 2000.
17. E. K. Wong, M. Chen, "A Robust Algorithm for Text Extraction in Color Video", in *Proc. ICME 2000*, 2000.
18. V. Wu, R. Manmatha, E. M. Riseman, "TextFinder: An Automatic System to Detect and Recognize Text In Images", *IEEE Trans. on Pattern Analysis and Machine Intelligence*, Vol. 21, No. 11, 1999.
19. Y. Zhong, H. Zangh, A. K. Jain, "Automatic Caption Localization in Compressed Video", *IEEE Transactions on Pattern Analysis and Machine Intelligence*, Vol. 22, N. 4, pp. 385-392, 2000.

Dialogue Scenes Detection in MPEG Movies: A Multi-expert Approach

Massimo De Santo[1], Gennaro Percannella[1], Carlo Sansone[2], and Mario Vento[2]

[1] Dipartimento di Ingegneria dell'Informazione e di Ingegneria Elettrica
Università di Salerno - Via P.te Don Melillo,1 I-84084, Fisciano (SA), Italy
{desanto,pergen}@unisa.it
[2] Dipartimento di Informatica e Sistemistica
Università di Napoli "Federico II"- Via Claudio, 21 I-80125 Napoli, Italy
{carlosan,vento}@unina.it

Abstract. In this paper we propose a method for the detection of dialogue scenes within movies. This task is of particular interest given the special semantic role played by dialogue based scenes in the most part of movies. The proposed approach firstly operates the segmentation of the video footage in shots, then each shot is classified as dialogue or not-dialogue by a Multi-Expert System (MES) and, finally, the individuated sequences of dialogue shots are aggregated in dialogue scenes by means of a suitable algorithm. The MES integrates three experts which consider different and complementary aspects of the same decision problem, so that the combination of the single decisions provides a performance that is better than that of any single expert. While the general approach of multiple experts is not new, its application to this specific problem is interesting and novel and the obtained results are encouraging.

1 Introduction

More and more videos are generated every day, mostly produced and stored in analog form. In spite of this, the trend is toward the total digitization of movies and video products given that the effective use of them is hindered by the difficulty of efficiently classifying and managing video data in the traditional analog format.

In the past few years, several algorithms have been presented in the scientific literature to allow an effective filtering, browsing, searching and retrieval of information in video databases. It is generally accepted that the first step toward an effective organization of the information in video databases consists in the segmentation of the video footage in shots, that are defined as the set of frames obtained through a continuous camera recording. Anyway, even if the individuation of shots represents a fundamental step, it is clear that this approach does not allow an effective non linear access to the video information. This is evident from at least two points of view: firstly, humans usually remember different events after they watched a movie, and hence they also think in terms of events during the retrieval process; secondly, a modern movie contains more than 2000 shots on average, which means

M. Tucci (Ed.): MDIC 2001, LNCS 2184, pp. 192–201, 2001.

that an intelligent video analysis program needs to process 2000 frames per movie to give a coherent representation.

Consequently, it is necessary to define units for accessing the video footage obtained by grouping semantically correlated shots. *Scene* is the term most used in the scientific literature to call this semantic unit. First approaches for detecting scenes (see for example [1, 2]) operate by simply clustering the shots according to the visual content of the most representative frames (also called key-frames). Anyway, the quoted techniques do not take into account any model for the scene, so the results are not always semantically coherent. In fact, it is worth noting that the way the shots are grouped in a scene generally depends on the type of scene under analysis as well as on the video genre. The scenes of a TV-news program are different from the scenes of a talk-show, of a documentary, of a movie. Hence, it is important to aggregate shots also considering a model for the scene. Several recent papers try to define models for scene detection, mainly in the field of TV-news, where effective and simple models can be defined. For example, in [3] a method based on a Hidden Markov Model to segment TV-news at various semantic levels it is presented, while in [4], Bertini et al. describe the use of multiple features for content-based indexing and retrieval of TV-news.

The same problem is much more complex when the movies domain is faced: there are much more different scene types and for each kind of scene different styles can be adopted depending on the movie Director. Interestingly enough, although scene analysis can be very useful for several purposes (let us think, for example, to the video abstraction and to the automatic classification of the video genre) only few papers have been presented on the problem of detection and characterization of scenes in movies. Among those, an interesting one is [5] where Saraceno et al. define some simple rules to group the shots of a movie according to some semantic types.

In this paper we present an original method for automatic detection of dialogue scenes within movies. This is a task of particular interest given the special semantic role played by dialogue based scenes in the most part of movies. The proposal is based on the use of multiple classifiers.

While the general approach of multiple experts is not new, its application to this specific problem is interesting and novel, and the obtained results are encouraging.

2   The Proposed Approach

Following the above discussion, the proposed approach starts with the segmentation of the video footage in shots. Then, it operates a characterization of each shot between dialogue or not-dialogue according to a multi-expert approach, where each decision system classifies a given shot on the basis of a particular description. The final result is obtained by combining the single decisions through suitable rules [6]. In this way, if the utilized experts consider different and complementary aspects of the same decision problem, the combination of the single decisions provides a performance that is better than that of any single expert. The aim is to take advantage of the strength of the single experts without being affected by their weaknesses through the adoption of an information fusion approach. Finally, the individuated sequences of shots are aggregated in dialogue scenes by means of a suitable algorithm.

It is worth considering that, in order to set up a system within the general framework we have just described, an important aspect is the characterization of the information source. It has to be noted that video sources are often provided in compressed form according to standards like MPEG. While the majority of the techniques for video segmentation process video in uncompressed form, a direct analysis in the compressed domain offers at least two advantages. First, the computational efficiency of the whole process is improved. Second, video compression is generally performed using signal processing techniques capable of deriving features for video segmentation, e.g., motion vectors in MPEG coding. Thus, such features become readily available for any parsing operation, and would have to be re-derived if a decoding step were applied. For these reasons, we perform the whole analysis of the video stream directly in the coded domain.

In summary, our method is based on the following ideas:

a) a scene is a group of semantically correlated shots;
b) *almost all* the shots belonging to a dialogue scene can be characterized as dialogue shots;
c) the shots belonging to the same dialogue scene are temporally adjacent.

From the previous observations it follows that the proposed algorithm can be structured according to three steps, as depicted in Fig. 1:

Step 1 - shot boundaries detection
Step 2 - dialogue / not-dialogue shot classification
Step 3 - shot grouping

A description of each of the quoted steps is given in the following subsections.

2.1   Shot Boundaries Detection

The problem of automatic detection of shot boundaries has been widely investigated in the recent years; hence, the scientific literature is rich of papers discussing approaches which allow us to reliably segment videos in shots both in the uncompressed and in the MPEG coded domain. For the purposes of this paper, we have implemented the technique described in [7] that is characterized by good performances both in terms of correct detection and of low computational requirements, since it operates directly on the compressed stream.

2.2   Dialogue/Not-Dialogue Shot Characterization

This classification is performed through the use of a multi-expert system. The reason inspiring the use of a multi-expert system lies in the experimental evidence that single experts, albeit very refined, fail to achieve an acceptable performance level. It happens that a recognition system adopts features and classification models which, as a whole, are not equally adequate for all the patterns. In this cases the efforts for reducing the errors are often too big and not justified by the relatively small performance improvements. The lack of a single expert system generally grows with the complexity of the considered classification problem, the number of the classes, the dimensionality of the feature space.

The idea of combining various experts with the aim of compensating the weakness of each single expert while preserving its own strength, has been recently widely investigated [8, 9, 10]. The rationale lies in the assumption that, by suitably combining the results of a set of experts according to a rule (combining rule), the performance obtained can be better than that of any single expert. The successful implementation of a multi-expert system implies the use of the most complementary experts as possible, and the definition of a combining rule for determining the most likely class a sample should be attributed to, given the class to which it is attributed by each single expert.

For the purpose of shot classification as dialogue or not, we introduce the following set of experts:

a) Face detection,
b) Camera motion estimation,
c) Audio classification,

which are integrated within the whole system as shown in Fig. 1.

Each expert of the system can be viewed as constituted by a sensor and a classifier as shown in the block diagram of Fig. 2. Each expert has two inputs: the MPEG video or audio stream and the complete list of the shots boundaries. The latter information is

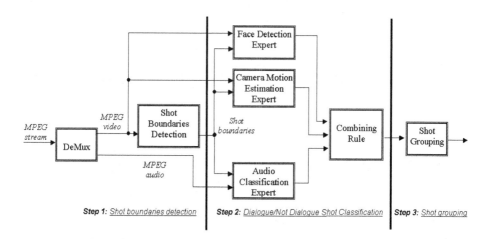

Fig. 1. Block Diagram of the System for Automatic Detection of Dialogue Scene.

used by the sensor to access and characterize the MPEG data at shot level. The output of the sensor is used by the classifier to perform the dialogue / not-dialogue shot classification. In our system we have integrated three experts whose sensors implement the algorithms described in [11] for face detection, in [12] for camera motion estimation and in [13] for audio stream classification, all working directly in the video/audio coded domain. It is worth noting that the outputs of the first sensor is correlated in a simple way to the output of the corresponding expert; in fact, the presence (absence) of a face implies a dialogue (not dialogue) shot. On the contrary, the sensor for camera motion estimation provides three estimates respectively for the zoom, tilt and pan rate for each P frame. Then, the mean and the standard deviation of the zoom, tilt and pan rate over each shot constitute the features vector used by a neural network to perform the shot classification. Finally, the sensor for audio classification uses the same feature vector defined in [13], but in our case the classification is carried out by a neural network trained to recognize only the dialogue and not-dialogue shot classes.

Then, the output of each single expert is combined according to a suitable combining rule (for a review of the most common used rules see [6]).

2.3   Shot Grouping

The final step of our approach provides to group in dialogue scenes the shots classified in the previous step. The rationale of the algorithm for shot grouping derives from the consideration that the shots belonging to a dialogue scene are

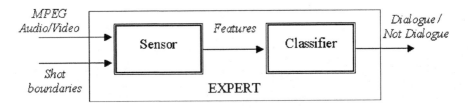

Fig. 2. Each Expert Can Be Viewed as Constituted by a Sensor and a Classifier.

temporally adjacent. Anyway, such observation have to be considered in a wide sense: in fact, dialogue scenes are generally constituted mostly by dialogue shots which sometimes are mixed with some shots which cannot be properly declared as dialogue ones. For instance, this is the typical situation of a dialogue scene characterized by two persons speaking, alternatively taken from the camera, so resulting in a sequence of dialogue shots; sometimes it happens that a shot taking no person, and/or with a silence pause, and/or with a rapid camera movement is inserted in the dialogue shots sequence. The same is true for the opposite situation with a dialogue shot in a not dialogue scene.

In a similar way, the shot grouping algorithm has to properly handle also the possible classification errors generated at step 2. In fact:

- a **false alarm** (i.e. a not dialogue shot classified as dialogue) might cause the declaration of an inexistent short dialogue scene, and
- a **missed detection** (i.e. a dialogue shot classified as not dialogue) might cause the partitioning of a dialogue scenes in two scenes.

Thus the shot grouping algorithm is implemented through a simple Finite State Machine (FSM) characterized by three states: the *dialogue scene* (D) and the *not dialogue scene* states (ND), both used to define the boundaries of the dialogue scenes, while the latter is the *probable dialogue scene* state (PD), purposefully introduced to deal with the aforementioned situations, that allows the transition from the D state to the ND state (and vice versa) only if at least three not-dialogue (dialogue) shots appear after the sequence of dialogue (not-dialogue) shots.

3   The Movie Database

It is well known in the field of Pattern Recognition that one of the most important steps toward a reliable training of a pattern classifier is represented by the use of a large database of samples. Furthermore, another important consideration in the construction of the database relies on the fact that its samples must be as much as possible representative of the world under study. Hence, in the construction of our database particular care has been taken to include a quite large representative of the major movie genres (action, comedy, drama, science fiction, fantasy, etc) in order to reproduce the high variability of the video characteristics over the different genres.

The considered video database consists of video footages obtained from 10 movies: it results in about 20 hours, corresponding to about 15000 shots.

All the video material used for the analysis was coded in Mpeg-1 format with the following parameters:

Video: constant bit-rate ranging between 1500 and 2000 kbps, 640x272 pixels;
Audio: Layer II, stereo, 44.1 kHz, 16 bits/sample, 224 kbps constant bit-rate.

The creation of the ground truth has been carried out by manually labeling each sample of the database according to the two classes, namely *dialogue* and *not-dialogue shot*. Although the meaning of the these classes is quite intuitive, classification "by hand" was not always a trivial task due to the intrinsic complexity and variability of movies. In fact, we noticed that some shots of the database were differently classified by different persons. In order to properly handle such kind of samples, the evaluation of the ground truth was carried out independently by three different persons. Then, each sample was classified on the basis of the choice of the majority among the three listeners. In Table 1 the list of the movies included in the database is shown, together with the genre, the year of production and the number of the samples of each movie belonging to the two classes. The classification of the movies in the database according to the appropriate genre has been accomplished by referring to the information available on the Internet Movie Database [15].

4   Experimental Results

In this section we report the results obtained at the 2nd and 3rd steps of the system. Note that we do not explicitly discuss the results of the shot segmentation level (1st step), since these are widely presented in the reference paper [7].

Table 1. The list of the movies included in the database, together with their genre, year of production and number of the samples belonging to the two classes.

Movie	Genre	Year	# Dialogue shots	# Not Dialogue shots
Mission Impossible II	Action	2000	1186	1353
The Matrix	Action/Sci-Fi	1999	1214	969
Chiedimi se sono felice	Comedy (Italian)	2000	624	278
Erin Brokovich	Drama	2000	963	386
Practical magic	Drama/Romance	1998	1239	255
Apt pupil	Drama/Thriller	1998	1051	268
True crime	Drama/Thriller	1998	1221	317
Sleepy Hollow	Horror	1999	917	739
Autumn in New York	Romance	2000	792	247
City of angels	Romance/Fantasy	1998	761	456
			9968	5268

In order to train the Audio and the Camera Motion experts, the whole database was split into three disjoint sets: a training set, made up of 50% of the database, a training-test set made up of 25% of the database, used to stop the learning process so as to avoid a possible overtraining (see [14]), and a test set, made up of the remaining 25%, used to test the classification ability of the nets. The neural architecture used for the classification stage of each expert was a Multi-Layer Perceptron (MLP) [14]. Several different classifiers have been experimented, by varying the number of hidden nodes for the MLP nets. The training phase was required also by the Face expert, in order to set-up the various parameters of the algorithm for face detection [11], with particular reference to the skin color module. In this case we used the same training, training-test and test sets defined for the other two experts. In Table 2 the best results of each expert obtained on the test set are shown.

Table 2. Recognition Rates Achieved by Different Experts on the Test Set.

Expert	Recognition Rate	Architecture	Size
Camera Motion	64%	Neural (MLP)	40 hidden
Audio	79%	Neural (MLP)	30 hidden
Face	70%	-	-

In Table 3 it is represented the *Coverage Table* evaluated on the test set, which reports the joint behavior of the three experts with respect to the shot classification task. In particular, the rows of this table represent the percentage of samples in the test set on which there were respectively three, two, one and zero experts which performed the correct classification.

Table 3. The Coverage Table: The four rows respectively report the percentage of samples in the test set on which three, two, one and zero experts performed the correct classification.

Correct Expert Classifications	Recognition Rate
3	49%
2	35%
1	13%
0	3%

From this table it is readily available the recognition rate achievable by employing the majority voting rule, for which the resulting decision depends on the majority of the votes: in fact, it suffices to consider the sum of the recognition rates of the first two rows of Table 3. Hence, by using this simple rule it is possible to achieve an overall recognition rate of 84% for the 2nd step of the system. It is worth noting that the multi-expert approach allows to obtain an improvement of 5% with respect to the best single expert (the Audio one – 79% correct classification).

In the 3rd module of the system the shots are aggregated in dialogue and not-dialogue scenes. This is realized by the simple FSM described previously. In Table 4 the performances of the whole system, in terms of missed detections and false alarms, are reported.

It has to be noted that the evaluation of these parameters was performed by considering as a correct detection a detected scene which is overlapped to the true scene at least for 50%; in Fig. 3 there are shown examples of a correct detection, a missed detection and a false alarm.

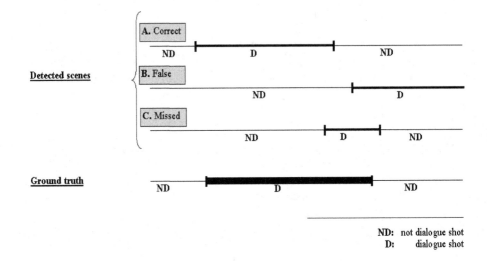

Fig. 3. Examples of: **A.** Correct Detection, **B.** A False Alarm and
C. A Missed Detection.

Table 4. Overall performance of the system in terms of missed detections and false alarms with respect to the dialogue scenes detection problem.

Performances	
Missed detections	9%
False alarms	7%

5   Conclusions and Future Work

In this work we have faced the problem of the dialogue scene detection within movies. The proposed approach is based on a Multi-Expert System constituted by three different experts which analyze the video and audio tracks of the movie directly in the MPEG coded domain. Although each expert is not characterized by optimal performances in the classification of the shots (this is due both to the errors of the sensor and of the classifier which constitute each expert), their combined use gives good performances even when a very simple combining rule is used. This confirms our initial hypothesis that the utilized experts consider different and complementary aspects of the same decision problem.

Current research is focused on improving the overall performance of the system by implementing the experts as classifiers able to yield also some information about the reliability of the classification [16], and by using more sophisticated combining rules. Actually, we are also exploring the possibility to extend the proposed approach to detect action scenes within movies.

References

1. M. M. Yeung, B. Liu, "Efficient matching and clustering of video shots", in Proc. IEEE ICIP'95, vol II, pp. 260-263.
2. A. Hanjalic, R. Lagendijk, J. Biemond, "Automated high-level movie segmentation for advanced video-retrieval systems", in IEEE Trans. on Circuits and Systems for Video Technology, vol. 9, No. 4, June 1999, pp. 580-588.
3. S. Boykin, A. Merlino, "Machine learning of event segmentation for news on demand", in Communications of the ACM, Feb. 2000, vol. 43, No. 2, pp. 35-41.
4. M. Bertini, A. Del Bimbo, P. Pala, "Content-based Indexing and Retrieval of TV-news", in Pattern Recognition Letters, 22, (2001), 503-516.
5. C. Saraceno, R. Leopardi, "Identification of Story Units in Audio-Visual Sequences by Joint Audio and Video Processing", in Proc. ICIP'98, pp. 363-367, 1998.
6. L. P. Cordella, P. Foggia, C. Sansone, F. Tortorella and M. Vento, Reliability Parameters to Improve Combination Strategies in Multi-Expert Systems, Pattern Analysis & Applications, Springer-Verlag, vol. 2, pp. 205–214, 1999.
7. S.C. Pei, Y.Z. Chou, "Efficient MPEG compressed video analysis using macroblock type information", in IEEE Trans. on Multimedia, pp. 321–333, Dec. 1999, Vol. 1, Issue: 4.
8. T.K. Ho, J.J. Hull, S.N. Srihari, "Decision Combination in Multiple Classifier Systems", IEEE Trans. on Pattern Analysis and Machine Intelligence 1994; 16(1): 66-75.
9. Y.S. Huang, C.Y. Suen, "A Method of Combining Multiple Experts for the Recognition of Unconstrained Handwritten Numerals", IEEE Transactions on Pattern Analysis and Machine Intelligence 1995; 17(1): 90-94.
10. J. Kittler, M. Hatef, R.P.W. Duin, J. Matas, "On Combining Classifiers", IEEE Trans. on PAMI, vol 20 n.3 March 1998.
11. H. Wang, S.F. Chang, "A Highly Efficient System for Automatic Face Region Detection in MPEG Video", IEEE Transactions on Circuits and Systems for Video Technology, vol. 7, no. 4, August 1997, pp. 615-628.
12. Y.P. Tan, D.D. Saur, S.R. Kulkarni, P.J. Ramadge, "Rapid Estimation of Camera Motion from Compressed Video with Application to Video Annotation", IEEE Transactions on Circuits and Systems for Video Technology, vol. 10, no. 1, February 2000, pp. 133-146.
13. M. De Santo, G. Percannella, C. Sansone, M. Vento, "Classifying Audio of Movies by a Multi-Expert System", to appear in IEEE Proc. of ICIAP 2001, September, Palermo, Italy.
14. R. Hecht-Nielsen, Neurocomputing. Addison-Wesley, Reading (MA), 1990.
15. http://www.imdb.com/
16. B. Ackermann, H. Bunke, "Combination of Classifiers on the Decision Level for Face Recognition". Tech. Rep. IAM-96–002, Institut für Informatik und angewandte Mathematik, Universität Bern, 1996.

A Proposal of a QoS Control Method for Digital Video Libraries

Yuka Kato and Katsuya Hakozaki

Graduate School of Information Systems
University of Electro-Communications
1-5-1 Chofugaoka, Chofu-shi, Tokyo 1828585 Japan
yuka@hako.is.uec.ac.jp

Abstract. Digital video libraries using IP networks have become a practical system from trial one. As a result, we need techniques providing data whose quality of service (QoS) satisfies user request. In this paper, we propose a QoS control method for digital video libraries, which made it possible to transport video according to user's system environment. In addition, we developed the experiment system using digital video transport system and conducted the experiment using the system. As a result, we found that a bandwidth control function on video servers improved QoS provided to users.

1 Introduction

As various sorts of service have been provided on the Internet, the idea providing all types of media including audio/video on the Internet has appeared. As a result, a digital library and a video library using IP (Internet Protocol) networks have become a practical system from a trial one. In order to develop the libraries, we need techniques providing data whose quality satisfies user request, as well as techniques searching multimedia data. Under such network environment using IP, users access to the libraries from various system environment and by various ways. For example, some users access them via a campus LAN using broad bandwidth from high performance PC. On the other hand, other users do them via a dial-up connection using narrow bandwidth from a PDA. Moreover, network condition always changes even if the users are under the same environment. For that reason, the library designer has to prepare a function providing multimedia data with adequate quality according to user's system condition.

At that time, we need to solve two problems in order to develop the function. One is how we probe user's system condition. The other is how we provide data of different quality as same content according to the condition. This paper proposes a Quality of Service (QoS) control method to solve these problems.

This method uses application QoS Management System (QMS)[1], which we have proposed as an application QoS management framework on IP networks. QMS has been designed in order to control application QoS of the whole system according to the management policies, when various services have been simultaneously provided on an IP network such as a campus LAN. We have implemented

M. Tucci (Ed.): MDIC 2001, LNCS 2184, pp. 202–212, 2001.

this application QoS management framework to a digital video library. As a result, we have made it possible to provide a video with quality required by a user. In the following chapter we will introduce QMS. Then we will apply QMS to digital video libraries in Chap.3. In Chap.4, we will describe the experiment system, and show the result of performance evaluation in Chap.5. After presenting related works of QMS in Chap.6, we will conclude the paper in Chap.7.

2   Application QoS Management System

2.1   Concepts

QMS has been designed for a purpose of adaptable QoS management for distributed multimedia applications. Its control target is application QoS. Therefore, we have provided the following concepts in designing QMS.

- Its control targets are application QoS.
- It adopts simple control methods without complicated modeling.
- It negotiates QoSes among many applications.

For these concepts, we designed QMS consisting of three types of module. These are *Notificator* module, *Manager* module and *Controller* module. QMS controls application QoS by communicating between these modules, which are deployed on distributed object environment such as CORBA (Common Object Request Broker Architecture)[2]. The function of each module is as follows:

- *Notificator* module: This module monitors each application QoS and detects the QoS degradation. This is implemented on client machines (ex. PCs and PDAs).
- *Manager* module: This module keeps QoS management policies and determines QoS control methods according to the policies. This is implemented on a management node (ex. a WS and a PC).
- *Controller* module: This module does the controls determined by *Manager* module. This is implemented on server machines (ex. WSs and PCs) and network equipment (ex. routers).

2.2   System Architecture

Figure 1 shows system architecture of QMS. Each module consists of several objects, and each control is done by communicating between these objects.

Notificator Module. One module exists on each application client. It consists of two types of objects. These are QoS Measurement Object (MSO) and QoS Detection Object (QDO). MSO measures QoS parameters of a target application. QDO detects the QoS degradation according to the QoS management policies. These objects monitor the QoS parameters while the user is getting the service. This module sends the detected results to *Manager* module. These events are the triggers for the QoS controls.

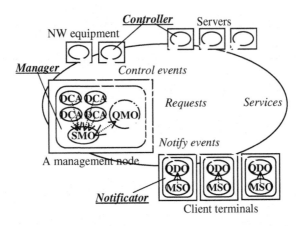

Fig. 1. System Architecture of QMS.

Manager Module. One module exists on each management scope. It consists of three types of objects. These are QoS Management Object (QMO), Data Collection Agent (DCA) and State Management Object (SMO). QMO keeps QoS management policies for each application and decides the control method. DCA collects various performance data for checking on system conditions. SMO keeps the collecting data as the system conditions.

Controller Module. When this module receives request event from *Manager* module, the control is done.

2.3   The Method Setting the QoS Management Policies

A QoS management policy of each application is set to *Manager* module. At that time, QoS negotiation among many applications is needed because there are many applications together in the QMS management scope. In this section, we describe the method setting the QoS management policies.

Concepts. The QoS management policy is set to QMS by the following two steps: (1) Define QoS of each application, and decide the control methods in an application level; (2) Determine the control priority in a network level according to the characteristics of the application traffic. The first step decides the control methods in an application level, such as a change of service level. The second step determines the control priority in a network level for negotiating QoS among many applications.

Control Targets. QoS control in QMS is adaptable measurement-based control. It adopts feedback type control methods without complicated modeling.

Table 1. Control Targets in an Application Level.

Control targets	Examples of control method
Change of the service level	Change of video transmission rate.
Load balancing	Change of a connection server.
Error correction	Use of redundant packets.
Change of the service	Change of a video to an image.

Table 2. Control Targets in a Network Level.

Control targets	Control methods
Throughput	Bandwidth guarantee. (RSVP etc.)
IP packet transfer delay	Weighted queuing.
IP packet jitter	Traffic shaping.
IP packet loss	Set discard priority. (DiffServ etc.)

Therefore, the control targets are the changeable elements in real time without stopping the system.

The control target in an application level is decided according to the observed QoS parameters, and the control method is decided according to this target. Table 1 shows the control targets in an application level. On the other hand, we adopt four types of control targets in a network level. These are throughput, IP packet transfer delay, IP packet jitter and IP packet loss. These parameters are end-to-end service qualities in the Internet[3]. For managing these QoS parameters, QMS does the network level controls as described in Table 2.

These control methods in Table 2 are determined according to the factors that degrade the control targets. As the factor of throughput degradation, there are a difference in end-to-end routes, performance of routers, the number of routers and link bandwidth. As the factor of IP packet transfer delay and jitter, there are the time searching routes and transfer delay on a circuit. As the factor of IP packet loss, there are buffer overflow of routers and transmission error on a circuit.

Application Classification. QMS determines the priority of network level control according to traffic characteristics of the application. These characteristics are classified using the traffic types and the requirement types of system response time[4]. These types are shown in Table 3 and Table 4. QoS parameters for block type applications are the time displaying an image, the time downloading a file and so on. Therefore, we use throughput as a quality parameter in a network level. QoS parameters for stream type applications are smoothness on movie, conversation delay and so on. Therefore, throughput, transfer delay, jitter and loss are all needed as quality parameters in a network level. In particular, jitter is very important. QoS parameters for transaction type applications are

Table 3. Application Classification According to Traffic Types.

Traffic types	Characteristics
Block type (B)	Large size information with low frequency.(ex. Images)
Stream type (S)	Middle size information periodically.(ex. Videos)
Transaction type (T)	Small size information irregularly.(ex. Commands)

Table 4. Application Classification According to Requirement Types of Response Time.

Requirement types	Characteristics
Real time (RT)	Need the time not exceeding 100 ms.(ex. Telephone).
Quasi real time (QRT)	Require the time not exceeding 10 s.(ex. WWW).
Non real time (NRT)	Allow the time more than 100 s.(ex. E-mail).

the time searching in a database, fail ratio of sending an e-mail and so on. Therefore, we use transfer delay and jitter as quality parameters in a network level. On the other hand, concerning requirement of response time, the control changing packet order is unsuitable for real time traffic applications. We use the control discarding packets for these applications.

Method Setting the Policies. The QoS management policy is set to QMS by the following two steps. First, we set feedback type control methods to QMS as application level controls. Second, QMS determines the priorities of network level controls according to traffic characteristics of the application. At that time, the rules for the determination are needed. We make the rules as the list of priority for each control target. This is shown in Table 5.

These priorities are determined according to the quality parameter for each traffic characteristic mentioned in Table 3 and Table 4. In this paper, we determine the priorities for 7 traffic types in Table 5, although there are 9 types

Table 5. The List of Priorities.

Traffic type	Bandwidth	Queuing	Shaping	Discard
B-RT	1	0	1	1
S-RT	0	0	0	0
T-RT	-	0	-	4
B-QRT	-	1	-	2
T-QRT	-	1	-	4
B-NRT	-	2	-	3
T-NRT	-	2	-	4

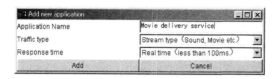

Fig. 2. The Window for Adding New Application.

Confirm/Change the policy of a bandwidth gurantee		
The priority	Application name	Need of the gurantee
1	Movie delivery service	O
2	WWW	O
3	E-mail	X
Target application	Movie delivery service ▼	
Change of the priority	Up	Down
Change of the need	On	Off
	Default	End

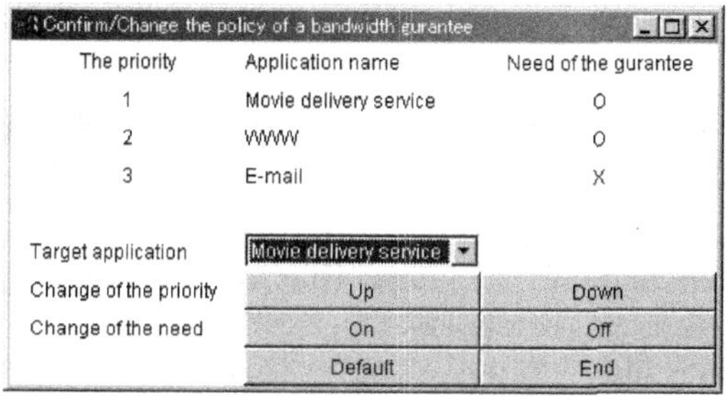

Fig. 3. The Window for Changing the Priority.

as combination of traffic types in Table 3 and Table 4. It is because there is no application whose type is S-NRT or S-QRT.

These are the priorities by default. Therefore, we need to change the order according to the system environment and the user conditions, if necessary.

An Implementation Example. We have developed the system setting QoS management policies to QMS by using Java language. Figure 2 and Fig.3 show the implementation examples.

When you add new application to a QMS management scope, you set the application name, the traffic type and the requirement type of response time to the window for adding new application (Fig.2). As a result, each priority of control in a network level is determined according to the lists of priority in Table 5. It is possible to check these priorities on the four types of windows (a bandwidth guarantee, packet transfer, shaping and packet discard) (ex. Fig.3). Moreover, you can change the orders on the windows if necessary. These priorities are set to the network equipment.

This system makes it possible to set QoS management policies to QMS easily by selecting traffic characteristics of applications from menus.

3   Applying QMS to Digital Video Libraries

We applied QMS to digital video libraries. As a result, it has become possible to transport video stream according to user's system environment. At that time, we needed two functions mentioned in Chap.1. One is a function probing system condition, and the other is a function changing services according to the condition. We explain each function in this section.

3.1 A Function Probing System Condition

In QMS, *Notificator* module detects QoS degradation, and *Manager* module monitors performance data in the management scope periodically and determines the providing service. In other words, QMS monitors system condition and determines providing services.

For digital video libraries, QMS monitors the video quality on the client machines, and provides the video service with adequate QoS. This video quality depends on application QoS for the users, for example, there are frame rate of the video and resolution. At that time, there are two types of method detecting QoS degradation on the client machines.

(1) We set QoS thresholds (such as packet loss ratio and delay) to *Notificator* module beforehand. QMS judges that QoS has degraded when the QoS parameters exceed the thresholds.

(2) We implement a function notifying user's QoS requests to QMS on client machines. Users detect QoS degradation, and they send the requests to QMS by using this function (such as a degradation button on a window). In this case, library users judge the QoS degradation.

QMS receiving the degradation event measures end-to-end available bandwidth between the client and the server, and requests to transport a video encoded into adequate rate.

3.2 A Function to Change the Providing Services According to the Condition

In QMS, Controller module does the QoS control when it receives the request event from *Manager* module. For digital video libraries, *Controller* module is implemented on the video library server and transports the video with adequate QoS for the users.

At that time, there are two types of method to change the providing services. These are as follows:

(1) On a video server, we provide several video files of the same content, which are encoded into different rate (such as 28 kbps, 56 kbps, 1.5 Mbps and 30 Mbps). This server selects a file of adequate rate according to a QMS request, and sends the file to clients. We need some mechanisms switching these files while viewing the video. Time stamps set by encode processes can be used for the mechanisms.

(2) By using a real-time encoder, a video server can change sending rate in real time according to a QMS request. Moreover, we can use a server function changing rate in real time if the server has such function. However, we need to prepare many real-time encoders for providing video services to many users simultaneously.

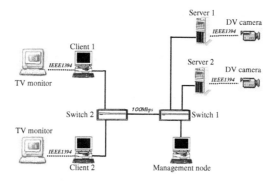

Fig. 4. System Architecture of the Experiment System.

4   Development of the Experiment System

We have developed an experiment system transporting a Digital Video (DV) in our laboratory, and have implemented QMS on the system. This is the prototype system of digital video libraries applying QMS. This has no database system and no stored video file; however, we can verify results of QoS control for digital video libraries applying QMS by using the prototype system.

As a DV transport system, we adopted DVTS (Digital Video Transport System)[5], which was developed by WIDE project[6] in Japan. DVTS makes it possible to develop a DV transport system easily at a low price by using IEEE1394 cards and digital video cameras, which are market products. As a method detecting QoS degradation, we adopted the method (2) in Sect.3.1. As a function changing providing services, we adopted the method (2) in Sect.3.2. In this experiment, we made the real-time DV transport function simulate the video library function. We show the system architecture in Fig.4.

There are 2 server machines (DVTS servers are implemented/ Pentium III 1GHz/ FreeBSD4.0), 2 client machines (DVTS clients are implemented/ Pentium III 1GHz/ FreeBSD4.0) and one management node (Pentium III 750MHz/ Windows2000). These are connected with each other in IP network (this bandwidth is 100 Mbps) using 2 switches (Layer 3 switches).

Manager module is implemented on the management node. In this system, users notify the video quality requests to *Manager* module by using the window detecting QoS degradation on a client machine. This is *Notificator* module. This window is shown in Fig.5.

These users can select favorite frame rate, buffer size and stream type (only video stream, only audio stream or both of them) by using a slide bar and buttons on the window. Then, the transport rate is notified to video servers. Consequently, QMS can change the transport rate in real time. At that time, we use the DVTS function changing transport rate and the function changing stream type. These are *Controller* modules.

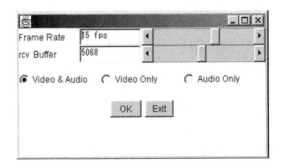

Fig. 5. The Window Detecting QoS Degradation.

5   Performance Evaluation

We evaluated video quality by using the experiment system. We compared video quality for system users with control (using the window in Fig.5) and that with no control. Figure 6 shows the experimental result.

As comparing movie 1 with movie 2, video quality of movie 1 is better than that of movie 2. At that time, both transport bandwidths in the network are about the same (about 10Mbps). However, video quality of movie 2 was worse since packet loss occurred on networks. This was because DVTS use about 35 Mbps in transporting a video without control. Digital video quality often becomes extremely worse by packet loss. Therefore, bandwidth control on video servers like this experiment is very important. Even if you provide data encoded into various rate, video quality becomes worse if you do not select adequate data. It is necessary to monitor the system condition at all times and to transport the video with adequate rate. By applying QMS to digital video libraries, these controls can be done.

6   Related Works

In this chapter, we introduce related works of QMS. Recently, from a viewpoint of the application QoS, a large number of studies have been made on system architecture suitable for QoS control and its control method. IETF has standardized RSVP[7], which has reserved end-to-end bandwidth on TCP/IP networks, and DiffServ[8], which has been a mechanism for TCP/IP networks to provide many QoS services flexibly. Moreover, the study of active network[9] has shown a technology for users to control networks actively. In addition, policy servers that have controlled network equipment according to the management policies have been produced on a commercial basis. These technologies and studies require descriptions of rules for each application. It means that we need decide the management policies beforehand. However, before the decision, we have to

Movie 1 (with control)   Movie 2 (no control)

Fig. 6. An Experimental Result.

solve the problems how we decide the policies and how the system negotiates the QoS among many applications, for managing the whole applications of the system according to the policies.

On the other hand, many studies have been made on control methods of which targets are end-to-end application QoS, such as The QoS broker[10] and Adaptive QoS management for multimedia applications in heterogeneous environments[11]. These research targets have been resource allocation methods and application QoS mapping methods. However, simple control methods are required for practical systems because architecture of the system is complicated and the estimate of fluctuations in the demand is difficult.

In order to solve these problems, we proposed QMS. This made it possible to manage whole applications according to the QoS management policies by using feedback type control methods without complicated modeling.

7 Conclusion

This paper proposed a QoS control method for digital video libraries. This method made it possible to transport video according to user's system environment by applying QMS to digital video libraries. In addition, we conducted the experiment using DV transport system. As a result, we found out that a bandwidth control function on video servers improved QoS provided to users.

References

1. Kato, Y. and Hakozaki, K.: Application QoS management for distributed computing systems. Proc. IEEE ICC'2001, Helsinki (2001)
2. Object Management Group: The Common Object Request Broker: Architecture and Specification. Object Management Group, Framingham, Massachusetts (1998)
3. Paxson, V.: Towards a framework for defining Internet performance metrics. Proc. INET'96 (1996) 3
4. Yamaguchi, H. et al.: Strategy for global megamedia network (GMN). Proc. APCC'97 (1997) 7-10
5. Ogawa, A., Kobayashi, K., Sugiura, K., Nakamura, O. and Murai, J.: Design and implementation of DV based video over RTP. Proc. Packet Video'2000, Italy (2000)
6. WIDE project: ⟨http://www.wide.ad.jp⟩.
7. Braden, R., Zhang, L., Berson, S., Herzog, S. and Jamin, S.: Resource reservation Protocol (RSVP). IETF RFC2205 (1997)
8. Brake, S., Black, D., Carlson, M., Davies, E., Wang, Z. and Weiss, W.: Architecture for differentiated services. IETF RFC2475 (1998)
9. Tennenhous, D. L., Smith, J. M., Sincoskie, W. D., Wetherall, D. J. and Minden, G. J.: A survey of active network research. IEEE Comm. Mag., Vol. 35, No. 1 (1997) 80-86
10. Nahrstedt, K. and Smith, J. M.: The QoS broker. IEEE MultiMedia, Vol. 2, No. 1 (1995) 53-67
11. Yamazaki, T. and Matsuda, J.: Adaptive QoS Management for Multimedia Applications in Heterogeneous Environments. IEICE Trans. Comm., Vol. D82-B, No. 11 (1999) 1801-1807

Enhanced Video Communication Using Gaze Correction with Simplified 3D Warping and Single Camera

Insuh Lee and Byeungwoo Jeon

School of Electrical and Computer Engineering
Sungkyunkwan University, Suwon, Korea
bjeon@yurim.skku.ac.kr
http://media.skku.ac.kr

Abstract. Under a video communication environment with single camera, the key problem to interfere user's natural feeling of conversation is its physical limitation to establish proper eye contact. This problem is caused by difficulty in aligning viewing directions of camera and user. We present a new approach to solve this problem using image-based warping technique. The main idea for our gaze correction is to generate an image captured by a virtual camera placed on the point which the user stares at. Our proposed method has two key components. The first one is to estimate the correction angle from the input images without supervision. The second one is the warping process to gaze-correct the input image. We show experimental results of gaze correction for situations which can occur in typical real communication environment.

1 Introduction

Video communication appears to be one of the most attractive ways which make face-to-face contact possible over long distances. Unfortunately, the natural feeling of eye-to-eye contact is currently hard to get since it is not easy to align the viewing direction of camera with the user's staring direction. This mismatch problem arises since the camera for video communication is generally placed above or at side of monitor screen which displays the person at the other side. Therefore the user cannot have a good eye contact, which greatly decreases natural feeling of conversation.

To overcome this problem, it is thinkable to physically embed a camera within monitor screen, however, this expensive approach is only applicable to large video conference system, but not to a personal video communication system, specially hand-held devices. Likewise an approach using stereo camera system to synthesize gaze-corrected image by interpolating views captured by two cameras is not acceptable either as a general solution for the same reason.

Our research here aims to generate a gaze-corrected image from input images themselves captured by single camera without user's supervision by effective and simple software-level method involving image-based modeling and rendering techniques. To do this, we have developed a method that virtually rotates camera viewing direction up to correction angle computed from input image. An overall block diagram of our approach is given in Fig. 1.

M. Tucci (Ed.): MDIC 2001, LNCS 2184, pp. 213–224, 2001.
© Springer-Verlag Berlin Heidelberg 2001

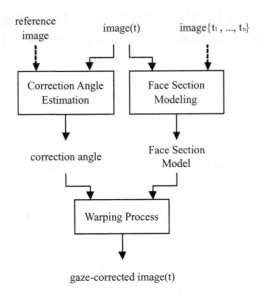

reference
image   image(t)   image{t₁ , ..., tₙ}

Correction Angle
Estimation

Face Section
Modeling

correction angle

Face Section
Model

Warping Process

gaze-corrected image(t)

Fig. 1. Overall Scheme of Proposed Method.

The proposed method consists of mainly two steps. As the first step, it estimates the correction angle between the camera viewing direction and user's staring direction from images. In the second step, we generate a new image by virtually rotating the user's face object in image by the correction angle computed in the first step to simulate the gaze-corrected image. For an inexpensive but still natural-looking rendering of rotated face object, we propose a simple face section model which has 3D shape information about face object. Face section model plays a key role in rendering natural gaze-corrected face object.

2   Correction Angle Estimation

We begin by considering a general situation in which a camera is placed above a display screen and one stares at the screen to see the other person over the network. Fig. 2(a) shows the geometric relation in this case. Note that the current configuration is simpler than the previous one[1] in that it can also model the case when the viewing direction of a camera viewpoint does not coincide with the direction of a user toward the camera. This tilt angle of the camera is denoted by ϕ in Fig. 2(b). The angle θ is the intervening angle between user's gaze toward the monitor and direction to the camera. If a camera were placed right on the spot at the screen which the user stares at and pointing at the user (that is, $\phi=0$), then there would be no mismatch between user's gaze direction and camera's viewing direction. The viewing direction mismatch causes poor eye contact and deteriorates feeling of natural face-to-face conversation to each other. The angle θ is directly related to the ratio of the distance H to L where H represents a distance of the user's staring point on the display screen to the center of camera lens and L represents a distance between the user's face, more specifically from user's eye, to the display screen.

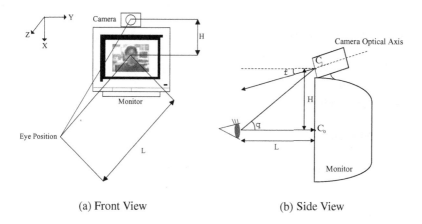

(a) Front View   (b) Side View

Fig. 2. Geometry of Configuration.

When the ratio is small, the user feels a good eye contact, but in the opposite case the user cannot. However, two factors L and H which determine the ratio are uncontrollable due to physical limitation such as screen size, and user's preference. To overcome this problem we rotate the input image using the viewing transform based on image warping to generate a gaze-corrected image for good eye contact. Such image warping requires the following:

1. The angle to rotate the source image to the destination image. Correction angle θ is given as:

$$\theta = tan^{-1}\frac{H}{L} \tag{1}$$

2. The depth value of the image, specifically of the face object to be used in the warping procedure

To find the correction angle, we assume a virtual camera placed at the user's staring point on display screen. Fig. 3 shows geometric relationship between the physical and virtual cameras. For simplicity, we assume that the virtual camera's optical center C_0 is equal to the world origin where its viewing direction normal is $(0, 0, 1)$ and the input camera's optical center C_1 lies on the world X-axis where its viewing direction normal is inclined by ϕ.

We now introduce how to automatically compute the correction angle θ from the images themselves. Now, we represent the image and the world using homogeneous coordinates: a location with Euclidean coordinates (X, Y, Z) is expressed by the column vector $\mathbf{P} = \begin{bmatrix} X\ Y\ Z\ 1 \end{bmatrix}^T$ and a location (x, y) on an image plane by $\mathbf{p} = \begin{bmatrix} x\ y\ 1 \end{bmatrix}^T$.

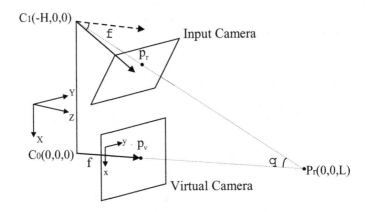

Fig. 3. Geometry of Virtual Camera.

Scalar multiples of these points will be written with a tilde, as $\hat{\mathbf{P}}$ and $\hat{\mathbf{p}}$. A camera is represented by a 3×4 homogeneous projection matrix of the form $\mathbf{\Phi} = [\mathbf{J} | -\mathbf{JC}]$ where the vector $\mathbf{C}$ represents the Euclidean position of the camera's optical center(either $\mathbf{C}_0$ or $\mathbf{C}_1$) and $\mathbf{J}$ is a 3×3 matrix which specifies the position and orientation of its image plane with respect to the world coordinate. The perspective projection equation[6] is

$$\hat{\mathbf{p}} = \mathbf{\Phi P} \qquad (2)$$

We now write the projection matrices, $\mathbf{\Phi}_0$ and $\mathbf{\Phi}_1$ which respectively represent the virtual and physical input cameras as:

$$
\begin{aligned}
\mathbf{\Phi}_0 &= \begin{bmatrix} f & 0 & 0 & 0 \\ 0 & f & 0 & 0 \\ 0 & 0 & 1 & 0 \end{bmatrix} \\
\mathbf{\Phi}_1 &= \begin{bmatrix} f\cos\phi & 0 & f\sin\phi & fH\cos\phi \\ 0 & f & 0 & 0 \\ -\sin\phi & 0 & \cos\phi & -H\sin\phi \end{bmatrix}
\end{aligned}
\qquad (3)
$$

where f represents camera's focal length.

In previous work[1], we assume that the eye is located on the Z-axis. In this paper, we lessen this constraint so that the eye can be off the Z-axis as in $\mathbf{P}_e$ in Fig. 4. The geometric relation in this case is as follows.

Let $\mathbf{P}_e = \begin{bmatrix} -H_e & 0 & L_e & 1 \end{bmatrix}^T$ be an arbitrary eye position in the world coordinate, $\mathbf{p}_e$, the projection point of $\mathbf{P}_e$. Scalar multiple of $\mathbf{p}_e$ is given as:

$$
\begin{aligned}
\hat{\mathbf{p}}_e &= \begin{bmatrix} B & 0 & 1 \end{bmatrix}^T \\
B &= \frac{f(H - H_e)\cos\phi + fL_e\sin\phi}{-(H - H_e)\sin\phi + L_e\cos\phi}
\end{aligned}
\qquad (4)
$$

From Eq. 4 we can find the correction angle θ:

$$\tan \theta = \frac{H - H_e}{Le}$$
$$= \frac{x_e \cos \phi - f \sin \phi}{x_e \sin \phi + f \cos \phi} \qquad (5)$$

where x_e indicates the x-value of $\hat{p}_e$ on image plane.

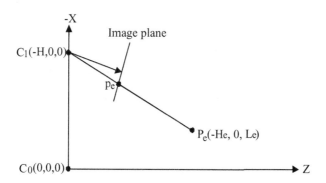

Fig. 4. Correction Angle Estimation with Arbitrary Eye Position $\mathbf{P}_e$.

If we know the camera tilt angle ϕ, we can compute the correction angle using Eq. 5. In case of mobile video communication device such as cellular phone or PDA, etc, the camera's tilt angle ϕ is almost 0. Thus the correction angle θ is computed in a simpler way:

$$\tan \theta = \frac{x_e}{f} \qquad (6)$$

Note that the reference image is not required since the correction angle θ is a function of x_e only. However, to enhance the accuracy of estimated correction angle, one can use a reference image which is obtained by letting the user stares directly at the monitor screen at an initialization step.

3   Facial Feature Search

In the previous section we show that if the eye position x_e is known in a given input image, we can compute the correction angle to rotate the input image. In this section we present a method to find the eye position in a given image and to track the user's eye position in video sequence to find the correction angle of each time. It is very important to find accurate positions, since reliable correction angle depends on them.

We use simple image processing techniques to find candidates that maximize the likelihood of being eyes. For this purpose, first we locate eyeballs in image sequence. First, we find facial region using color and motion cues, and subsequently the eyeball position is located within the facial region.

To identify facial region, we use skin color cue first. Although the probabilistic or adaptive color models may be introduced, we use a simple color model transformation below that needs no multiplication for a search independent of lighting condition:

$$diff = R - 128$$

$$\begin{bmatrix} R' \\ G' \\ B' \\ 1 \end{bmatrix} = \begin{bmatrix} 0 & 0 & 0 & 128 \\ 0 & 1 & 0 & -diff \\ 0 & 0 & 1 & -diff \\ 0 & 0 & 0 & 1 \end{bmatrix} \begin{bmatrix} R \\ G \\ B \\ 1 \end{bmatrix} \tag{7}$$

We use two color elements (G', B') instead of (R, G, B). A Pixel whose modified color components (G', B') satisfy the relation in Eq. 7 is identified as belonging to a potential facial region. $(k_G^-, k_G^+, k_B^-, k_B^+)$ are constants defining skin color tones.

$$k_G^- < G' < k_G^+$$
$$k_B^- < B' < k_B^+ \tag{8}$$

The potential face region identified using Eq. 8 can contain background regions which happen to have color similar to skin. Those extra regions are discarded by subsequent motion-based search: since the background doesn't change over times, any region which does not change over times is discarded by checking the relation in Eq. 9 where $I(x, y)$ stands for the image intensity at a pixel location (x, y).

$$\frac{dI(x, y)}{dt} > k_m \tag{9}$$

Once the facial region is identified, we can efficiently look for the eye location. We use the edge and color information around the eyes in the region detected in face region search step.

Having determined the eye position in the images, it is possible to easily track the eye positions using a number of windows on the face which is a unit for template matching via correlation as in Fig. 5. Four tracking window are initialized around the eyes. Registration of the windows from one frame to the next is accomplished by minimizing the correlation over translating, rotating, and scaling parameters. Given an image $I(x, y, t)$ at time t, we want to find motion parameter μ which minimizes $O(\mu)$:

$$O(\mu) = \sum_{(x,y) \in window} \left[I(g(x, y, \mu), t) - I(x, y, t - 1) \right]^2 \tag{10}$$

where $g(x, y, \mu)$ is a motion parameterized by μ which represents translation, rotation, and scaling.

Fig. 5. Initialized Correlation Windows.

4   Face Shape Approximation

To obtain more realistic rendering of face after the gaze correction, we need to know depth values of face object. Now, we describe 3D face section modeling using structure from motion(SfM) technique using multiple morphable model. Many solutions have been proposed to solve the SfM problem based on the most influential work done by Kanade[3] who proposed the factorization technique for rigid objects and orthographic projection. As an extension work of Kanade's method, we use multiple morphable model proposed by Bregler[4] and Blanz[8] as shape vector to represent face shape appropriately. This is main difference of our work compared to the previous SfM solutions.

The 3D section model in each frame is a linear combination of a set of m shape vectors. We represent the geometry of the section model $\mathbf{S}_{mod}$ with a shape vector $\mathbf{S}_i$ which is a $3 \times n$ matrix describing n points. The shape of a section model is a linear combination(morphing) of this shape vector set.

$$\mathbf{S}_{mod} = \sum_{i=1}^{m} a_i \mathbf{S}_i, \quad \sum_{i=1}^{m} a_i = 1 \qquad (11)$$

Under an orthographic projection, the n points of a S_{mod} are projected into 2D image points $p_i(x_i, y_i)$:

$$\begin{bmatrix} x_1 \ x_2 \ \cdots \ x_n \\ y_1 \ y_2 \ \cdots \ y_n \end{bmatrix} = \mathbf{R} \cdot \mathbf{S}_{mod} + \mathbf{T}$$

$$\mathbf{R} = \begin{bmatrix} r_1 \ r_2 \ r_3 \\ r_4 \ r_5 \ r_6 \end{bmatrix} \qquad (12)$$

$\mathbf{R}$ is the rotation matrix and $\mathbf{T}$ is the translation matrix. As in Kanade[3], we eliminate $\mathbf{T}$ by subtracting the mean of all 2D points, and assume that $\mathbf{S}_{mod}$ is centered at the origin. We can rewrite the linear combination in Eq. 11 as a matrix form:

$$\begin{bmatrix} x_1 & x_2 & \dots & x_n \\ y_1 & y_2 & \dots & y_n \end{bmatrix} = \begin{bmatrix} a_i \mathbf{R} & \dots & a_m \mathbf{R} \end{bmatrix} \cdot \begin{bmatrix} \mathbf{S}_1 \\ \mathbf{S}_2 \\ \dots \\ \mathbf{S}_m \end{bmatrix} \tag{13}$$

We add a temporal index to each 2D point, and denote the tracked points in frame t as (x_i^t, y_i^t). We assume 2D point tracking data over N frames and represent them in the tracking matrix $\mathbf{W}$:

$$\mathbf{W} = \begin{bmatrix} x_1^1 & \dots & x_n^1 \\ y_1^1 & \dots & y_n^1 \\ x_1^2 & \dots & x_n^2 \\ y_1^2 & \dots & y_n^2 \\ & \dots & \\ x_1^N & \dots & x_n^N \\ y_1^N & \dots & y_n^N \end{bmatrix} \tag{14}$$

Now we can rewrite tracking data matrix $\mathbf{W}$ using Eq. 13:

$$\mathbf{W} = \mathbf{Q} \cdot \mathbf{B}$$
$$= \begin{bmatrix} a_1^1 \mathbf{R}^1 & \dots & a_m^1 \mathbf{R}^1 \\ a_1^2 \mathbf{R}^2 & \dots & a_m^2 \mathbf{R}^2 \\ & \dots & \\ a_1^N \mathbf{R}^N & \dots & a_m^N \mathbf{R}^N \end{bmatrix} \cdot \begin{bmatrix} \mathbf{S}_1 \\ \mathbf{S}_2 \\ \dots \\ \mathbf{S}_m \end{bmatrix} \tag{15}$$

Eq. 15 shows that the tracking matrix W has rank $3m$ and can be factored into 2 matrixes. Q has the face pose R^t and weighting coefficients $a_1^t, \dots, a_m^t$. The shape matrix B has the m shape vectors. The factorization can be done using singular value decomposition(SVD) by considering only the first $3m$ singular vectors and singular values (first $3m$ columns in U, D, V) [7]:

$$\mathbf{SVD} : \mathbf{W} = \hat{\mathbf{U}} \cdot \hat{\mathbf{D}} \cdot \hat{\mathbf{V}}^T = \hat{\mathbf{Q}} \cdot \hat{\mathbf{B}} \tag{16}$$

Now we extract the rotation matrix R and shape vector coefficient a_i from $\hat{Q}$. If the 2 rows of $\hat{Q}$ that correspond to one single time frame t, namely rows $2t - 1$ and $2t$, then:

$$\mathbf{q}^t = \begin{bmatrix} a_1^t \mathbf{R}^t & \dots & a_m^t \mathbf{R}^t \end{bmatrix}$$
$$= \begin{bmatrix} a_1 r_1 & a_1 r_2 & a_1 r_3 & \dots & a_m r_1 & a_m r_2 & a_m r_3 \\ a_1 r_4 & a_1 r_5 & a_1 r_6 & \dots & a_m r_4 & a_m r_5 & a_m r_6 \end{bmatrix} \tag{17}$$

We can reorder the elements of q^t into a new matrix $\bar{q}^t$:

$$\overline{q}^t = \begin{bmatrix} a_1r_1 & a_1r_2 & a_1r_3 & a_1r_4 & a_1r_5 & a_1r_6 \\ a_2r_1 & a_2r_2 & a_2r_3 & a_2r_4 & a_2r_5 & a_2r_6 \\ & & \cdots & & & \\ a_mr_1 & a_mr_2 & a_mr_3 & a_mr_4 & a_mr_5 & a_mr_6 \end{bmatrix}$$

$$= \begin{bmatrix} a_1 \\ a_2 \\ a_3 \\ a_4 \\ a_5 \\ a_6 \end{bmatrix} \cdot \begin{bmatrix} r_1 & r_2 & r_3 & r_4 & r_5 & r_6 \end{bmatrix} \tag{18}$$

Eq. 18 shows that $\overline{q}^t$ can be factored into the pose and shape vector coefficients by SVD. We apply the reordering and factorization to all time blocks of $\hat{Q}$.

Given 2D tracking matrix W, we can estimate a non-rigid 3D shape matrix with m degrees of freedom, the corresponding pose, and weighting coefficients for each frame.

Now we further simplify the face section on facial plane using a large arc of radius r as shown in Fig. 6. A selected region around the eye is curve-fitted using arc shape as in Fig. 6. There are two reasons for this: one is by the notion that one may generate gaze-corrected image only for the horizontal strip containing eye area since that is the most critical area which gives most cues of gaze direction. In experiment, we observed that people seldom noticed any artifacts when the gaze correction was performed only on the horizontal strip containing eyes. The other reason comes from a practical requirement of reducing the computation as low as possible.

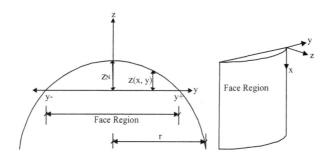

Fig. 6. A Simplified Arc-Shaped Face Section Model.

According to model in Fig. 6, the depth value of a pixel at (x, y) on the input image, denoted by $z(x, y)$ is calculated as;

$$z(x, y) = Z_N - r + \sqrt{r^2 - y^2}$$
$$r = \frac{z_N^2 + (y^+)^2}{2Z_N} \tag{19}$$

Z_N is the height of nose in z-direction, and y^+ is the half of the face width.

Finally, the gaze-corrected image is obtained by warping(rotating) the input image by the correction angle computed using eye position searching[1][2][9]. To perform the rotation and to get a natural looking image, we find new vertex points of the meshes reconstructed in face section modeling after warping:

$$\tilde{p}_{new} = \Phi_1 \mathbf{R} \mathbf{P}_{mesh} \tag{20}$$

where $\tilde{p}_{new}$ represents warped image points of $\mathbf{P}_{mesh}$ in world using rotation matrix $\mathbf{R}$.

There are no holes which are potentially significant warping artifact in the output images since we perform interpolation using mesh warping procedure. Moreover there is no fold which is another warping artifact since meshes have depth value. We use conventional Z-buffer algorithm to prevent fold appearance.

5   Experiment

We present the results of the proposed method applied to face images in different conditions. We capture facial images with a CCD camera having a focal length f=8mm. We set 3D meshes only on the neighboring region around eyes to minimize computation time.

Fig.7 shows eye position determined by proposed method. In Fig. 8, when the camera tilt angle ϕ is = 8 degree, we found the correction angle(θ =6 degree). Using the correction angle we rotate the input image to obtain the gaze-corrected image using SfM based method. The result image Fig. 8(b) shows much better eye contact than Fig. 8(a). Fig. 9 shows another case corrected by the proposed simple section model method where the camera tilt angle is 10 degree. We find the correction angle is 8 degree and the result image in Fig. 9(a) shows our gaze correction method works well wherever the user's eye are located at. Fig. 10 shows a sequential view of the results corrected using SfM based method. Images in the first row are input images and images in the second row are the corrected images. Since the face section model used in our system has 3D information about the face, we can also feel natural eye contacts as can be seen in the result images in Fig. 10 where the correction angles is 8-10 degree.

6   Conclusion and Future Work

In this paper we present a simple approach for gaze correction using only one camera to overcome poor eye-contact problem in typical desktop video communication environment. The system estimates the correction angle automatically and rotates the input image by the estimated correction angle using the face section model to generate gaze corrected image. The requirement on computation is low, therefore, it can be applied to real-time application.

Acknowledgments

This work was supported by grant No.1999-2-515-001-5 from the Basic Research Program of the Korea Science and Engineering Foundation.

Fig. 7. Eye Position.

(a) Input Image   (b) Gaze-Corrected Image

Fig. 8. Result 1: ϕ =8 degree, θ =6 degree.

(a) Input Image   (b) Gaze-Corrected Image

Fig. 9. Result 2: ϕ =10 degree, θ =8 degree.

Fig. 10. Sequential View of Input (Top) and Corrected Images (Bottom).

References

1. I. Lee and B. Jeon: Three-dimensional Mesh Warping for Natural Eye-to-Eye Contact in Internet Video Communication. Proc. of Visual Communication and Image Processing(VCIP 00), vol.4067, pp. 308-315, 2000.
2. I. Lee and B. Jeon: Gaze-Correction using Simplified 3D Mesh Warping. Proc. of Visual Communication and Image Processing(VCIP 01), vol.4310, pp. 595-602, 2001.
3. C. Tomasi and T. kanade: Shape and Motion from Image Stream under orthography: A Factorization Method. Int. Journal of Computer Vision, 9(2):137-154, Nov., 1992.
4. C. Bregler, A. Hertzmann, and H. Biermann: Recovering Non-Rigid 3D Shape from Image Streams. Proc. of Computer Vision and Pattern Recognition 2000(CVPR2000), vol. 2, pp. 690 -696, 2000.
5. B. K. Horn: Robot Vision. The MIT Press, Cambridge, 1986.
6. A. M. Tekalp: Digital Video Processing. Prentice Hall, 1995.
7. W. Press, S. Teukolsky, W. Vetterling, and B. Flannery: Numerical Recipes in C. Cambridge University Press, pp. 59-70, 1996.
8. V. Blanz and T. Vetter: A Morphable Model for the Synthesis of 3D Faces. Proc. of SIG-GRAPH'99, pp. 187-194, 1999.
9. G. Wolberg: Digital Image Warping. IEEE Computer Society Press, 1990.

Author Index

Lecture Notes in Computer Science

For information about Vols. 1–2084
please contact your bookseller or Springer-Verlag